Unrelenting

When Safe was the Exception

~ A Memoir ~

Brian Francis

Unrelenting

This is a work of narrative nonfiction. The events are portrayed to the best of the author's memory. While all the stories in this book are true, some names and identifying details have been changed to protect the privacy of some of the people involved.

ISBN (eBook): 978-1-968563-26-4
ISBN (Paperback): 978-1-968563-27-1
ISBN (Hardcover): 978-1-968563-28-8

Dedication

Dedicated to the memory of Charlie Francis

We are better for having known you,

and we continue to see your goodness after all these long years.

You would still be proud of us.

We Miss You.

Acknowledgement

I wish to give heartfelt thanks as well as to acknowledge the assistance and the input of the following people, all of whom had an influence on the way in which the story of this part of my life eventually came to appear on the pages of this book: Chuckie Peterson, Alycia Francis, Margo Davis, Colleen Curtis, Richard Sprague, Stephanie Pattison, Nat Latos, Lantz Simpson, Robin Bahr Casey, Susan Z. Witter, S.M. Clark, Michael F. Suss, Michael W. Jolin, PhD; Faith Trudel, Richard Trudel, Rosemary Adam, Donna Lauzon, James Wells, Jeffrey Stiglitz, Lindsay Cornelius, and Jeremie Ruby-Strauss.

Brian Francis

Contents

Unrelenting

A Note on Location

"The power of location lies in its ability to provide us with the opportunities and experiences that shape our identity."

— Roy T. Bennett

I grew up in the small town of Blackstone, Massachusetts. At the time I was living there, it boasted a population of around 6,000 people. It was a mix of mostly Irish, French-Canadian, and Polish residents whose ancestors had settled the town in the 1660s and incorporated it in 1845. Before them, the Nipmuk tribe had lived there. Geographically, Blackstone is situated on the state line of Massachusetts and Rhode Island. The city of Woonsocket, RI, was within walking distance from where we lived. Reportedly, the Blackstone River was the birthplace of the Industrial Revolution in the United States, and it flowed through our little town. Blackstone had once served as a railroad hub for the New York and New England Railroad. I can remember three distinct houses that we lived in, in town, but we lived in two of them before I was five years old.

Preface

*"I began to think better than I had before about the commonplace need,
alive in all of us, to make large sense of things in the very moment,
even as experience is overtaking us."*

- Vivian Gornick

To quote a great comedian: "I was born at a very early age." I had (at least at the time, I thought) a somewhat normal upbringing, but in 1976, our entire family endured a horrific event. I later realized the rest of my life was affected, to a huge degree, by this seemingly singular event and by the apparently separate events that both preceded and followed it. After reflecting on this traumatic occurrence, I came to realize that it was not an isolated problem or even the primary symptom of our dysfunctional family narrative. It was a grotesque and explosive symptom of a larger process... an illness. Our family was ill.

As I set about putting my memories to paper, I was able to identify several moments that have stood out along the arc of my life—rites of passage, if you will. These are moments that helped me to understand who I am and how I got to be that person. We humans have a lot of rites of passage. Some of the more common ones in American life are going on a first date, getting a driver's license, and graduating from high school. To this list I added the moment when I realized my upbringing was not normal, as well as when I decided to do something to halt the generational legacy of violence and trauma. The horrific event I mentioned earlier represents another one of those major milestones. The date of that was September 10, 1976. It was the definitive end of my childhood—my sudden coming of age.

My mother victimized me for the better part of my first eighteen years. Domestic violence traumatizes children who witness it, and violence perpetrated by an adult against a child multiplies the collective trauma of a household filled with violence. I survived, but how? It is a question I'm asked frequently. Looking back, I can see the varied ways I tried to maintain some sense of normalcy... some sense of sanity. I tried forgetting the past, but that simply did not work. I tried forgiving those who played the villains of my childhood, but this process gave only brief respite from the torture I could not forget. I took advantage of distractions whenever I could, but ultimately, I found that the act of giving was the secret. I had to give, to find peace.

I thought joining the armed forces would be a means of giving, but I eventually realized this was just another temporary escape. It was merely another distraction that brought me right back to my troubling baseline—full circle, as they say. I learned a lot from that distraction, though. I found parts of the military hierarchy too reminiscent of the abuses I suffered at my mother's hand. I learned that there are healthy ways to live in a hierarchy as well as unhealthy ways. That knowledge led me farther down the path to peace, but it was still not what I needed. I tried self-employment, turning my paternally derived and somewhat unique work ethic—Dad didn't have an excuse not to work and never made one—and skillset (He taught me basic mechanics and engineering—covering numerous disciplines) into a way to give to others. I was often too generous, and that was not financially sustainable. Then, in a motor vehicle accident, I suffered an injury that was made worse by two more accidents in rapid succession. This opened my eyes to the field of nursing. Through nursing—specifically psychiatric nursing—I felt as though I'd found the path to healing—one that allowed me to give and still get paid.

The effects of this violence on certain of my family members helps to support the premise that personality disorders may be passed from one generation to another. My mother's father displayed many of the behaviors I saw in my mother. My sister Lori displayed many of my mother's negative behavioral traits. There may be a genetic predisposition, but these traits were also probably learned—nature and nurture. Ultimately, I do not believe that the events I witnessed and experienced made me who I am. However, I believe that how I chose to deal with those events has certainly contributed to me being the person I am today.

I have made and continue to make comparisons between the people in my life—especially my parents. One's prejudices against me, while inexplicable, were so patently obvious while the other was so caring and loving. I needed to analyze that dichotomy to make sense of it. I've also made comparisons between my siblings and how the violence in our household may have been more intensely and more obviously targeted toward one or two individuals over the others. Nonetheless, it involved all seven humans who lived together—at some point or another—under that roof. How it affected each of us so differently speaks to the nebulous and subjective nature of abuse.

In 2004, my mother wrote and self-published a book describing her early life in a series of anecdotes. I have referenced this book as an adjunct to my memories of the tales she told. In 2010, my sister Lori also self-published a book in which she describes several of the same events I have explored in these pages. Many times, her version of our shared experiences is vastly different from the way my mother, my older sisters, and I remember those same things. Within these pages, I have drawn comparisons to the different telling of these tales.

This is a memoir and as such, it relies upon my memories of certain events. We all know that human memory is fallible, and I claim no exception. I have taken many steps, though, to ensure that every aspect of my story is as true as possible, and that individual privacy is protected where needed. Any misrepresentation is completely unintentional. I have sought permission to use some names and have changed other names that were not already a part of public records. The locales and some other aspects of the events about which I write are integral to the stories as I remember them. Those details have remained and were consciously unaltered; thus, it is conceivable that despite my efforts to hide some identities, those who may know me, my family members, or may know of the more fantastic bits of our family's experiences might be able to connect dots and my efforts to protect certain identities may be compromised. For any transgressions of this stripe, which may develop, I humbly apologize.

Dad

*"My father gave me the greatest gift anyone
could give another person – he believed in me."*

—*Jim Valvano*

Without question, the guiding force, inspiration, and influence that helped most in shaping me as a person was and is my father. I had a very special (some would say unique) relationship with him. Being the only boy in a family of five children had provided a kind of privilege for me. Dad never seemed to mind me tagging along with him— wherever he was going. He worked away from home a lot, but I made it a point to spend as much time with him as possible when he was home. Starting from the time I was a very little boy, I was a weekend tag-along and near-constant companion with that man. On Saturday mornings, he took me with him to a "greasy spoon" train car diner when he went there for coffee. I went with him to junkyards, where he collected used parts for car repairs. I visited the mills in which he worked during the week. I knew most of his friends and associates, and they knew me—mostly as "Charlie's boy."

When I was about six or seven years old, Dad obtained a giant, antique, upright piano. He had a friend transport it to our house, and they backed up their truck to the bulkhead that led to our basement. He, and several guys that he knew, manhandled that beast down the bulkhead steps and set it against the stairs connecting the basement and the living area above. No one knew this right away, but the truck had run over and broken the clay tile pipe that connected the house's drainage to the cesspool in the backyard. Once the drains (and toilet) began to back up, Dad knew it had to be dug up and replaced. He began digging in the afternoon, but he lost the natural light long before the job was done. He asked me to hold an automotive trouble light for him so that he could see what he was doing. We were at that job for several hours. It was autumn, and the nights were cold. He often remarked that he was in awe of the resilience I showed that night. He brought it up many times in the years that followed. From that point forward, I was his "bestest helper"... "The best what est!" I spent more time with him between ages six and sixteen than any of my siblings.

It is to that man and his memory that this book is dedicated.

One

"True peace is not merely the absence of tension;
it is the presence of justice."

—*Dr. Martin Luther King Jr.*

I didn't always know the reasons for Mom's behavior. I'd get punished without really knowing why. I would often find myself kneeling in the southeast corner of our kitchen and staring at the pink-magenta painted walls, where they joined. With my body still, my mind would often take off. I might imagine myself flying over the house and surrounding woods at sunset. I remember one such instance when I was just a little boy – maybe nine or ten years old. In my mind's eye, I was able to stretch out my legs and spread my arms. I was free of restraints, and there was no inflicted pain if I moved. I fancied myself drawing my knees and arms in, to my tummy, to spring open like a switchblade knife, propelling me ever more quickly. I was in a different world... a fantastic world where open space was king. Maybe my idea of open space was not the same as it might have been for a grown-up, but I would enjoy those imaginary flights – sweeping big circles above the house. I'd seen the next-door neighbor's house and all the bulldozers and other heavy equipment in their yard—I wondered why some of them were yellow or green and some were brown. The place across the street used to be a bar, but a nice old man bought it and worked at turning it into a home for his family. When I was in this corner, I would have this kind of imagined flight and other adventures on a regular basis.

Suddenly my head was slammed from behind. The force of the blow bounced my forehead and nose off one of the walls making up the corner. Tears welled up in my eyes from the pain, and also from the frustration—knowing I had inadvertently extended my own punishment. My momentary lapse in focus meant I would not be getting up anytime soon.

"Kneel up!" came the command.

I had drifted into my alternate reality, and I had lowered my guard. I had also lowered my butt, and it had touched my heels.

"Fifteen more minutes!"

All kids have to do this, I told myself. Long after the pain of my nose hitting the wall had gone away, my tears of frustration kept flowing.

"You want to cry? I'll give you something to cry about. Maybe another half hour will dry those tears."

In my friends' houses, kneeling in the corner was not like this. My friends might get sent to the corner for five or ten minutes. It wasn't hours on end. Even if bare knees on a linoleum floor could be construed as non-violent punishment, my mother's cruel version was torture. My initial punishment was supposed to be thirty minutes in the corner for some ill-defined infraction… and I wasn't supposed to move. What she really meant was for me to spend thirty minutes in absolute, silent stillness—"kneeling up" with my full weight on my knees and with hands clasped behind my back, like a soldier awaiting execution.

By resting my buttocks on my feet, I relieved a considerable amount of pressure on my knees. Sometimes I did this deliberately to relieve the pain, which was always a risky move. If Mom caught me doing so, it always meant more time kneeling in the "Attention!" position. I'd learned by experience that anything but statuary stillness resulted in additional time in the corner. Scratching an itch—fifteen extra minutes. Saying I'm thirsty—an extra thirty minutes. Shifting weight from side to side, breathing the wrong way, looking at the clock, asking to go to the bathroom, humming—all meant more time on my knees. I *was* usually very well-behaved and, on that day, I was trying really hard to do what I was supposed to do. I was occupying my brain with my imaginary flight, so I wouldn't move my skinny little body. I had failed and would have to pay the price.

While I was in the corner, my younger sister Lori came into the kitchen and seated herself at the kitchen table to do her homework. I could always tell it was her without looking. Even Mom, who seemed to really like Lori, sometimes referred to her as "motor mouth" or "chatterbox" due to the nearly incessant stream of chatter emanating from her mouth. When referring to Lori, Mom would sometimes recite a little poem that was a modification she had made to Helen Cowles LeCron's *Little Charlie Chipmunk*.

She did this, I think, to shame Lori. Mom used several phrases and would also modify song lyrics or poems when addressing us. She may have thought she was being cute, or funny. It was not always obvious to us as children, but as we matured, some of us came to realize just how cruel her comments had been.

For Lori, homework was probably almost as torturous as kneeling in the corner was for me. Somehow, I knew she had decided to exact revenge for something I may have said or done to her at some point in the past. What or when seemed completely unimportant—I never really knew what she was thinking, anyway. From somewhere behind me and to the left I heard my mother coming down the hall and back into the kitchen. Before she could do anything, Lori blurted out:

"Ma! He made a face at me!"

That was enough for more time in the corner. I hadn't even looked in her direction, but experience had taught me that arguing only guaranteed an even longer punishment.

I had already been in the corner for over an hour. With the added fifteen minutes for letting my butt touch my heels, the extra thirty minutes I got for crying, and the extra twenty minutes I got for supposedly making a face at Lori, I knew I was in for a long stretch. My entire afternoon would be spent silently staring at the corner. I needed a new game to play in my mind. There was a texture that had been sprayed onto the wall before it was painted, so I began trying to make out patterns in it. There was a lion eating a cloud. Maybe that little bit was a lady's dress standing by... a pile of dog poop? I could see some weird combinations. Then I thought about looking at the same shapes and trying to see something different. The frequency of my visits to that corner meant that some of those patterns became indelibly etched upon my memory.

As for Lori, after numerous check-ins with Mom and at least as many corrections to her work, she finally appeared to be done with her homework. She flew off to her room and returned a few minutes later, bounding across the kitchen toward the back door that was behind me. Out she went into the world, and the rest of the world didn't have the courtesy of a warning she was approaching. The house became silent. Not totally silent, because the radio—tuned to WLKW (Mom's favorite easy listening radio station)—was still droning out Andy Williams and Percy Faith. Although I couldn't see her, I could hear Mom making dinner preparations diagonally across from my position. It was a return to simple, pleasant, suburban background noise. I went back to my made-up game of identifying the shapes in the wall texture. Fifteen minutes likely ticked by. I thought *I'm doing it! I'm passing my punishment time.*

At the edge of my awareness, I heard it coming. Like the hum of an advancing mosquito, and promising to be just as annoying, Lori was returning from who-knows-where and getting closer. The Chatterbox was back. Immediately behind my position and to the right was a window, and beyond that was the back door. Because it was warm, both were open on that day. From my corner, I could easily hear the voices of anyone on the sidewalk—before they could ascend the concrete steps to the back door. Lori was not alone. There was a moment of quiet again, then—BLAM! Lori threw the screen door open and knocked the inner door into one of the dining chairs. As startling as that was, I stayed quiet. Mom yelled at her for a moment, but then I heard Lori's voice again, undeterred and without a hint of remorse—"Can Piper and I play Barbies in my room?"

Mom didn't usually allow playing indoors when it was nice enough to play outdoors. For whatever reason, Mom made an exception and approved the request.

"My mom says we can play in my room... Come on in."

Lori invited the neighbor girl in. It wasn't very common for any of us to want friends over because it was a restrictive and unhappy environment, so this was already a little weird. Piper was a year older than Lori and was a bit of a stick-in-the-mud. She and Lori had a relationship that was constantly in flux. They would play together, then fight and be angry with each other for a while, and then they'd make up and the cycle repeated. The two girls came into the kitchen. I heard the sniggering begin. At first, they were whispering to each other—not particularly quietly. They had not moved more than a few feet inside the door when they began to giggle. I took a chance and slowly turned my head to the left. In my arc of vision, Mom came into sight first. She still had her back to me. I turned a few degrees more and Lori's eyes locked onto mine. She burst out laughing and Piper joined her. Humiliated, I turned my face back to the corner. I could feel the tears welling up. Mom let it go on for a lot longer than I would have hoped. Maybe it only seemed to drag on that long because I was the subject of her shaming. Eventually, she admonished the girls that if they weren't going to go upstairs and play, they would have to go back outside. Off they went, giggling and cavorting to Lori's bedroom, while I remained kneeling in the corner. Mom did nothing to comfort me. I was there, after all, to be humiliated. That was the entire point.

I was still in the corner—almost an hour later— when Piper had to leave to go home for her supper. Her exit did not have the same feeling as her arrival because, not being a very good hostess, Lori had allowed her to come downstairs by herself. Without Lori's instigation, Piper didn't laugh at me as she passed through the kitchen. I remembered once hearing her brother screaming when he had been locked into one of their dad's outbuildings—so perhaps she didn't really recognize humiliation of a sibling as being that out of the ordinary. When I was eventually allowed to get up—just before Dad got home—it was difficult for me to walk normally for several minutes. After nearly three hours of kneeling, my knees had taken on a dark red color with a purplish tinge. I knew from my many trips to that corner that they would remain sore for days.

Two

"All happy families resemble one another,
but each unhappy family is unhappy in its own way."

—Leo Tolstoy

Our immediate family consisted of Mom, Dad and (in birth order) Faith, Chuckie (birth name was Charline, after my dad), me, Lori, and Wendy. There are sixteen years between Faith and Wendy. Mom described hers and Dad's first home together as a "cold water flat" in Blackstone (it was, in fact, a tenement in the long block building in which she and her siblings were mostly raised). They moved to Uxbridge, Massachusetts at some point in late 1952 or early 1953, and in 1954 (according to Faith), Mom and Dad moved into an apartment for a short time along with the two girls (ages two and three) before buying the house in which I spent my first years.

Faith was the oldest and was (obviously) named after my mother. Her hair was nearly as black as Mom's, but she had started seeing white hair on her head while just in her teens. She had a slightly daintier version of Dad's nose and wore thick, "Coke-bottle" glasses. She was prettier than I think she believed, and was slightly taller than Chuckie. When my youngest sister Wendy came along, Faith willingly babysat her. She became a second, more sensitive and attentive mother to her. Chuckie had been similarly more of a parent for me, even though she was only eight years old when I was new to the family. Faith was meek and non-aggressive.

Faith and Chuckie were a study in opposites. When they were teens, Chuckie was a wild hippy, Faith was reserved. Where Chuckie was unabashed in her approach to life, Faith was a quiet homebody. She was determined, from a young age, to have a family and live happily ever after. For a short while after nursing school, and before she eloped, I had (involuntarily) shared my bedroom with her. It was also Faith who had inadvertently given me my first glimpse of a naked female. I was, perhaps, five or six years old and had innocently opened an unlocked bathroom door. Faith had just stepped out of the shower. She was fourteen or fifteen years old and let out a shriek that everyone up and down the street heard. Sorry Faith! I couldn't figure out (at the time) what might have happened to her penis.

I knew that I had two older sisters. However, in my early childhood, it seemed there was only one – Chuckie. There are photos of me with both Faith and Chuckie, but I really do not remember Faith being a part of my day-to-day life until I was a little over five. My memories before age five are limited. I was told that my sister Lori came along a couple of months after my second birthday – I don't remember that. I also do not remember interactions with her until about the same time as those with Faith and most of those memories are vague and intermittent until a few years later, still.

While I was technically a middle child, there were enough years between Chuckie and me that I could have been considered the oldest child in the second grouping. Lori is twenty-six months my junior. She had a poor ability to concentrate and was not good with details. There was a wiry goofiness to her physical movements. She was, to my mind, jealous, contrary, obstinate and had a psychopathic and malicious fascination with other people's pain and suffering. She appeared to have no moral objections to lying or exaggerating and she did so to make herself look better or for no obvious reason at all. She was also my default playmate for many years.

Lori and I were not meant to get along. She was, as far as my other sisters and I were concerned, Mom's clear favorite. She had skinny legs, knobby knees, frizzy hair and a penchant for embellishing the truth, or fabricating situations and/or events to such a degree that they were just beyond the realm of believability. Hyperbole was her modus operandi. The entire family referred to these fantasies as 'Lori Stories'. If they made her seem more important or substituted her for someone else and gained her a little extra pity or glory, it was that much better for her. As she grew older, her process became more elaborate and pathological. It seemed Lori really believed these tales as the truth and would get terribly upset if any of us refuted her version. She also appeared to thrive on creating discontent, even if there was nothing she might obviously gain by doing so. She thought nothing of telling an outright lie to one person about a third person that would then cause a row between the others. I never understood that.

One year I was given a chord organ as a Christmas present. The unit sat on a folded cardboard "stand" that was decorated with black stripes on a white background – like a zebra. My journey into the world of music began with that organ. It came with a small booklet of sheet music which allowed me to teach myself those tunes. As I became more familiar with those pre-written songs, I began attempting to recreate other tunes. Chuckie would help me as we tried, together, to replicate TV show theme songs. Jealously, Lori would reach between my hands or between Chuckie's hands and mine and would purposely hit as many keys as possible. Noise inserted into music. Chaos inserted into order. It was a direct reflection of the contentious relationship between Lori and me.

Wendy is the youngest sibling. She was an adorable baby and toddler. I had a habit of lying on my stomach on the living room floor, to read, or to do homework. Wendy would hop onto my back and ride me as though she was riding a bucking bronco, except I wasn't moving. As she got older this proved to be hazardous to my breathing – she would stand up and then flop down, throwing all her weight onto my back. It would knock the wind out of me. She inadvertently gave several of us nicknames that are still occasionally used. Of course, this was mostly due to her not being able to pronounce the real names properly.

She would sometimes call out to Faith – especially early on – as "Shae". This name hung on for probably close to a year. As her speech skills improved, the names changed. Wendy learned a second iteration of Faith's name from Dad. To differentiate between my mother and my oldest sister, he would call Mom "Faith" and he'd call the younger "Faith Ann". Wendy turned this into "Thaith-Ann", but she'd add "My oh-nee" (my only). There was a memorable night when the entire family went to the drive-in. We had a 1962 Pontiac Grand Safari station wagon – a cavernous monstrosity of a car. It had three rows of forward-facing seats. Faith and Chuckie were in the very back seat, Lori and I were in the middle row, and Mom and Dad were in the front. Wendy kept asking to move. "My wanna see Mummy"… "My wanna see my oh-nee Thaith Ann"… "My wanna see Mummy". She was not getting sleepy, as Mom had predicted, and all this movement was too much for the parents. We waited until the second feature started and then made our exit from the drive-in.

Mom tried to teach Wendy how to say "Chuckie" but she just couldn't. Mom said: "That's okay, just call her 'dum-dum', instead". When Wendy did say "dum-dum" Mom roared with laughter, which just reinforced the slur and encouraged Wendy to continue to use this moniker – it lasted a full 2 years. For a while, Chuckie wore it as a badge of honor. She even signed a couple of birthday cards as "Dum – Dum". To this day, it bothers Chuckie that Mom did that. She considers this to be another of our mother's power trips. Mom just didn't care how much her words hurt.

For me, Wendy couldn't quite understand that there were two syllables in my name. She began with "Ben". Here was another instance of Dad furthering Wendy's malapropisms: in the mill where he worked, the maintenance guy's name was Ben, and he was called for mechanical issues arising in the equipment. When a call came over the intercom, the individual calling out to him would say "Ben... Ben, mechanical". Dad heard Wendy call me Ben and then related the story. Now the nickname became "Ben-Ben Mechanical" which lasts to this day. Chuckie calls me Ben, but I do NOT call her Dum-Dum.

The one exception was Lori, whose name Wendy was more closely able to pronounce. The first version was "Oree" as little kids often have difficulty with the initial L. We tried to extend the use of it by calling after her: "Oree – Oree – Oreeeee" but that just didn't stick. The initial "L" sound is easy to learn, and Wendy did so in rather short order. This small, simple thing caused Lori to be very jealous of the rest of us.

By far, though, Chuckie and I were consistently closest. We played together (or she would entertain me) and we were temperamentally most similar among the Francis kids. She introduced me to sewing, knitting, drawing and other art forms. She shared in many of my successes. I remember a poster she helped me create for school where I needed to show a way to be safe from fire. My poster won me the top grade in my class. She also helped me to sound out themes from TV shows on the little chord organ. We learned to make each other laugh. If there was a bratty prank a young kid could pull on his older sister, Chuckie was my most frequently chosen victim (Faith would have cried and complained, right away, to Mom).

I had an air rifle that didn't have a designed projectile. It just made a sound as the slightly compressed air was released through the gun's barrel. If I first shoved the end of that barrel into the dirt, the plug of dirt would fly out with the released air blast. Chuckie liked to sunbathe and would slather baby oil on her exposed skin. I aimed the dirt-plugged air rifle into the sky directly above her and it rained dusty dirt onto her oil drenched skin. Oh, was she angry! I ran, but back then, Chuckie was faster. I paid for my dastardly deed – Chuckie would pin me down on the ground and tickle me until I couldn't catch my breath. I don't think she ever tattled to Mom about what I did. But she never forgot it, either.

If I had a bad dream, Chuckie was the first (and only) person I ran to. She was a fan of the soap opera *Dark Shadows* (1966–71) and to spend time with her, I would sit beside her on the sofa and watch it as well. That show was filled with ghosts and vampires. I remember one of these events quite vividly. Chuckie slept in the top bunk in another room and when that nightmare left me shaking and fighting for breath, I managed to make record time across the hall and up into her bed. Mom heard all the noise but was deaf to the legitimate concerns of a big sister and the frightened pleas of a little boy. Chuckie got a tongue lashing and I got a spanking while being ushered back to my bed. Needless to say, I wasn't allowed to watch *Dark Shadows* anymore. When I tried to watch from the hallway just outside the living room, she'd chase me out of the area. I'd then pull a fast one: with the way our house was built, I could (barely) reach the ceiling of the main floor by climbing up a few steps in the stairway to the upper floor and leaning forward with my body stretched out, and bracing myself on the ceiling where the hall met the stairwell, I would peer around the corner from way up high.

She'd sometimes pretend not to notice me, and I was able to watch some more *Dark Shadows*.

The two of us challenged our parents (in many different ways) to extremes. I often showed that I could out-do Mom. I tended to coast through school with little or no effort. She always had to work to accomplish anything. I once brought home a report card that was nearly all As. She got upset, saying, "How do you do this? You never bring home your books!" I would beat her at board games, and she would behave like a small child – often throwing a minor tantrum and stopping all play.

Chuckie was always incredibly popular – something Mom never was (she probably put on an air of superiority among her peers, so no one liked her). Mom wanted Chuckie to cut her hair short – she kept it long. She wanted Chuckie to be some sort of executive, so Chuckie proclaimed she wanted to be a hairdresser. Mom simply could not dictate Chuckie's actions and that frustrated her. They had two very different views of the world, and Chuckie was just as stubborn as Mom – and possibly more so. It essentially came down to her being jealous of us.

With Dad, a challenge from one of us was not something to denigrate or dismiss. I think we both respected him, and knew we could learn things from him. What we knew he could teach us was not the kind of stuff you'd find in a book. For instance: Dad and I restored a 1963 Pontiac Grand Prix together.

That iteration of the Grand Prix was based on the Pontiac Catalina body. I noticed that the taillight assembly on the Catalina was in the same location as a removable block on the Grand Prix body. When I suggested we could add the Catalina tail lights to the Grand Prix, and make it unique without any major body work, he said, "I don't know if you're right, but I'll see if I can get a pair of those, and we'll try it." They fit just fine, and he praised me (and bragged to his friends) for having thought about it.

To some who observed his behavior, it might have appeared that he favored Chuckie and me, which increased the resentment Mom seemed to hold against us. Our parents, being very different people, reacted to our challenges differently. With Dad, our world expanded. He never tried to influence us or impose his will on us. With Mom, we ended up frustrating her (more than the other three children) and we bore the lion's share of her wrath.

In our adult years, Chuckie told me that she knew she had been a bratty, defiant child and that she felt responsible for worsening the difficult relationship I had with Mom. In other words, by the time I was beginning to get into trouble with her, Mom thought she was adept in curbing my behavior because of her experiences with Chuckie. There may have been a degree of truth in this, but I never connected it in that way. I always laid the responsibility for the abuse solely on my mother.

Chuckie apologized for her part in the dynamic, but the closest to an apology I ever got from Mom was, "I did the best I could with you kids. You didn't come with an instruction manual."

Three

"Family dysfunction rolls down from generation to generation, like a fire in the woods, taking down everything in its path until one person in one generation has the courage to turn and face the flames."

—*Terry Real*

In late November of 1950 an iconic storm developed over the eastern United States. It packed hurricane-force winds, with gusts up to 108 mph, rainfall up to six inches and more than sixty inches of snow in West Virginia. It would come to be labeled "The Great Thanksgiving Day Storm," and it is almost always included in meteorologists' top ten lists of all-time greatest storms. It was responsible for the deaths of at least 383 people and caused widespread power outages, affecting twenty-two states. That storm's effects on Blackstone were not really felt until the following Friday. On that Thanksgiving Day, November 23rd, another major storm saw its beginning – but this was not the type of storm that meteorologists may have watched for. On that day my parents were married in St. Paul's Catholic Church. My mother was four months pregnant with their first child – my oldest sister Faith. Mom's sister Rose and my father's brother-in-law Arthur were the witnesses.

When a warm front collides with a cold front, meteorologists label the result an occluded front. In some cases, the cold overpowers the warm front, creating a cold occluded front. This occurrence can bring damaging storms, like that 1950 Thanksgiving Day storm. My mother was the more forceful partner in the marriage – she was the cold front. Dad was a contributing partner – the warm front. Their relationship was certainly stormy. To me, it was worthwhile investigating their pasts to try and make sense of the part of their relationship that I shared with them. I looked to their families for clues.

My father, Charlie, was born in 1928 to James (who turned sixty-eight years old that year) and Mabel (who was forty-one). Not a planned pregnancy, I'm sure. My best estimate as to when Grandpa Jim and Grandma Mabel were married (if they were married) is about 1913. There was a son, James, who was born in 1914 and only lived for about a year. Dad had two older sisters (Ruth and Helen) and an older half-brother (George – Mabel's son from another relationship). Jim died when my dad was just eight years old. Mabel died when he was not quite sixteen. With only his older sisters watching out for him, he got into trouble with the law. After being arrested (for probably the second time), he entered service in the U.S. Navy for the very last part of World War II. He was just seventeen years old.

My mother, Faith, was born in 1932, the result of at least the ninth pregnancy for her parents. She and her siblings were raised in abject poverty. Four of the siblings had died before I was born and a fifth (her sister Rita) died when I was quite young – before the time where I have any real memory. This left sisters Dottie, Rose, Mary, Shirley and brother Rene (the family pronounced his name "Rain'-nee") and their spouses as the extended family with whom I was most familiar. She was not the youngest but was easily the smallest in stature of all the siblings. She had jet-black hair and the irises in her eyes were so dark as to render the whites bluish. They remained so until late in her life. Both French and English were spoken in their childhood home because both of her parents had been born in Canada. Mom was always able to speak and understand that particular variation of the French language.

As both of my mother's parents were Quebecois (French-Canadian), by birth, they were "Memere" and "Pepere" to all their grandkids ("Mem-May and Pep-Pay" were the pronunciations we learned). Memere's name, given by her adoptive parents, was Maximillienne but she was baptized Rosanna. She was the only grandparent I ever knew. Pepere's given name was Guillaume (William or Bill were also used) and he was twelve years Memere's senior. They were married on 10 October 1916 – less than seven weeks after Memere's fifteenth birthday. Pepere was twenty-seven at the time. One reason (if not the only reason) for the marriage was to provide Pepere a means to avoid conscription into the Canadian Corps for service in WWI (his brother served and was killed in action).

My mother loathed her father. However, she apparently came by her personality issues honestly (as the saying goes). Later in her life, my mother self-published a memoir, of sorts. Reading this allowed me to discover just how much she was like him. If I had switched names and personal pronouns, the individual she described as her father could have been her. Pepere was a mean, exacting and vengeful man. He was also highly prone to drinking, which was one personal attribute that she eschewed. Mom would describe the old man's meanness while being totally oblivious to her own. I remember hearing, from her, one anecdote which involved the old codger strolling through the neighborhood, walking stick in hand. When he spied some kids playing in their own yard, he rapped their fence with his stick – for no reason other than to startle them. He was just that mean.

Other stories I heard over time describe a man with obsessive-compulsive tendencies. He always required a clean, white shirt and pressed trousers for himself. Although his children were in rough-looking hand-me-downs, he insisted upon looking neat and clean. He would remove nails from wood scraps found at construction sites, straighten the nails, and then divide them into coffee cans or jars according to their sizes. Then he then buried them in the backyard according to a matrix which could be accessed via a number of paces and in directions that only he knew. He also ensured his firewood was always cut to exactly the same length by measuring each piece.

Mom also recalled some of Pepere's positive traits. She would occasionally tell us how inventive he could be. One anecdote involved the family's radio. It simply would not work if they just manipulated the knobs and dials on the front. Pepere had somehow figured out that if he removed the innards from the case and re-inserted them – backwards – that he could make the radio work. She claimed he had apprenticed and trained to be a jeweler. That he could fix watches and clocks. All the positive stories included the caveat, "Of course, he could only do this when he wasn't drunk." It may have been that "Jack of all trades" talent he shared with Pepere that first attracted her to my dad.

Although Mom and Dad were married on the 23rd of November, my sisters and I had erroneously thought it was the 25th. One rainy day, when I was about seven years old, Chuckie, Faith and I were at the kitchen table looking at some of the wedding photos taken on that November day in 1950. I noticed dates printed in the border of the old black-and-white photos. They were all dated December 1, 1950. When

I asked what that date was for, Chuckie and Faith began giggling. When I asked why, Faith said to me:

"It takes nine months to have a baby."

Puzzled, I said, "So?"

She went on to say, "Mom and Dad were married on the twenty-fifth of November in 1950. Count forward nine months."

I did as she advised. I was still young and was a bit slow at this counting of months.

"...December twenty-fifth... January twenty-fifth..."

I kept going.

"June twenty-fifth... July twenty-fifth... August twenty-fifth. That's nine months,"

I proudly proclaimed. Chuckie could no longer hold in the laughter, and it made her snort. This made Faith laugh, too. What was I missing? I didn't think I had done it wrong and said so. Chuckie calmed down enough to tell me that I wasn't the reason they were laughing. Begging to be let in on the secret, I shook Faith's arm.

"What's so funny?" I asked.

Both knew I was good with remembering dates – even as a youngster. Chuckie asked, "When is Faith's birthday?"

"April twenty-fifth... Why is that funny?"

Chuckie continued, "April twenty-fifth of what year?"

I knew this answer and quickly blurted out, "1951."

The two teenagers burst out in another laughing fit. I was getting angry, now.

"WHAT???" I insisted.

This time Faith calmed down enough to have me go back over the dates. What was it Faith had said? "It takes nine months to have a baby."

"Nine months would have been Aug... wait a minute! How come you were born in only five months?" I asked Faith.

When she calmed down from yet another fit of laughter, she then tried to explain how that could have happened in a way a seven-year-old would understand, but without disclosing any salacious details. I wanted further explanations. I needed to know details, but the girls were done. They felt as though they had already told me more than they should have. To start shutting down the conversation, Chuckie said, "Don't say anything to Mom. She'll get really mad."

"Should I ask Dad how that happened?"

Both girls simultaneously and emphatically said, "No!"

I had just been let in on part of some strange little secret that they had obviously figured out some time ago. That was just mean, though. Letting me know part of something and then telling me that the only way for me to understand the rest wasn't allowed.

This would not do.

I was curious, but I had also learned early on how difficult my mother could be. Several years went by before I said anything to her about this "secret." I knew how it could happen, but I guess I wanted to know how she reconciled Faith's date of birth with her wedding date – considering her Catholic ideals. Both of my older sisters had moved out of the house by the time I finally confronted Mom about these inconsistent dates. I tried to be tactful when I confronted her with the math, but at eleven or twelve I had all the tact of a sledgehammer. Mom's family was Catholic and quite devout, so the idea that she had premarital relations ran counter to the beliefs she professed. I was pushing her to reveal that she was flawed.

Mom was quick to respond, though. She told me that the marriage "must have been in 1949" (it wasn't). She explained,

"The reason the photos show a 1950 date is because we waited to develop them. The camera place doesn't know – or care – when the pictures are taken.

35

They can only print the date they actually process the film. Faith was not conceived out of wedlock."

Now, I wasn't asking her to explain where babies come from. I was, however, asking about information she apparently felt was private. It was really none of my business. She didn't look at me when she was explaining all of this. I felt reasonably certain she was telling a fib.

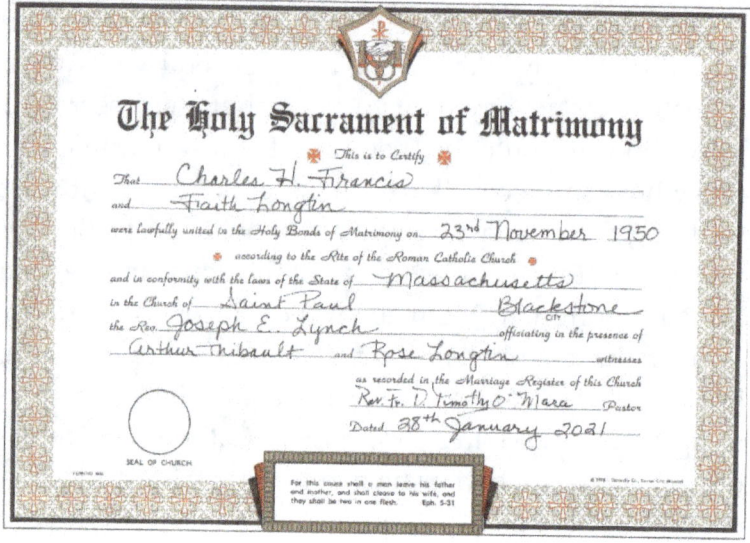

A copy of my parent's Wedding Certificate provided by St. Paul's Catholic Church. When I recently asked Faith about their wedding date, she responded "November 1949". Chuckie and I had understood the date to be November 25th. The records do not lie, though. Thanksgiving Day, 1950.

I was beginning to understand that my mother's unwavering need to be right every time was of utmost importance to her. Admitting that I learned this tendency from her is not easy for me. When I have recognized it, I have tried to accept that I can be wrong without that making me a bad person. The behavior was so ingrained, so much a part of me, that I have not always recognized when I was heading down that same path. All those years of severe reinforcement are difficult to ignore, at times.

I guess I've always compared. I have compared my parents to each other and to other parents. I've compared my sisters to each other. It seems a totally normal thing to do. When I was going through puberty, I once compared my hand size to that of a friend of the same age. I was sure my hands were bigger. Of course, he called me out. He said, "Prove it." We put our hands up, palm to palm. His fingers and thumb extended beyond mine. Defeated, but not willing to be wrong, I tried to reframe the comparison. I insisted that the comparison should be limited to the parts of our hand that were not fingers or thumb. I was acting as I had seen my mother act.

Four

"I've learned that people will forget what you said, people will forget what you did, but people will never forget how you made them feel."

—*Maya Angelou*

With Dad as the primary (and often the sole) breadwinner, it seemed he was often away from home, and this was true – most of the time. With the hours he worked (sometimes more than 16 hours a day) or with the distance he had to travel from home, he was often gone by the time I rose to go to school in the morning. He often arrived home late at night. Consequently, I had a lot of time to interact with Mom. This was not always bad.

Mom had grown up during the Great Depression. She was one of the three youngest siblings in a large Catholic family. Memere's adoptive parents were the LaRoses, who owned a "block house" in the Waterford neighborhood of Blackstone. Because of Pepere's affinity for drink, their housing was often in flux or in jeopardy. Eventually they moved into one of the apartments in the LaRoses' block house, and this is where she grew up.

Mom recorded a lot of anecdotes from her childhood in her 2004 book. She titled the book *Anecdotes from the Depression*. Among these anecdotes are stories about having to share beds with siblings and having to deal with chimney fires from the old wood stove, among many others. A considerable point of focus was on their poverty and their frequent lack of adequate food and clothing. One story she relayed to me when I was an adult (she did not write about this) had to do with hygiene. Mom was always insistent about our dental hygiene, but she had false teeth (uppers) as far back as I could remember. I once asked her about that, and her response was quite a story. She had often spoken of the vanity of her older sister Dottie. For reasons I do not remember, Mom said Dottie was the only sibling who had a toothbrush. Mom was relegated to disinfecting (in boiling water) Dottie's cast-off toothbrushes so that she could have one. Mom said her teeth suffered because of this. Her story concluded with, "So, Dottie's the only one of us who still has her own teeth."

She often poked fun at Dottie for her bridgework. As a kid, I didn't understand the reference, but as she continually mentioned Dottie's teeth and I heard these comments as an adult, I understood the reference as well as Mom's envy. There were several anecdotes, in the book, detailing her memories of her father, but kind words for him were mostly absent. Most of her fondest memories revolved around interactions with her mother, her siblings, and the kids in the neighborhood.

Mom was a superb student. She went to St. Paul's Catholic School through the 8th grade and then attended high school at the (now defunct) Blackstone High School. Once in the public-school system, she blossomed. It was not a physical blossoming – physically, she was referred to (sometimes by herself) as the runt of her family. I don't think she ever really passed the five-foot mark. Academically though, she was a giant. Recently, some of her report cards were put on display in the Blackstone Historical Society Museum. She had earned straight A's throughout high school and graduated as Valedictorian of the BHS Class of 1949. She was awarded the DAR (Daughters of the American Revolution) Good Citizen award that year.

Although the only one of the Longtin siblings to graduate from high school, and despite her doing so well in her academic pursuits, college eluded her. She met my father Charlie while she was still in high school. He was a good-looking young man with wavy auburn hair, bright blue eyes, and an infectious smile who had been in the Navy near the end of the Great War. Back then, he had tried to teach her to drive in his prized 1938 Packard. She had some difficulty and banged the car into a stone wall. When he brought her home that day, Pepere noticed the damage to the car's front passenger fender. He chastised my dad for trying to teach her to drive and told him to go inside. He then set about to fix the damage his daughter had caused to Dad's car. He used a whole lot of wax and elbow grease to soften the paint and then banged out the dented fender. Dad always said it looked "as good as new" after that.

Due, in part, to the poverty under which she had been raised, Mom developed a bitterness toward almost all aspects of her young life, but her resilience shone with the inventiveness and creativity born of all that negativity. For instance: she could always find a game or activity to keep us busy on particularly cold or wet afternoons when playing outdoors was not really an option. "Button, button… who's got the button?" was a game we often played under those conditions. She would go through her tin of buttons and come out with a large one. Threading cotton twine through the holes and tying it off in a loop of about a foot in diameter, she created a toy. After winding the button up (and twisting the string stretched between two small fingers), she would instruct us to pull our hands away from each other and the button would spin. With accordion-like movement, the button's spinning motion could be sustained for as long as the child's attention could be maintained.

Her memories of poverty also drove her to avoid returning to that financial state under any condition. To outside observers, we never showed any signs of deprivation. Mom did whatever she could to ensure that no one ever suspected we were going without, as she had. We were always clothed and fed. Dad did whatever he could to provide financial stability for the household. He adored Mom and was always complimentary toward her and her sisters. Mom ran the checkbook and tasked herself with getting the maximum for the minimum. She had to make whatever money Dad brought home go as far as possible. I can remember summertime Kool-Aid being diluted to the point where it tasted like slightly sweet water with no other flavor and just enough color to make it different. If she got low on milk, she'd mix up powdered milk for us (which tasted yucky). Thinly sliced luncheon meat between slices of white bread was a bit of a respite from the peanut butter and jelly sandwiches we usually took to school. She had learned the ways to mask poverty. We may have been dirt poor, at times, but she never let us feel the way she apparently had as a kid.

Mom was the driving force behind some very family-centric activities. She would instigate a Sunday family drive and thought it was important for our immediate family to eat together – at least once a week. We knew our extended family well because Mom ensured we had regular contact with them. We'd visit Memere and Aunt Mary (because she lived with Memere) on a regular basis. She encouraged playing board games and card games. She had a full-time job keeping us occupied, and for a majority of the time, she was successful. When she was not, skirmishes would break out and her role changed to that of referee and/or intermediary.

During the winter of 1966–67, I noticed Mom really putting on some weight. She was getting fat, and I said so. At seven years old, I was not wise in the ways of diplomacy, but Mom thought I was being funny or cute, and she laughed it off. She would be really tired a lot of the time, too. She spent more and more time on the sofa with a book in her hands. Someone may have told me, but the idea of pregnancy and its eventual outcome were lost on my wee little brain. Then, one spring day, we were left with just Chuckie and Faith babysitting Lori and me. Dad and Mom were gone. Faith continually tried to explain to me about Mom having another child. I didn't get it.

After a couple of days without Mom, Chuckie told me that Dad, who had been home with us outside his work hours, was going to bring her and the baby home. I remember the day very clearly. The baby was born on a Friday, and I think Mom brought her home on Sunday. Dad pulled our family car into the driveway, a white 1962 Chevy Nova II. Lori and I were at the kitchen window, peering out. Mom got out of the passenger side and was wearing a knee-length green woolen coat. She was remarkably slimmer than when I had last seen her. She had a bundle in her arms and as she came into the house, we were all agog. She uncovered the baby's face and I remember seeing a lot of black hair. We were all introduced to our new baby sister: Wendy. She was tiny and remained asleep during all this hubbub.

Not all of us got a turn holding our new sister. Faith was particularly enamored, and she was trusted to hold the new sibling without Mom's supervision. Chuckie was not. I remember being scared I would drop her, an anxiety apparently shared by Mom. I kind of held her, but Mom never fully released her grasp on the infant. I think Lori was made to sit down and was then allowed to hold Wendy without the helicopter oversight I had. Mom doted on her newest and was ever vigilant when it came to her being protective of that child. She was as tender towards her as any mother could be. As an adult, Chuckie remembered a similar show of tenderness when I was brought home. This was contrasted with Lori's arrival, when there was less of a fuss made. None of us ever really knew why Lori's arrival was different from that of Wendy or me. The next time any of us would see that degree of maternal tenderness was when her first grandchild, Faith's daughter Jennifer, came along four years later. The tenderness waned with subsequent grandchildren. While she was generally—and genuinely—fond of most infants and some toddlers, she was also not as loving toward others. She barely recognized the existence of Chuckie's son. When her youngest grandchild, Brendan, came along, she was mostly hands-off. She was, however, taken by surprise when he put his arms out to greet her at their very first meeting. He was eleven months old.

Mom tried to keep herself fit in many different ways. She was fond of walking. I can remember, from about the time I was five or six years old, I would sometimes go for walks with her and sometimes Lori would go, as well. Mom would try to explain the varying things we'd find about which we would question her. She was a bit of a loner, though, and she preferred to walk alone. At the same time, I remember watching as she tuned in to watch Jack LaLanne on television. She'd go through all the exercises he'd describe and demonstrate, while standing in front of the television in the living room. Along with exercise, Jack LaLanne also promoted good nutrition. She bought vitamins and supplements which she occasionally shared with us.

Outside Jack LaLanne's TV program, I remember Mom regularly visiting the local YMCA. There, she swam and played volleyball. The Y (by which it was most often referred) also gave her the opportunity to participate in a favorite activity: singing. Although not formally trained, Mom could carry a tune and could often be caught singing along with a favorite crooner on the radio or on the record player. She joined a choral group at the Y. They would sing at nursing homes and go Christmas caroling. (She even let Chuckie go with her a few times, as she was old enough and interested enough in singing.) We were encouraged to sing along with Christmas records. I remember her being enamored of certain Broadway musicals, and she had several original cast recordings (*South Pacific, Camelot, The Music Man, Hello Dolly!* and *My Fair Lady* were all represented in her music library). She bought a boxed set of Beethoven's nine symphonies (Joseph Krips / London Symphony Orchestra) that became my gateway to the world of classical music. Whether intentional or not, Mom opened my mind to music.

Reading was another favorite pastime for Mom. She read novels and history. She fostered a love of reading in all of us. Our house was built with a fireplace in the living room. On either side of the fireplace were bookshelves on which she kept many books. Among them was a three-volume, leather-bound set of *A Thousand and One Tales* (*The Arabian Nights*) that had been printed in 1865. The set was a gift to my mother, from a family friend named Earl Wheelock, on the occasion of my birth. Both Chuckie and I read these books at every opportunity. Mom had also purchased a 1966 set of *The Encyclopaedia Britannica* that most of us used for school. I used to just take down a random volume from the shelf and search through it to see what there was to learn. Mom's love of books and learning, in general, was infectious—for some of us, anyway. I never really knew Faith to consider reading as recreational, and Lori seemed to have no interest at all.

For a time when I was eight or maybe nine years old, Mom dabbled in local politics. She got herself elected or appointed to the Blackstone Parks and Recreation Committee. While executing the duties associated with that committee, she secured funding to install a set of monkey bars at Roosevelt Park, behind the Town Hall. She and Dad and I assembled them, setting the feet in concrete. I'm sure I wasn't too much help because I wanted to climb on them. (If I remember correctly, Lori also played on them while we were putting them together.)

As a young person, I was incredibly impressed with and curious about the world around me. I think Mom saw this and genuinely attempted to foster my curiosity. I would pester her for books or tools that might help me to increase my knowledge of our surroundings and of our place in the universe. Some of those things, like a microscope or my own tape recorder, she refused, but there were a few tools she did give me with which I could—and did—learn more. She (reluctantly) gave me a chemistry set, which Dad augmented with stuff from the textile mill's dye mixing lab. She was afraid I'd cause a house fire or create something toxic, so there were a lot of conditions and caveats to my use of the chemistry set. She got me a kit that allowed me to build a weather station (she also included a weather balloon that she must have purchased separately). I think the tool she gave me (after a lot of haranguing) that I found to be the most educational was a telescope. It was not a terribly powerful one, but it allowed me to see some of the surface features of the moon. What made this even more fun, useful, and educational was a subscription to *Scientific American* magazine. On the back cover of the magazine, each month, was a region-specific sky map. Mom would take me out to the front yard after sundown, and we'd try to find and point out the visible planets and constellations. We would take turns looking through the telescope. Each month, with the arrival of the magazine, we'd have a unique view of the heavens, and I gained a better understanding of the cosmos. It was always a disappointment if the skies were cloudy on the night the magazine arrived, but we usually made up the session on the next clear night. Each monthly front yard session was a rare moment shared solely between her and me.

When I was around nine, Mom decided she wanted (or needed) to return to the workforce. To do so meant doing something she had never successfully done before: driving a car. She began with driving lessons from Dad. The first time she took the exam, she failed. Apparently, the officer conducting her exam was not impressed by her just slowing down and rolling through a stop sign. It was not her fault, she proclaimed, because Dad never said not to do that. Nevertheless, she persevered and got her license. Afterward, she carted us all over, and I'm sure Dad was relieved to no longer be the sole licensed driver. That same year Dad bought a new Ford F-250 four-wheel-drive pickup truck. Mom hadn't driven any vehicle with a manual shift since the single attempt with the 1938 Packard. The truck had a three-speed transmission with a compound low gear that Dad called a "Granny Low." The truck was delivered to our driveway while Dad was at work. Mom decided she would go check it out. She put the key in the ignition and turned it... the truck had been left in gear, and it lurched forward as the starter engaged. It frightened her, and she never tried that again.

When I was about ten or eleven years old, and our high school marching band began to grow, the music teacher encouraged parents to form a Band Booster Association. Mom volunteered and took on some accounting duties. People within the organization got to know her and, truth be told, saw a very different person than her family saw. They saw a friendly, competent mother of five—a person dedicated to the success of the band. She didn't drink or smoke and did not socialize. She didn't follow sports. The Band Boosters represented almost the only social outlet she had. She did a little sewing and attempted other craft projects. I really don't know if she maintained any outlets for self-care.

All of this would make Mom appear to be a semi-normal suburban mother/housewife from the '50s, '60s, and '70s. While it was a part of who she was, it was not this person with whom her husband and children interacted. It was as if there was some dark veil between our home and the rest of the world.

Silence from perpetrators, witnesses, and victims creates and perpetuates the hidden nature of abuse. Later in life, shame and embarrassment play their part in keeping the abuse a secret. At the time, we all believed that the way we were treated, at home, was the same as other children were treated in their homes by their parents, although this was not the case. Even today, I have a hard time recalling the positive qualities about my mother because my memories primarily involve how badly she made me feel. That over-arching feeling mostly obscures my memories of the better parts of my upbringing.

Five

"Even a dog knows the difference between being kicked or tripped over."

—*Justice Oliver Wendell Holmes, Jr.*

Without boundaries, we can have little or no focus. Boundaries may be physical, like fences, walls, doors, and a roof. They may also be invisible constructs, such as time. Like other children, I learned about the world around me by experimentation, exploration, and testing boundaries—both physical and constructed. My parents (mostly Mom) constructed the boundaries and the rules to which I was subjected. Whether I felt they were just or not, I had to abide by these limits or face the brutal consequences. Decades later, when I became a parent, I considered the rules I put in place for my son as a means to help keep him safe while he learned to be a functioning human. Whether designed for the child's safety or for capricious and arbitrary reasons, rules and boundaries still define the limits of any child's world. Here's another area where Chuckie and I were like each other and not like our siblings. They mostly stopped testing boundaries—Chuckie and I did not. The possible exception was Lori. Lori tested, but seldom experienced the reinforcement of boundaries the rest of us did. Her experience was different.

One afternoon, while we were raking leaves in the backyard, I heard Lori saying to Mom that something "sucked." It wasn't a foreign adjective to me, as I heard the phrase used regularly when at school. I figured (at the time) this meant it was an acceptable means to describe a less-than-positive situation. Shortly afterward, I tested the water by repeating the same phrase. Mom dropped her rake and quickly moved toward me. She reached out, grabbed me by the earlobe, and marched me into the house, where she proceeded to wash my mouth out with soap while simultaneously lecturing me about inappropriate language. I tried to argue that Lori had used the exact same phrase just moments before I uttered it. There was no explanation and no backing down. The boundary was different for Lori than it was for me. I never figured out how to consistently tell when the boundaries varied—and by how much.

In our household, discipline was administered inconsistently, disproportionately, inequitably, and often harshly. How we were punished, for what, and to what degree could never be truly predicted. The only predictable aspect for me, at least, was that I could (and should) expect to be punished. As a result, discipline was not effective, and my respect for my mother waned. Sure, I was scared to do anything wrong. The problem I grappled with came to be: what is wrong... what is right... and when? There were times I did things and got away with them right under her nose—like going into the garden, picking and eating a strawberry right in front of her. Other times, similar behavior drew blood—like going into the garden for a couple of fresh green beans and receiving a fist (aimed at my ear, I think) in the nose. Because the severity of punishments was inconsistent and, especially in retrospect, highly inequitable, I began looking for some reason or pattern or circumstance that would help to explain my experience. I was having a lot of difficulty making sense of the so-called discipline I experienced early in my life until I broadened the scope of my observations.

With the difference in Faith's and Chuckie's ages being almost exactly a year, and with them both being teenaged girls, I expected they would be treated similarly. Mom would often buy them the exact items of clothing from a travelling salesman named Joe Rowe—dresses, corduroy pants, blouses—all the same or very similar. Since they were essentially the same size and the clothing was so similar, mistakes were bound to happen. It didn't seem to matter who was complaining or which one of them might have the other's item in hand. Mom would pretty consistently take Faith's side, giving Chuckie a tongue-lashing and sometimes physically punishing her or even grounding her. I don't recall Faith getting the same degree of discipline—ever. There was no realistic, consistent enforcement of boundaries that any of us could predict. The only pattern here seemed to be that Mom had pre-decided that one of us was nearly always wrong and the other was nearly always the victim, with little attention given to the truth.

Our extended family seemed to know to be cautious. Before visiting our house, my cousins would be warned:

"You're going to visit your Aunt Faith. You know how strict she is—you need to be on your best behavior."

I never saw her hit any of my cousins, but during a family cookout hosted at our house when I was around eleven or twelve, I did see her grab the earlobe of one of my older cousins and drag him across the yard. I remember feeling embarrassed. I was embarrassed because she was my mother, but I knew I didn't have any degree of control over what was happening. I felt his pain, though.

Through some of the experiences of myself and Chuckie, I began to see some semblance of a pattern. This pattern was one of prejudgment—and sometimes, discipline crossing the line into abuse. Parents are not the only ones who create constructs—children create constructs of their own. Child abuse relates directly to the meanings assigned to the constructs of justice and injustice. The inequity in the administration of discipline in my youth has given me an exaggerated awareness, as an adult, when it comes to right and wrong, fair and unfair. The variability in the severity of punishments doled out by my mother has made me hypersensitive about fairness as an adult. My adult sense of justice became skewed because of the injustices I suffered as a kid. Abuse absolutely changes a person—and that change is irreversible.

The acts of violence in our house were myriad. It may have been generational, and corporal punishment may have been more socially acceptable in the 1960s and 1970s, but as we later learned, it truly was considerably worse in our household than it was in others. I can remember the feeling that my ear was going to be separated from my head and end up in my mother's hand on more than one occasion. There were times when a tiny tear appeared at the point of connection between the lobe and the side of my face, bleeding ever so slightly. I was grateful my hair was cut short as a youngster, because I had seen my mother physically dragging a couple of my sisters around using a fistful of their hair. Her hair being mostly straight, I don't think she understood the challenges of grooming the curly hair most of us inherited from Dad. Chuckie described (and I saw this also with Lori) my mother getting frustrated with her squirming due to the discomfort of having knotted hair caught in and pulled by a hairbrush. Mom would try to correct the squirming behavior by hitting her victim on the head with the hairbrush. On multiple occasions, she hit with sufficient force to break the brush. Further punishment was sure to ensue because it was obviously Chuckie's (or Lori's) fault that the brush now needed replacement.

Mom was usually very careful not to leave visible injuries. She rarely made contact above the shoulders. This told me that somewhere deep inside her, she knew that what she was doing was wrong. It was not socially acceptable—even then. Because my hair was kept short, I was mostly spared headshots. When I was older and allowed to grow my hair longer, a ruler or a toy taken up as a weapon might find its mark on the back of my head. I frequently caught a balled-up fist on the ear. When I once described that form of punishment as "boxing my ears," she quickly corrected me. She stated that if she had boxed my ear, it would have been with an open palm, and I would have experienced excruciating pain. Didn't the fist cause excruciating pain?

I remember one occasion when I was about ten years old, where Chuckie had somehow crossed the ever-moving and invisible line Mom had established between behaviors that were "barely acceptable" and those she considered "wrong." Mom was red-faced and screaming at Chuckie, who had backed up as far as she was able by standing against the kitchen wall beside the back door. In an instant, the situation escalated. Mom had wound up and had her arm fully extended out to her side. She then brought it around in an open-handed roundhouse slap, leaving a red imprint of her right hand on Chuckie's left cheek. There was a loud smack followed by a dull thud as Chuckie's head struck the wall. Suddenly, there were no other sounds. People will often describe silence as hearing nothing but crickets. This was even quieter than that. It was as if time took a pause and nothing else happened for what seemed like an eternity, although I'm sure it was mere seconds.

That slap had almost knocked Chuckie unconscious, and she began to slowly slide down the wall behind her, dazed. Mom lifted her back up by the collar on her clothing, grabbing and pulling hair along with the clothes. I thought she was going for the knockout punch, but she ultimately just yelled some more and shoved Chuckie, who found her way out the door. I had been crouched on the stairs off the hallway, terrified by what I was witnessing. Chuckie and Mom were close to the same size, but in that moment, Mom's bullying behavior made my sister seem small... so very small.

Chuckie ran into the woods to cry and hide until it was nearly dark outside. Upon her return, neither she nor Mom spoke a word. Chuckie said it was the hardest Mom had ever hit her. She thought Mom had some sense of guilt when she saw that Chuckie's cheek still bore the red imprint of her hand upon her return from the woods some hours later. Nothing more about the incident was ever said. To this day, Chuckie cannot remember what provoked it—but the violence is remembered. If ever proof was needed against the efficacy of corporal punishment, this incident stands as a prime example. What did all that physical violence accomplish?

Maybe a year after that altercation, when I was about eleven, Chuckie was subjected to another gruesome, disgusting, and deranged punishment. Faith, Lori, and I all witnessed this episode. We were all assigned weekly chores. They rotated, too, so none of us got complacent or burned out on any one task. It also helped to avoid complaints of favoritism. One sibling was assigned to wash dishes, another to dry. One was assigned to take out the garbage (food scraps) and the trash (paper, cardboard, cans) on a nightly basis. (The two youngest were not yet part of this rotation.) The trash was collected in a brown paper grocery bag, with the top folded over to make a lip. This helped keep the bag open. It was kept under the sink. The garbage was kept on the counter. Mom had a dark greenish-blue, triangular rubber container about one and a half inches deep, which she would line with a piece of waxed paper. She deposited eggshells, kitchen scraps, and coffee grounds into this container. We collected it separately because Mr. Zarichny came by once a week and gathered that stuff to feed his pigs. We would each do our assigned task for the week, then rotate to a new one. Switching midweek was not allowed, even with both parties in agreement.

Faith and I were on dishes that week, and Chuckie was on garbage and trash duty. Chuckie had failed to take out the garbage after dinner two nights in a row. As a not-so-subtle reminder, Mom threatened to make her eat it if she forgot again. Innocently enough, she did. The following morning at breakfast, Mom set our places at the table, but instead of a cereal bowl, she set the garbage container in Chuckie's place. Once we were all seated, Mom came up behind her, pulled her head back by her hair, and force-fed her the garbage. She mercilessly shoved handfuls of coffee grounds and eggshells—mixed with tears—into Chuckie's mouth. There was no other breakfast for her. Chuckie had to go to school with her morning meal consisting only of the bits of garbage she had unwillingly ingested. Of course, Mom didn't want anyone outside the home to know, so Chuckie was directed to wash her face before heading off to school. I had no appetite after that and asked if I could skip breakfast. Mom had no sympathy for Chuckie, and none of the rest of us could either. Request denied.

In 1966, the year after we moved to our new home, Chuckie was fourteen years old and growing more rebellious with every beating and every restriction. It seemed to be inversely proportional— the more Mom tried to dampen Chuckie's enthusiasm for life, the more Chuckie resisted, pushing buttons and defying rules. For some reason long forgotten, Mom had grounded her (once again). With only a few days of her punishment remaining, Faith knew Chuckie was chomping at the bit to be free again and hatched a plan. She needed some new stockings but was too lazy to go into town to get them herself. With a promise to keep it secret and a little extra cash as a bribe, she convinced Chuckie to go.

Waiting until both Mom and Dad were out of the house, Chuckie took her bike and headed down the road. Along the way, she was attacked and bitten by a neighbor's German Shepherd named Butch. He was usually chained up, but unluckily for Chuckie, he was loose that day. Butch sank his canines deep into her left thigh. I can remember those marks on her leg—four circular scars that intrigued me years after the event. Luckily for her, our next-door neighbor Mr. Robinson happened to be driving by at that very moment. He grabbed a shovel from the back of his car and whacked the dog to get him off Chuckie, then picked her up and rushed her to the hospital. It was not the last time he would perform this kind of role for our family.

Once Faith learned that Chuckie was in the ER, she quickly and totally reneged on her promise and gleefully informed Mom that Chuckie was out on her bike. Faith lied and claimed it was despite her efforts to keep Chuckie confined. Mom was furious. She and Dad went to the hospital, but Dad was not allowed to utter a word. Chuckie later said, "I figured she must have lectured him before they even came in and threatened him within an inch of his life."

Mom threw such a tantrum that she came very close to being physically removed from the premises. She was telling the doctors she could take care of Chuckie at home—that she didn't need to be there. She cursed up a storm at Chuckie for having broken her grounding. Chuckie tried to tell her that she was doing Faith a favor and then got smacked for lying. Needless to say, Faith may have gotten some satisfaction from seeing Chuckie punished (they were always at odds with each other), but she was out both her bribe money and the money for the stockings. Chuckie kept Faith's money, figuring she had gotten her just desserts for being a snitch, and now she had to go get her stockings herself.

Mom continued to threaten Chuckie with all sorts of additional punishments when a doctor tried to intervene. He was told, in no uncertain terms, where he could go. She even tried to take Chuckie out without her being treated. (In today's healthcare system, if a mother reacted that way to a child, that parent would be removed, and Child Protective Services would be contacted.) The wounds required stitches, and she likely was prescribed antibiotics— Mom couldn't have provided that kind of care. What she could (and did) do was to ground Chuckie for another three months with no TV and no telephone privileges. Rather than nurture her daughter in an hour of need, she belittled, embarrassed, and further punished her.

Chuckie had a kind of last laugh in this situation. Mom had already signed her up (and paid) for Girl Scout camp, which started soon after. Mom's sister Mary was the assigned chaperone, so Mom felt reasonably assured that Chuckie would not enjoy the camp. This assumption was wrong. The whole idea of Girl Scout Camp was for all the girls to have fun. If Mom had tried to get Aunt Mary to single Chuckie out, it would have been too obvious. With no children of her own, Aunt Mary often took us to events outside the home. I suspect she did it not only to help her sister—relieving her of the burden of caring for a child or two—but also because she genuinely seemed to enjoy seeing us have fun. She was stern, but not mean. Aside from not being allowed to swim in the lake because of her wounds and having latrine duty for the majority of her time at camp, Chuckie had a lot of fun over those two weeks. How could she not? She was away from Mom.

Six

*"Children should not be burdened with making us, happy, nor blamed
for making us sad or angry.
Children are not responsible for how we feel. We are."*

—*Larissa Dann*

During her early teens, Chuckie had repeatedly asked to use Mom's sewing machine, only to be met with denial, threats, and belittlement. Dad, who had witnessed this cycle too many times, saw her growing disappointment and frustration. He decided she needed a sewing machine of her own. While working a second job at the Singer company to supplement his mill income, he managed to get Chuckie a used machine and, in doing so, set her on the path to becoming the textile artist she is today.

I'm sure she felt special—perhaps even more so because Mom became jealous. It wasn't that Chuckie's machine was newer or better (it was neither); it was that it was equivalent. That fact alone seemed to offend Mom. She had lost the power to limit Chuckie's learning of the craft, even if she could still control access to her own machine.

Chuckie began sewing gifts for others and making her own clothes. I still remember a set of suspender shorts she made for my Teddy bear from some blue, grey, and black plaid material. Mom was offended. She had been the only person in the house who could sew, and now that identity was threatened. But Dad had made it clear: the sewing machine belonged to Chuckie.

Chuckie's skills quickly surpassed Mom's, but that didn't stop Mom from trying to exert control. She threatened to withhold the machine as punishment. Though it was heavy and not easy to move or hide, Mom found a way. The foot pedal was detachable— and she began removing it, rendering the machine unusable. I remember Dad stepping in at one point and saying the machine was Chuckie's, not hers, and that the foot pedal needed to be returned. I don't recall exactly how that played out, but when I asked Chuckie years later, she said Mom refused to give it back outright. Instead, she reduced the punishment— from two weeks without the pedal to two days. She needed to save face. To return it immediately would have been to admit she was wrong.

Mom was frugal—painfully so. I understand that her poverty-stricken childhood likely shaped this, driving her to avoid wasting anything, especially food. But woe to the child who didn't like what was served. In our household, Dad loved liver, Chuckie mostly did, and Mom tolerated it. The rest of us despised it. I gagged every time and looked for any way — short of swallowing — to get rid of it.

Mom didn't tolerate complaints. If we forced ourselves to vomit to avoid eating something, she would threaten us with having to eat our own vomit. (To her credit — or maybe to our relief — I never saw her carry out this particular threat.) If we didn't like what was on our plate, we had to sit at the table until we did. Depending on the meal, one or more of us might be stuck there an hour or more after everyone else had gone, staring at cold, congealed leftovers we still refused to eat.

To this day, I go out of my way to avoid vomiting — regardless of the reason. Maybe that habit traces back to those childhood threats.

Steak was another ordeal. The way Mom cooked it, you needed a serrated knife just to make a dent. She'd fry it so long and so hard that cutting it left dust — sawdust — on the plate. I called it steakdust. It may sound like a cliché, but her steak was exactly like leather.

Then there was the cereal saga. In the 1960s and '70s, some cereals included a toy in the box. I once wanted a toy that came in boxes of Count Chocula. I'd never tried the cereal before, but once I did, I realized I hated it. That didn't matter. I had to eat it every morning until the box was empty. Lori liked the cereal and offered to eat it instead, but Mom said, "You wanted it. You will eat it."

Lesson learned. I stuck with what I knew after that. Even now, as an adult, I order the same thing every time I visit a restaurant—something familiar, something safe.

Seven

*"If you are silent about your pain,
they'll kill you and say you enjoyed it."*

—Zora Neale Hurston

Consciously or not, Mom was an expert at inducing stress. Kneeling in a corner for hours was stressful. Watching my older sister get force-fed garbage or beaten to the brink of unconsciousness was definitely stressful. The constant fear of being beaten myself, the confusion of never fully understanding the rules or boundaries to avoid punishment, the relentless tension of listening to Mom and Dad fight—these were all stressors. And the common denominator was always our mother.

Her ability to impose psychological pressure on her children was as damaging as the physical punishments she inflicted. Stress didn't leave visible bruises, but it left its own kind of scars. And emotional pain, unlike broken skin or a black eye, didn't scab over and fade—it lingered. My mother also weaponized embarrassment, humiliation, and public mortification as part of her parenting strategy. Often, I felt she hated me.

What had I done to deserve that kind of treatment from the woman who gave birth to me? Even the act of being born came with condemnation, as though I had chosen my birth weight or the timing of my arrival.

Years later, when I was an adult living on the opposite side of the country, I called Mom with exciting news—my son had just been born. Brendan, her youngest grandchild, had arrived. When I called to share the moment, I told her:

"He weighed nine pounds, six ounces—just like me."

Her response came sharp and immediate:

"You weighed nine pounds, six and a *half* ounces!"

It wasn't a correction—it was a retort. Her tone was biting, like she couldn't resist the urge to assert herself even in that moment. She couldn't be outdone.

If we used a word or phrase Mom didn't approve of, we might have our mouths washed out with soap. And while many children of that generation endured that punishment, Mom's version was something else entirely. Her method was violent—often leading to split lips, injured tongues, or scraped cheeks. I'm surprised she never broke our teeth with how aggressively she shoved the bar of soap in and out of our mouths.

Lori, in her own clever way, once tried to reclaim control over the punishment. After saying something Mom deemed inappropriate, she was ordered to the bathroom to retrieve the bar of soap. She came back to the kitchen with an unused bar of green Lux soap, stopped just out of Mom's reach, took a massive bite out of it, chewed, swallowed, and said, "See? I *like* to eat soap!"

For that, she got slapped.

Induced stress wasn't incidental—it was another weapon in Mom's arsenal. Promises were never reliable. There were always caveats, many of them undisclosed. A deal might sound clear, like "If you do the dishes all week, you can go to the movies on Saturday." But come Saturday, she'd change the terms: "I had to remind you on Tuesday, so that doesn't count."

As we got older—especially me—the punishments evolved. What once was a swat on the bottom became a strike with a weapon. Kneeling in a corner, being grounded for long stretches, losing privileges—these were common. But under Mom's hand, these typical forms of discipline became prolonged and extreme. She took away television, telephone access, bicycles, toys, favorite activities— and she kept them for weeks or even months.

What made it worse was the inconsistency. The goalposts were always moving. The same action could earn a slap one day and be ignored the next. Siblings were rarely punished equally for the same offense. We never knew what might spark her anger or how severe the fallout would be. The volatility made everything feel unsafe.

I could have learned to accept it, to resign myself to the hopelessness of the situation—but I didn't. More often than not, the unpredictability and injustice made me want to fight back.

Eight

"Crying is how your heart speaks when your lips can't explain the pain you feel."

—*Ankita*

A slap was not a spanking, and spankings were not always beatings. Slaps were usually one-off—quick, sharp, and over. Spankings lasted longer. Beatings were worse still: more prolonged, more brutal, and often involved a weapon. I'm not exactly sure how old I was when I got my first real "spanking," though I'd guess around five or six. Most of the spankings I received quickly escalated into rabid, furious beatings. Sometimes it seemed her rage only grew mid-punishment, intensifying the pain without truly satisfying her need to vent whatever fury she was carrying.

Chuckie has said she had similar experiences. Like most of the discipline I endured, I don't remember the supposed offenses—but I remember the beatings. They became so frequent and so expected that we only learned to adapt our reactions. Faith would start crying even before the first strike. Lori did too, but she often flailed her arms around like a makeshift shield, as if to slow or deflect the blows. Chuckie and I responded differently—we resisted the urge to react at all. That might be why we got it the worst. Our stillness probably read as defiance.

To add insult to injury, Mom didn't hesitate to embarrass me publicly. A slap on the butt wasn't nearly as effective, in her view, as coupling it with humiliation. She would pull down my pants in public and "warm my bottom," as she put it. I remember one school event—probably when I was nine or ten— where she did just that in front of some classmates. I don't remember what I had done wrong, but they all saw the violence, the tears, and my bare backside. I never saw her do that to Lori, but I do know Lori witnessed, on more than one occasion, my public bare-bottom spankings.

Even the *threat* of that kind of punishment became its own form of control. The possibility of humiliation was its own shadow looming over everything.

Nine

*"That feeling you get in your stomach when
you get rejected is like all the butterflies just died."*

— *Unknown*

I remember, when I was just six years old, trying to appease my mother's malevolent tendencies by bringing her bouquets of flowers I'd picked from our backyard and the woods. One day, during our first summer in the new house, I ventured deep into the forest behind it. The fiddlehead ferns were just beginning to emerge from the humus, and I remember being creeped out by their curled shapes. Near the bed of a small, seasonal stream, I found a cluster of beautiful, sweet-smelling, unusually shaped blossoms. I picked six or seven of them and began the uphill trek back to the house, clutching them tightly in my small fist.

Later, I learned they were called "Lady Slippers"—a wild variety of orchid.

When I reached the house, I quietly stepped into the kitchen, carefully hiding the bouquet behind my back. Mom stood at the counter with her back to me. I said softly:

"I have a surprise for you."

She turned toward me with a scowl. Her mouth didn't smile or frown—it simply flattened, expressionless. Her plucked eyebrows arched over a furrowed brow, and her dark eyes held no emotion. I froze, staring.

"What is it, Brian? I'm busy."

Jolted from my trance, I proudly presented the delicate flowers.

"Flowers! For you!" I said excitedly, holding them out.

"Brian! Those are illegal to pick. Don't ever pick those again!"

There was no "thank you." No warmth. No kind words. Chastisement was my only reward. Still, despite receiving no smile, no hug, no appreciation of any kind, I kept trying. I brought her different types of flowers each time. In my childish mind, I thought I had simply picked the wrong kind.

We had some bearded irises growing in the front yard. When they bloomed, I picked some for her. I got slapped. More rejection followed when I offered her tiger lilies. Then came the lilacs. We had a bush in front of the house, but the woody stems were tough to snap, so Chuckie helped me. We were both punished.

"You should have known better," Mom scolded her. Chuckie was older, after all.

The punishment didn't end there. That spring turned into a long-term reminder. The lilac bush rarely bloomed again after that. For years afterward, Mom never missed a chance to remind me that my picking the flowers was why the lilac had stopped blossoming. Her words turned into emotional punishment.

As a child, I believed that anything colorful counted as a flower. So I brought her skunk cabbage, blackberry blossoms, milkweed, violets—even dandelions. Sometimes, my bouquets made it into a jelly jar with a little water. Usually, they disappeared quickly. Other times, they never made it to the jar at all—I'd be chastised or punished before that could happen.

I remember once she asked me why I kept giving her flowers.

Caught off guard, I replied, "Because you're pretty."

I didn't actually believe it, and maybe she sensed that. Her response?

"Oh."

Eventually, I gave up. I never picked lady slipper orchids again.

Ten

"*The places of childhood are always etched on the memory with great power and clarity.*"

—*Jill Ker Conway*

When we moved into the new house on Blackstone Street in the fall of 1965, the two upstairs rooms weren't finished. Both still had exposed studs and rafters, with foil-backed insulation visible between them. The floors were nothing more than planks laid across the joists. One of those rooms was intended to be the master bedroom. It was slightly larger and sat above the living room. For reasons no one seems to remember, my two older sisters were made to share the smaller room, while I—alone—was given the larger one. My parents chose a smaller, finished room downstairs, likely for the sake of completed walls, ceilings, and flooring.

I remember being quite excited. My room was, in reality, the largest in the house. I loved the space— but I quickly learned to dread bedtime.

For the first few years, I slept on an aluminum cot with a foam rubber mattress. It creaked loudly when I so much as rolled over. Because my room was directly over the living room and the floors were bare planks, every shift or squeak echoed below. If Mom was watching TV—which she usually was—any sound from my bed would prompt her to yell, "Go to sleep!" A second noise might earn a harsher warning—or even a spanking. If there was a third creak? That meant a full beating.

The springs and foam mattress gave under me, and being positioned on my stomach for the spanking meant each hit forced my body down into the bed. I was a scrawny child, and I remember how each blow seemed to bend my back unnaturally. My face would press deeper into the old chicken-feather pillow Pepere had made, and it became hard to breathe. Like a swimmer, I had to time my breaths for the upstroke. Sometimes it was just a few smacks; other times, the spanking dragged on. That was the punishment for moving in bed. If I was caught getting *out* of bed— well, you can imagine the consequences.

In 1969, our family dynamic shifted. Faith graduated from high school, worked that summer at a bakery, and then left for nursing school. With her departure, Lori moved into the upstairs room with Chuckie, and Wendy got the downstairs room to herself. That fall, I finally got a real bed. I hadn't minded the cot before; I had no comparison. But now I had a proper bed—with box springs and a twin mattress—which, unfortunately, also creaked. The added cushioning gave me a little more grace, but the beatings didn't stop.

Dad knew about them. Sometimes, after Mom gave her first warning, he would call out a softer one himself. I thought he was just siding with her. But later, I realized he was buying me one more chance to stay safe. The expression about "thin walls" applied more to floors in that house—I could always hear when people were talking in the room below, even if I couldn't make out the exact words. And I could always tell who was speaking.

One night, when I was about ten, I moved in bed and heard Mom call out my name: "Brian!" Then I heard Dad's voice take over the conversation. A few minutes later, the stairwell light clicked on, and I heard his heavy footsteps on the stairs. He had never hit me before, but in that moment, I was terrified.

His shadow appeared at the top of the stairs, and I watched as he rounded the corner and stepped into my room. Backlit by the stairwell light, I could tell it was him, though I couldn't see his face. He spoke softly in the darkness, telling me I needed to stay still and be quiet. Then he sat on the edge of my little bed, leaned close, and whispered:

"Now cry like I'm hitting you."

He began to slap the side of the mattress with his big paw. I caught on instantly, crying out in pretend pain.

Three... four... five slaps.

Then he whispered again. "This is the only time I can do this. Don't ever tell anyone."

He winked and, in a louder, firm voice said, "Now go to sleep."

Loud enough for Mom to hear.

Eleven

"Never look down on anybody unless you're helping him up."

—Jesse Jackson

Dad often kept a slew of cars in various states of repair in our backyard. Some were long-term projects, others were there just for parts. Over the years at our Blackstone Street address, I saw as few as three or four behind the workshop—and at one point, as many as thirty-two. I would often sit for hours in one of those cars, pretending to drive. It was a mix of my love for solitary play, my dad's passion for cars, and my vivid imagination. By age seven or eight, I already understood the basics of shifting gears and recognized how engine RPMs changed when upshifting or downshifting. Every Matchbox car I owned had its own soundtrack. When Mom overheard the sounds I made during play, she thought I was pretending there were endless gears. I tried explaining that it wasn't about quantity—it was about the transition between gears. But she didn't get it.

As I got older and could grasp more technical concepts, Dad taught me the differences between gasoline and diesel engines. He even explained the various types of diesel engines used in different vehicles. A Mack truck, for instance, might have a Mack diesel, or it could be fitted with a Caterpillar, Cummins, or Detroit diesel. By age ten, I could tell the difference by ear between a Detroit diesel and a Cummins or Caterpillar. The Detroit diesel had a very distinct sound and was often used in Greyhound buses. I mimicked that sound all the time. It didn't matter whether I was "driving" a 1951 Buick coupe, a 1961 Rambler wagon, or a 1964 Chevy Impala SS—in my world, they all ran on Detroit diesel.

To my young mind, sitting alone meant you were driving. After all, that's what Dad did when he went to work. Naturally, then, any time I was sitting by myself, it was a perfect moment to pretend I was behind the wheel. Besides the old cars in the backyard, one of the best places to sit alone was the bathroom. It seemed like the perfect substitute for a driver's seat. Long after nature's call had passed, I'd stay seated—driving the toilet. My mom and sisters found it hilarious that I'd go through full gear shifts while behind that locked door. I got teased plenty, but I didn't care. I was having a blast.

One evening, while negotiating a winding, hilly city street in my Detroit diesel-powered tractor trailer (still in the bathroom), someone knocked on the door. Someone else clearly needed the facilities. After I finished my business and parked my truck, I left the bathroom—but continued driving through the house instead. I dropped my head, focused on my imaginary dashboard, and shifted through the gears from room to room. Down the hall and into the kitchen, I picked up speed. A quick right, then left, dodging the kitchen table and chairs—complete with screeching tire sounds. I put the hammer down.

Wearing a baseball cap with the brim low, I didn't have much visibility. Suddenly, *crack*. My head collided with something that made a crunching sound. I looked up to find one of the panes of glass in the back door spider-webbed with cracks. Mom, busy cooking dinner, turned to see what had happened. Her expression twisted into fury. If her hands hadn't been full with dinner prep, I would've gotten a beating on the spot.

"Jesus Christ, Brian! What the hell were you doing? You just wait 'til your father sees that!"

Because of her Catholic background, Mom rarely took the Lord's name in vain. I tried to explain it was an accident, but she wouldn't hear it. Calmly, and with a terrifying finality, she took the leather strap out and laid it on the counter like she was following a recipe.

Dad was due home any minute. My stomach churned. I'd escaped an immediate beating, but I was panicking about what was to come. I went to the living room and sat on the sofa, watching the back door. Anxiety doesn't quite cover what I felt.

Eventually, I heard the door open.

"What the hell happened here?" Dad asked.

I crept out from the living room and hovered at the edge of the hall. Mom, in one of the most bitter tones I'd ever heard, responded,

"Why don't you ask your son?"

Then she pushed the leather strap across the counter toward him, like a gambler going all in. Dad looked at me and asked how I'd broken the glass. Staring at the floor, I took a deep breath and quietly said,

"I hit it with my head."

He knelt down and motioned for me to come over. He still hadn't touched the strap.

"Did you hurt yourself?"

"No."

"What were you doing?"

(Long pause.)

"I was driving."

"What were you driving?"

"A big truck."

"Gas or diesel?"

By now, Mom's face was crimson. She looked like a cartoon villain—steam practically puffing from her ears, veins bulging in her neck. She shoved the strap closer to Dad. But he ignored it.

"Diesel," I said.

His eyes lit up and he smiled.

"What kind?"

"Detroit diesel."

"Can you make the sound?"

I made the sound. He laughed.

"Very good!" he said. "Very good. Next time, be more careful—you could've been badly cut. Tomorrow, you can help me fix it. Okay?"

I nodded and threw my arms around him. The wave of relief was overwhelming.

Thoughts flooded my mind. *Why couldn't my mother be like this? Why did she always want to punish me? Why did she seem to enjoy hurting me?*

The next day was Saturday. Dad didn't have to work. He bought a pane of glass from the hardware store and showed me how to cut it and putty the frame. By the time we were done, the door looked as good as new.

I didn't know it then, but I had just received another powerful lesson in compassionate parenting.

Twelve

*"It is a mysterious thing, the loss of faith-as mysterious as faith itself.
Like faith, it is ultimately not rooted in logic;
it is a change in the climate of the mind."*

—George Orwell

Unlike several of my elementary school chums, I did not attend Catholic school. None of us in the family did. As Mom once explained, Catholic school was expensive, and we simply couldn't afford it. (In her 2010 book, Lori claimed she had attended St. Paul's Catholic School, though she had not.) To a devout Catholic like my mother, this meant we needed religious education elsewhere—specifically, Catechism training. It was a sort of supplemental schooling held on Saturday mornings. Every Catholic family in Blackstone (which made up a huge portion of the town's population) sent their children to Catechism classes—either at St. Theresa's or St. Paul's—if they were enrolled in the public school system.

Our instructor wasn't a nun, as one might have expected, but Miss Cunningham, the elementary school librarian. She had been old when she substituted for some of Chuckie's classes, and by the time I knew her, she was ancient. She wore her jet-black dyed beehive hair like a helmet, sported cat-eye glasses, and carried the unmistakable scent of old lady—too much perfume chased by mothballs.

I was enrolled in Catechism at St. Paul's once I'd made my First Communion. Every Saturday, for over a year, I went to the St. Paul's parish school, which was situated right next to the church.

A little local trivia: the church was built directly on the state line between Massachusetts and Rhode Island. The convent and part of the church building were in Blackstone, while the school and the rest of the building stood in North Smithfield, Rhode Island.

There were no buses, so every Saturday Dad had to drive me. Our neighbors, the Robinsons, had two kids: Nick, a year ahead of me in school, and Piper, a year ahead of Lori. Nick and I were both enrolled in Catechism at St. Paul's at the same time. Many of the kids there were also my public school classmates. Catechism used roughly the same class groupings—if we were in second grade together in school, we were together again on Saturdays.

Lori was just as difficult a playmate as she was a sibling—obstinate, argumentative, and constantly contrary. She distorted facts, invented stories to suit her in-the-moment needs, demanded special treatment, and was regularly enabled by Mom, who let her get away with far more than she allowed Chuckie or me. I'm sure Lori felt entitled. She made promises she didn't keep, insulted people freely, and absolutely could not be trusted with a secret. If Faith was the bane of Chuckie's existence, Lori certainly filled that role for mine—and then some.

One day, after Lori and Piper got into a fight during the week, her brother Nick decided to get revenge—on me. As we were leaving Catechism one Saturday, he cornered me and landed several punches to my stomach, knocking the wind out of me. I doubled over, gasping, leaning against the building.

"Tell your sister she better be nicer to my sister," he growled.

I'd had enough. I was already struggling with Catechism's content—it all felt too magical to accept as reality. I hated memorizing the lines of Mass responses (the Church had just transitioned to vernacular Masses, so Latin was no longer taught to kids. Ironically, that was the one thing I *wished* I had gotten to learn). And I loathed the fact that my Saturday mornings were now spoken for. I think Dad resented having to give up his time as well to shuttle me there and back. And it wasn't like I had other downtime—Mass on Sunday mornings, public school Monday through Friday... every single morning from September to June was taken.

Though Mom still went to church every Sunday, we later referred to this period as her "Agnostic Phase." She had begun questioning her beliefs. Truth be told, I got lucky. After getting beaten up by the neighbor kid on church property—for something my sister had done—I was thoroughly convinced that no benevolent, all-seeing deity was watching over anything.

That same Saturday, I came home and approached my mother as she sat on the sofa, nose buried in a Leon Uris novel.

"Mom?"

"Yes, Brian?"

"Do I have to keep going to church and Catechism?"

She placed the book down and looked at me. There was a pause.

"Why?"

"I just don't believe this stuff," I said, fidgeting. I didn't mention the beating.

And then, something unexpected happened.

"Well, Brian, if you don't want to go, then you don't have to go. That doesn't mean you can sleep in on the weekends—I'll still expect you to get up with your sisters and do your assigned chores—but you don't have to go to church if you don't want to."

My mother didn't do a lot of kind things for me, but this—this was the pinnacle of her parenting. I was eight years old and felt like I had just been paroled. The weight of an invisible burden lifted off my chest. I became an atheist in 1968 and haven't wavered since.

Eventually, Mom found her way back to her faith and left the agnostic period behind. But from then on, religion became something of a sore spot between us. For that moment, though, I quietly celebrated.

When Lori found out I was no longer required to attend, she immediately went to Mom and asked if she could stop going too.

Mom asked her one simple question:

"Do you believe in God?"

Lori said yes.

"Then you need to keep going," Mom replied.

And that was that. It was the very first time I found something I could opt out of—something Lori couldn't mimic, hijack, or mock. One victory in a row.

Thirteen

"If love does not know how to give and take without restrictions,
it is not love,
but a transaction that never fails to lay stress on a plus and a minus."

—Emma Goldman

During the summer of '69, I started spending more time with my friend Kevin, who lived just down the street. His dad and mine knew each other. Kevin had a brand-new, gold-colored, five-speed Schwinn Spider bike. Oh, how I envied him for that bike. Kevin was a few months younger than I was, but we had been in school together since kindergarten. I wasn't allowed to ride my bike on the street until I turned ten, so Kevin would ride up to our house and we'd stick to riding around the yard. He sometimes let me try his bike out, but he had no interest in riding the one I had. It technically belonged to Faith, who hardly used it anymore, but Kevin dismissed it as "...a girl's bike." I learned to ride a bike with hand brakes on Kevin's Schwinn but never dared to try changing gears. I begged Mom to let me ride on the street with Kevin, but the rule was hard and fast.

That Christmas, I got a brand-new Spider bike. I don't remember the brand—it wasn't one of the big names—but that didn't matter. It was sparkly purple, with hand brakes, high-rise handlebars, a banana seat, and white-wall tires. It had three speeds and... wow! Was it shiny. I tried to ride it right there in the living room. I was so excited that no other present even mattered.

Of course, Mom made sure Lori had a brand-new bike too. Hers was a girl's Spider bike made by Murray—light blue, with training wheels, high-rise handlebars, and a banana seat. The comparisons started immediately:

"Why did he get a three-speed bike?"

"Why does he have special brakes?" and so on.

In a rare moment of rebuke, Mom told Lori, "Stop trying to compare. Brian is a boy and he's older."

It wasn't a major defense, but it felt good to have her *kind of* take my side—again.

I was about to turn ten in just over a month. I figured the new bike might mean I'd finally get to ride on the street. I hadn't even fully formed the question in my head when Mom answered it anyway:

"This does NOT mean you get to ride in the street."

Dad said, "For Chrissakes, Faith. He's almost ten. Let him ride it. He knows the rules of the road."

It was rare for Dad to contradict one of Mom's overbearing rules in front of us. I'm sure he paid for that afterward—just as I did. Mom doubled down. If I brought up the issue again before my birthday, I'd have to wait an additional month for each time it was mentioned before being allowed to ride outside the yard. I could ride in the driveway and in the backyard. If I didn't like that, I could give the bike back. If I was caught outside the yard with my bike— or someone else's—I'd lose the bike and be grounded for three months.

Dad shook his head. Later, he offered to take both Lori and me to a park so we could ride our new bikes.

One day, while I was on the phone with Kevin, I told him I'd gotten the new bike but couldn't ride it on the road until after my birthday. I was in the living room, and Mom was in the kitchen—opposite ends of the house—but she still heard me. She reminded me I was not to talk about it or I'd have to wait another month. It was just a warning, but the message was clear: there would be zero tolerance. I hadn't even said anything about whether the rule was fair—just mentioned the facts—and still, I was walking the line.

That's when I began to feel the need to keep secrets from my mother. I learned to talk quietly around her or make sure she wasn't nearby. I started lying. I had already figured out how to make myself scarce and avoid unnecessary contact. If her goal was to keep me out of her life, she was succeeding. And I didn't mourn that. I had my dad and his cars. I had friends at school. I had Chuckie. And now—I had my bike.

I was beginning to understand her. I was beginning to understand *hate*.

As a strange little side note: Lori didn't have to wait until she was ten to ride on the street. In fact, the prior fall—when she was still nine—Mom gave her permission to ride a short stretch of Blackstone Street, up and down a few houses in each direction. Her birthday was in March, so I noticed the discrepancy. I brought it up. Mom's reply?

"It's not your job to make the rules. If you don't want to lose your bike, don't bring this up again."

Fourteen

"Without music, life would be a mistake."

— *Friedrich Nietzsche*

For kids my age, we attended John F. Kennedy Elementary School from kindergarten through fourth grade. Near the end of our fourth-grade school year, a fifth grader came to our classroom to show off his band instrument. Miss McCooey introduced the student as Stephen Clark. He brought his shiny gold saxophone with him and sat down to play at the front of our class. He was an awkward-looking kid with dark hair and glasses, but he did a wonderful job playing that saxophone. I really didn't understand why he was there or why he played for us. That would change in the fall.

Just to the west of Blackstone was a small town called Millville. Sometime in the previous few years, the school boards of both Blackstone and Millville had gotten together and decided to create a regional school district. They built a brand-new Junior-Senior High School, and it opened for classes in the fall of 1970. The old high school, on Main Street, was now going to be home to Blackstone's fourth, fifth, and sixth graders. It had been renamed the Augustine F. Maloney School, after a teacher and principal. That old high school was the same one from which my mother and both of my older sisters had graduated (Mom was in the class of '49, Faith in the class of '69, and Chuckie in the class of '70). Chuckie had the distinction of being part of the very last graduating class from Blackstone High School. She had also been part of the first kindergarten class in Blackstone and was in the last eighth grade class at John F. Kennedy Elementary School.

At the beginning of the 1970–1971 school year, I was in a new (to me) school. The building was old and cold and had a funny smell to it. After being on only one level at JFK, it was a new experience to climb the well-worn oak staircases to get to some of our different classes. Going to different classes in different rooms was also new. After settling into our new space and learning how to navigate the old building, we began classes in earnest. The old high school building was right down the street from Dad's sister Ruth's house, and I took advantage of that proximity on occasion.

One day in the fall of 1970, we were directed to the gymnasium for an assembly. We were going to have the opportunity to try a musical instrument and to play in a band. This gymnasium had green-painted bleachers all along one wall, and all the kids from all three grades were seated in that space. There was a lot of noise, and it was hard to hear what the adults were saying.

Eventually, there was order. Different adults were allowing all those interested (and a few who were not) to try any instrument we wanted. There were saxophones like Stephen Clark's, trumpets, flutes, trombones, and clarinets. The last one appealed to me most. I decided I wanted to learn to play the clarinet. Dad referred to that instrument as a "licorice stick," a name made famous by Benny Goodman. Yup! This one. I got some papers to bring home. Mom said:

"No. We can't afford that. You'd probably ruin it anyway. You have no musical talent—you sing off key."

When I persisted, she added, "See what your father says."

Dad came home later than usual that night. It was almost my bedtime by the time he got home. He was exhausted and asked if what I wanted could wait. While I didn't want to wait, the official deadline was still weeks away. We agreed to talk about it over the weekend.

Dad was already working on a car in the backyard when I got up on Saturday. As soon as I finished my breakfast, I went down to help him out. He was catching me up on what he'd been able to do with the project so far. He had two cars that were very similar—one was a two-door 1962 Chevy Impala SS, and the other was a four-door 1963 Chevy Bel Air. They were both black with red interiors. The Impala's engine was shot, but the Bel Air had a sweet-running six-cylinder engine. Since the Impala was the nicer car, he had decided to put the '63 engine into the '62.

The first phase was already done, and the good engine sat on the ground near the engine hoist. He had maneuvered the Impala under the chain hoist and had begun disassembly. We needed to remove the hood, and for that job, he needed my help (or so he said).

Once the hood came off, we got the power steering pump and the alternator off, and then proceeded to remove the motor mount bolts. Dad worked on the passenger side, and I was on the driver's side. He was stronger and had longer arms, so his motor mount bolt came off quickly. He was on to disconnecting the exhaust manifold. I brought up the clarinet. He said:

"A licorice stick? I had hoped you'd learn the accordion like Myron Floren…"

(Dad was a huge Lawrence Welk fan, and Mr. Floren, dubbed "The Happy Norwegian," was a frequent guest on the show.)

"…but if you want to learn the licorice stick, that's okay too… they both play the polka."

Now came the hard part.

"Mom said we can't afford it."

"Hmmm… we'll have to see what we can do," Dad said.

"I have the papers from the school. They said we could rent one."

"Brian, if you want to play an instrument, we'll find a way. If I have to work another job so you can do it, I will."

Mom was not impressed. I'm sure her hope in deferring to Dad was that he and the arts were quite far apart and he wouldn't think twice about my little "whim." He often quipped that he could "…only play two things: the comb (wrapped in wax paper and sounding like a kazoo) and the radio." I'm sure she thought he would consider my musical aspirations ridiculous and that would be the end of it. Once again, though, Dad had usurped her dictatorial commands, and I was getting to try something just for me.

Mom went to a meeting at the school (without me, which was weird—all the other kids went with their parents) to find out about the instruments. She came home with my clarinet. It was a used instrument, but it was new to me and so very intriguing. All those silver keys against the jet-black body... how exciting! I started to put together the five pieces it came in and Mom got upset.

"You'll break it. Wait until you're shown how."

It wasn't rocket science. There were a couple of alignment things I needed to learn, but the pieces could only go together in a certain order. You could put it together in a way it wouldn't play, but it would have taken some real force to break it. Nonetheless, to appease her, I stopped. When it was bedtime, I began to ascend the stairs with the clarinet under my arm, but of course, my mother insisted I leave it downstairs. This was going to be a tug of war. She wasn't going to relinquish any more control than was absolutely necessary—and certainly not before she absolutely had to.

Mrs. Bartch was the middle school music teacher. We met in a room next to the old gym (it may have been a locker room), and she taught us how to put together our instruments. The first squeaks and squawks that emanated from that clarinet were truly awful... not unlike fingernails dragged down a chalkboard. We persisted and progressed.

Mom didn't like this whole arrangement. She couldn't take the clarinet away because I needed to practice. She wouldn't break it because it was expensive. In short, she had no means of regulating me with the clarinet. This predicament caused her to really work at a way she could eke out some modicum of control. She decided to push from the other side. Practice time now became mandatory and, per her schedule, it usually fell at the exact time a favorite after-school television show aired.

I learned that it was her intent to push me to the point I would want to quit. At first, I bucked a little, but the more I practiced, the better I got (surprising how that works). I got to a point where Mrs. Bartch said I had exceeded her ability to teach me more—I needed a private teacher.

Once again, Mom was faced with an added expense related to me. Once again, she balked. She went to the school and spoke with Mrs. Bartch. Mom tried to convince her I wasn't anything exceptional and couldn't she just continue things as they were? Mrs. Bartch was able to prevail, and Mom reluctantly relented. She had driven me to excel by trying to punish me, and it was coming back to bite her.

She gave me instructions to ask, at my next music rehearsal, where I might get the private lessons Mrs. Bartch had recommended. This led to my first encounter with Mr. Thomas Hessney.

Tom Hessney was a tall man who appeared to be of Mediterranean or Middle Eastern descent. His great mop of hair was jet black, as was his neatly trimmed goatee. His eyes were dark, piercing, and yet full of life. They also bulged considerably. He had big white teeth that shone whenever he smiled… and he smiled a lot. He had recently been hired to be the head of the music department at the new Blackstone-Millville Regional Junior Senior High School. He had graduated college four years prior, so he was a young man, full of hope and full of energy. He had come to the Maloney School that day with the specific intent of meeting myself and a few other promising music students. There was Stephen Clark with his saxophone, and both my friends Chris and Kevin, who were learning their way around the trumpet. There may have been others, but these were the ones I knew. He told me Mrs. Bartch thought I needed a private teacher, and he could be that, for me. I was given his phone number to pass on to my parents.

For the rest of that school year and on into summer vacation, I visited Mr. Hessney's home in Woonsocket every weekend. He charged my parents five dollars for a half-hour lesson. I was advancing by leaps and bounds. By fall, I was ready for the next step. I was devouring new music and learning more about music theory. This was a great distraction from the stuff at home. Mr. Hessney was a patient but demanding teacher. We formed a friendship that lingers to this day.

As my fifth-grade school year came to a close, I learned our class was going to attend school in the new Junior-Senior High School for our sixth year. It was a stopgap measure on the part of the school board. St. Paul's Parochial School had closed its doors, and there was an influx of former Catholic school students into Blackstone's public-school system. As it turned out, it was not a precedent-setting move, and it was the only year they did it. Still, I was going to be a student in the new school. I remember asking Mrs. Bartch if she would still be our music teacher. She told me she would not, but that we'd be working with Mr. Hessney. I had no idea what to expect. We had been just a loosely coordinated bunch of kids under Mrs. Bartch. We had not really played anything together—no pieces of music or concerts or other kinds of performance—so I had no understanding about what lay ahead.

I felt special because I already knew Mr. Hessney, and he told us that we would be a part of the Junior High band, even though we were sixth graders. I played second clarinet in the band that year, and we performed in a Christmas concert. Both of my parents came. I was so proud of myself. My mother told me that Dad was too unrefined to understand or to enjoy the music being made by a bunch of eleven-to-fourteen-year-old kids. She said, "There were a lot of squeaks and sour notes."

I guess that was her way of congratulating me. Did she enjoy it? I doubt it. I honestly don't know what Dad thought, other than him being proud of me. We didn't stay to listen to the portion of the concert where the high school band performed but went home so I could be in bed on time. Mr. Hessney was making a name for himself in Blackstone. I was a part of what he was doing, and while Mom knew that, she seldom acknowledged it. The world of performing music was foreign to her, but she did not want to admit that. I was doing something she never did—or could do.

I continued private lessons with Mr. Hessney through the summer between sixth and seventh grade. When the new school year began, Mr. Hessney told me I was getting beyond his skill set for teaching clarinet (he was trained as a brass player—primarily on the trumpet) and he suggested a new private teacher. He had set up a studio in Woonsocket and had hired a young clarinet player, who had just graduated from college. He was hoping to break into teaching and felt working at Mr. Hessney's music studio would be a good place to get his foot in the door. His name was Russ Arnold. Russ rubbed me the wrong way with his exuberance and general demeanor. Something about him seemed false and superficial. He spoke with a slight lisp and had a gap between his front teeth. He and I would meet for my lesson once a week, and I was not advancing adequately, according to his standards. I complained to Mr. Hessney that I didn't like the man. He asked me to give it a little more time. I did.

When seventh grade began, I was fully expecting to be a part of the Junior High band, but I felt as though I belonged there now, as an official seventh grader. Shortly into the new school year, Mr. Hessney selected some of us to be moved into the Senior High band. Stephen Clark (who preferred to be called simply 'Clark') and I were among those pushed forward. Talk about daunting—and exciting! I was still in the second clarinet section, and that made me feel awkward, as there were older students who were lower in the hierarchy by virtue of Mr. Hessney's instincts and his subjective assessment. He announced that we would have auditions just prior to the Christmas concert to determine placement on a more objective basis. I had never auditioned, and after learning about what was involved, I was petrified.

I did well in those auditions and earned the second chair in the second clarinet section as a seventh grader. There were three students in the first clarinet section who were all two to three years ahead of me. Tim McQuade, an eighth grader, was the first chair in the second section, and Adam Ranslow, another seventh grader, was the third chair. The guys in the first clarinet section—Ben, Archy, and Leo—stayed in their respective seats until they graduated, with only a rare re-ordering between Archy and Leo on a couple of occasions. Ben was three years ahead of me and was the first chair in the first clarinet section until he graduated. Both he and Archy became music teachers. Mr. Hessney was a real-life Glenn Holland (*Mr. Holland's Opus*) who inspired several of his students to go on to teach and write and perform. We were lucky to have known him.

Fifteen

"Nothing compares to the simple pleasure of a bike ride."

—*John F. Kennedy*

With my ever-expanding automotive knowledge, I spent an increasing amount of time with Dad. More time with him increased my knowledge and my value to him as a helper. From the time I was eleven or twelve, he began giving me a little money when I helped him with a job. The amounts varied from a quarter to a dollar, and for really big jobs I could earn five dollars. With Dad regularly bringing cars home to work on, there was also a chance to find the coins previous occupants had lost in the seats. For a while, I kept my money in my room. I'd spend a little, on occasion, on some sweets or a model, but I was mostly saving it. I had a bank account that had been started by my parents. I would deposit any birthday money I received from my godparents or Memere into my account. I began putting my meager earnings in, as well. I had a card that I needed to take with me to the bank for any transactions. They would mark it appropriately (deposit or withdrawal) whenever I went in. In my fourteenth summer, I took on added work wherever I could (mowing lawns at the cemetery, working for the neighbor guy) and I put my money into my bank account. I was driven. I wanted a new ten-speed bicycle.

Faith had met Dickie when they were both employed at the Archway cookie bakery. Dickie was not very tall—maybe 5 feet 6 inches, at the most. He was a robust kind of guy, though, with a quirky sense of humor. He had served two tours of duty in Vietnam while a part of the United States Marine Corps and had been decorated with a Bronze Star and two Purple Heart medals. He had lost the 4th and 5th fingers from his left hand but still managed to play the guitar and entertain Lori, Wendy, and me. He was fond of camping and had invited me along several times. He was the coolest brother-in-law a kid could have.

In August of that year, Dickie asked me if I'd like to go camping with him and his brother over the upcoming long Labor Day weekend. I readily answered yes, and the planning began. Then a flyer came in the mail. Child's World was a major toy store chain in New England in the '70s and the flyer was advertising a Labor Day weekend sale. In the Child's World flyer was a Huffy 26" ten-speed bicycle for $99 (its regular price was $149). I had exactly $100 in my bank account. I asked Dad if he could front me the additional amount needed for sales tax. I also asked if he would go to Child's World and pick up the bike, with my money, since I was going to be camping on the weekend it would be on sale. I felt as though I was imposing a great deal upon him. Nevertheless, he agreed, and I withdrew $99 and turned over the cash to Dad. I had no experience that would have allowed me to hold that much cash, and I remember thinking I was rich!

Dickie, his younger brother Danny, and I went camping that weekend. Several days without having to deal with Lori or worry about being punished by Mom made for a wonderful reprieve. Dickie had his dad's aluminum rowboat and the place they picked had a little island in a pond near Ken Blake's farm… across the street from the Old Quaker Meeting House in Blackstone. We took enough food for a small army. That trip stands out as the only time I have ever consumed frogs' legs (yuck). On Sunday morning, Dickie and I were awakened by his brother's screams emanating from somewhere on the water. We hurriedly dressed and ran down to the water's edge. Out on the lake was Danny, sitting in the boat. He was taking bucket after bucket of cold pond water and dousing himself with it. With each bucket came a howling "Whoooooo-Hooooo!" Dickie and I laughed over that for many years. Monday came, and it was time to break camp. We paddled back to the car and loaded everything up. They brought me home before going to their respective homes.

As we pulled into the Blackstone Street driveway, before I even got out of the car, I could see it there. Leaning over on its kickstand in the driveway, behind the family car. My new bike. When I got close to it, I could not believe my eyes. It was not a Huffy 26″ ten-speed. It was a 27″ Columbia ten-speed with center-pull brakes, a tire pump, and a water bottle. In today's high-tech bicycle market, it would not be considered anywhere near top-of-the-line, but in 1974 it most definitely was. This bicycle, even then, carried a price tag considerably higher than the $99 I had given Dad. Probably at least double that amount.

"Was THIS the one on sale?" I asked.

"No. I got this at Darling's bike shop, in Woonsocket." Dad replied.

"…and it was $100?"

"No. It was a bit more than that…"

"But I didn't have that much to spend."

"That's okay. You worked really hard to save up what you did, and I thought you should be rewarded for that… but don't tell your mother." he said with a wink.

Dad urged me to get on it and take a spin but only after I relieved Dickie of my camping stuff. I did as I was told. The bike was a dream. I gave Dad a big old hug. I couldn't come up with enough ways to thank him. I offered to work for free to compensate him for the additional money and his response was, "We'll see."

Of course, the day could not remain positive and festive. I took the bike out on an extended ride, and upon my return, Lori asked if she could ride it. I could barely reach the pedals on this bike, and it was a boy's frame. That was not, however, my primary reason for not wanting her to ride it. It was mine! I had just gotten it. I had saved my money to buy it. Lori had squandered all the money she received as gifts from her birthday and Easter. She used up her allowance as soon as she got it. She had spent all the money she had found in Dad's cars (he once offered to match what she found if she could dig out another dollar from one particular car's seats. She did, and he held up his end of the bargain). She had only the minimum dollar amount in her bank account. She began to wail and cry and tattled to Mom that I would not let her ride my bike.

Mom directed me to let her ride it. Dad jumped in, "That's a boy's bike and it's too big for her. She'll hurt herself and probably damage the bike Brian has worked and saved for."

Once again, the wheels of injustice and inequity turned rather quickly in Mom's mind. She turned to him almost without losing a beat and said, "You bought him that—go and buy her one too."

She said this in front of both Lori and me. Dad wasn't going down without a fight, though. He spoke quickly and forcibly, "I didn't buy that bike for him. He saved his money, and he paid for it. I just went to pick it up."

(Obviously, she didn't know he had upgraded on my behalf). Mom refused to be swayed. If I got a new bike, Lori was going to get one too.

Lori had always been a clumsy girl. She'd trip over shadows and bump into sunlight. In one instance, she somehow fell off her Spyder-style bicycle on the left side and yet managed to get her left armpit pinched by the chain on the opposite side of the bike. She was so goofy that she became a source of entertainment for the rest of us. Of course, the more she made us laugh, the more she wanted to do so. Dad had loved her, as he had all of us, but he was always very wary when it came to Lori. On one occasion, while working on the roof of the shed, he had asked if I could go up and nail down the tar paper. He was afraid he'd fall through the cobbled-together roof and wanted me to do it, as I was lighter (truth be told, methinks my dad was afraid of heights). Half-jokingly I suggested he ask Lori. He gave me a look. Then he said:

"I can't ask Lori to do this. I love her, but I just can't trust her."

I have the feeling that Dad got my upgraded bicycle on credit. He knew the guys at Darling's bike shop, and they were probably willing to work with him. He couldn't do it for the entire purchase price of yet another bike. He also knew Mom was not going to back down at all. He went out to Rogeski's, the only other bike shop around. He got her a basic girl's ten-speed. The brand name was Vista. He probably needed to get that one entirely on credit. Once again, Lori got something she didn't earn by whining and crying. She knew Mom was supporting her all the way, too. I felt bitter and resentful. I wanted, so badly, to denigrate the lesser machine she received. I started talking about the differences. It had side-pull brakes, which were the simplest variety of hand brakes on the market... Dad caught me and said:

"Don't point out that it's not as nice as yours. She doesn't have a clue about the difference between the kinds of brakes. Neither does your mother. Let her think she's got the same. You and I both know you've got a better bike, and you do because you earned it. You don't need to brag. Just... let it be."

That was enough, and I did as he suggested. I made a mental note, however, and have not forgotten it. I also never told anyone that he had done those things. Mom simply didn't care that I had the initiative, perseverance, and discipline to save up and buy a bike for myself. She didn't know Dad had put any money toward it. She was hell-bent on keeping me from feeling special, or even just accomplished.

Sixteen

*"Hark! Along the street there comes, a blare of bugles,
a ruffle of drums, hats off! The flag is passing by."*

—*Dad's version of the first stanza of 'The Flag Goes By'*
Henry Holcomb Bennett

Along with rehearsals for performance in concerts, Tom Hessney had set up a marching band at our high school. For the eight years prior to his coming to Blackstone, both during and after college, he had taught drum corps in upstate New York, so he had the background. Our school's first marching band uniforms consisted of black pants and shoes that we supplied, a yellow windbreaker jacket, and a black beret (our school colors were purple and gold—not black and gold). We made do with what we had, though, and began bringing more and more music to our sleepy little towns. We began by performing in a Memorial Day parade in Blackstone. They hadn't had a parade in 27 years. Tom Hessney had a big hand in getting the tradition going again. In fact, he single-handedly started the parade. He approached Boy Scout and Girl Scout leadership, police and fire departments, and got it going. This was a way of giving back to the homeowners in both towns who were unhappy with the property tax increases necessary to build the new school. It was a huge hit.

Late in the 1973–74 school year, we received word that we had been accepted to take part in the 1975 National Cherry Blossom Festival in Washington, DC. If I recall correctly, we had not performed outside Massachusetts and Rhode Island. The furthest away we had gone was a parade in Newport. Now we were going to Washington, DC? This was awesome! While it was about a year away, marching band practice now took over nearly all of our in-school rehearsal time, and we added after-school and weekend rehearsals as well. We rehearsed in the parking lot. We rehearsed in the music room, on the stage, and in the gymnasium. One of the high school physics teachers, Ed Parker, volunteered to help out. He had been a drill sergeant in the Air Force and had a totally commanding presence. We began work on a field presentation that was quite intricate. We were also working on a street maneuver called an echelon corner. We would be finishing our parade schedule for the current year, but we were gearing up to go south.

We needed better uniforms. We were going to be on the national stage and also on TV. The yellow windbreakers were just not going to cut it. We also needed money to get us there and back. Our fundraising activities were like nothing the school district had seen. We sold calendars and candy. We did 'Walk-A-Thons' where we got pledges by the mile. To my best recollection, we had two ten-mile Walk-A-Thons, and I had either the most money pledged or the second most for both events. A Band Booster organization was formed and—surprise of surprises—my mother volunteered to help with bookkeeping.

As the school year came to its conclusion, another music event took center stage. The University of Rhode Island was offering a two-week summer music camp. There was no way I was going to get to go. It was just too much money. Tom Hessney had somehow secured funding to help out six of the band members with the tuition (in the form of a scholarship). I was offered one of the six scholarships and had a two-week respite from the turmoil at home. Mike Suss, Archy, Clark, and several other kids from our school attended. One of the girls, Maureen, was the subject of Clark's fancy. He was in love with her. To my knowledge, they never dated. Every day, for two straight weeks, everything around us was music, music, music. I made new friends, got to try an instrument nobody in Blackstone played (bassoon), I got to watch some older teenagers go streaking (it was still a thing), and so much more. I got lessons from and performed in a wind band directed by Frank Marinaccio, who was the Principal Clarinetist with the Rhode Island Philharmonic Orchestra at the time. Music was opening doors in front of me that I could not have imagined were real.

We weren't home from camp very long when we started getting very serious about the marching band. We marched all over the school grounds. Music rehearsals were usually separate from the marching practice. We were allowed to play while marching—occasionally, though—to keep our minds in the game. March for twenty or thirty minutes, then we'd march and play. Between Mr. Hessney, Mr. Parker, and a few other adults, we were taught a lot, but it was done so well that most of us didn't realize just how much we were getting accomplished. We stayed with it as school started up again. As fall turned to winter, it came time for us to cash in on all the fundraising we had done. We got some samples from which we could choose our new uniforms.

The time between deciding, ordering, and receiving our new uniforms was a blur to me. There was so much happening. Once they arrived, however, things started getting more and more exciting. We were feeling really good about ourselves. Confidence was very high. We learned that our school was going to be judged in the large school category. That meant, as Tom Hessney explained, that we would be in direct competition with some of the largest schools in the country. This was a decided disadvantage. One of the reasons we were considered a large school was because our student body was greater than 600, which was true (by a very small margin). But our 600 students were in grades seven through twelve. Many of those schools we competed against were 600-plus students in grades ten through twelve. The schools in that category were well-funded and well-established. He warned us that this was the first time we would be venturing outside New England and that the national stage was quite different from that to which we had become accustomed. He repeatedly told us not to get our hopes up. We were doing this to gain experience. We had all seen the parades on television. The schools performing were the best; they were top-tier schools, and we now had a chance to learn by being in the same competition with them.

We completed a few more fundraising events through the winter and as spring approached, we started really feeling like we were ready. We rehearsed and rehearsed and rehearsed. We would be traveling from Blackstone to Washington, DC by bus—four of them, in fact. We were staying at the National 4-H headquarters; in retrospect, it wasn't a hotel, but it really wasn't bad, either. I thought of it as a kind of barracks. None of us cared. We got to go sightseeing and I had my first Dinner Theater experience: we saw *Guys and Dolls* at a place called the Harlequin Theater. One of our band members experienced a seizure on our first night in the 4-H center. It caused a bit of excitement, but she ended up being okay and persevered through the competition.

The parade and competition were to be held Saturday, the fifth of April. Esther Rolle, the actress from the TV show *Good Times*, was the parade marshal. We were awakened early that morning and assembled outside well before dawn. The weather was frigid. Reeds were freezing, the poor kids with brass instruments risked major skin issues if they didn't keep their mouthpieces warmed. Flute players were worried about the skin below their lower lips. Some of the kids could use gloves, but that just didn't work for the rest of us, so we had gloves without fingertips. We assembled and got our final pep talk from Tom. He had poured his heart and soul into prepping us. We were as ready to do this as we could be. There was not a single kid in that band who was willing to be the one to disappoint him. We wanted to go.

The street upon which we were assembled was cold and dark. When the word was finally given, we all came to attention, adjusted our spacing and alignment, and stood at the ready. Then, following the drum major's whistle, the drum section began the street riff. Adrenaline rush! We began marching in place—marking time—to the beat of the drums. Then our drum major got the word to progress down the street. We began to move, but we couldn't quite tell where we were going. Left, right... left, right... marching... take a right here... a left... still the streets were dark. Left, right... left, right... marching blindly to the repetitive monotony of the drummers' street beat... Left, right... left... Suddenly, we found ourselves marching into an incredibly brightly lit section of road... left, right... left, right... The sun had not fully risen, but we were ready to begin the National Cherry Blossom Festival Parade in the nation's capital. We were a bunch of kids from an unknown corner of Massachusetts marching with school bands from all over the United States.

We came to a stop and got a few minutes to make last-minute adjustments to our uniforms and our instruments. The adults were all hovering and making final checks. Up and down the rows of kids in their new uniforms and their cold fingers desperately grasping their frozen instruments, the adults checked in with all of us and helped a few. Then we got the word. It was our time. We marched into a square playing our hearts out and perfectly executed that echelon turn we had so feverishly rehearsed right in front of the reviewing stand. We got a huge round of applause from the gathered masses as we were announced. We were all so scared that no one made a mistake. Then we began playing again and marched the rest of the parade route down Constitution Avenue, turning every corner like some odd, multi-layered zipper and with such precision! That afternoon, we took part in the field competition. Again, we did our very best out on that field.

When all was done, we gathered to watch the award ceremony with all the other bands from all across the country. Tom Hessney was one proud man. He told us how proud he was of all of us and then reiterated that we should not be disappointed if we came away without an award. It was the experience that mattered, and the reward was that we had given our all and done a good job. When they got to announcing the winners in the large school band category, we knew it would be conducted similarly to the other divisions. "Honorable Mention" would be awarded first, then third place, second place, and then the winner. We didn't get Honorable Mention. Our hearts sank a bit. When we weren't mentioned for the third or second place awards, some of the band members were upset to the point of tears. We knew we couldn't have come into our very first National competition as total neophytes and win. What a great experience it had been, though. Some of the kids had begun getting ready to leave, when, over the announcing system:

"In the large school category…"

The voice over the loudspeakers droned…

"…the first-place award goes to…"

We were beginning to get our stuff and head back to the Four-H center when we heard something oddly familiar:

"…the Blackstone-Millville Regional Charger Band, from Blackstone, Massachusetts!"

"What? Did they just say… US???"

Our drum major and the color guard captain went with Tom Hessney to collect the plaque. There were tears and shouts of joy. What an experience! Our very first time on the National stage. Some of the band members thought they were dreaming. We had exceeded all of our own expectations, and we had certainly done credit to the organizers and teachers. The next day we got to do a little sightseeing. Many of the band members attended church at the National Cathedral. Monday morning, we boarded the buses for our trip home. The plaque was passed around so we could all touch it and get a nice, close look at it. It was a great ride.

The sun had recently set as our caravan approached the Rhode Island / Massachusetts state line. We had taken a bit of a backward way in, following RI highway 146. In the distance, some flashing lights could be seen. We figured there had been an accident, and we would likely be delayed. As we crossed the state line, we saw the source of all the lights: every police car, fire engine, and every vehicle with a flashing light from either town was lined up on both sides of the highway. Horns, sirens, and whistles were sounding. We proceeded—with our escort—down Central Street in Millville and on to the high school in Blackstone. At the entry to the school there were two fire department ladder trucks with the ladders raised toward each other, like a triumphal arch. There were television crews with cameras and, despite it being after 9 PM, there was a throng of people from all over the area. The buses pulled up in front of the school and we began to disembark.

My mother later wrote a letter to the editor of the local newspaper, *The Woonsocket Call*, saying that she had not seen that many people gathered in our little corner of the world since VE Day, when World War Two ended in Europe and our boys were heading home. Approximately 2,000 people had gathered to greet us. From this point forward, Mr. Thomas Hessney would have whatever he wanted in the way of funding for his music program. He, virtually single-handedly, had put Blackstone and Millville on the national map.

Over the next couple of years, the band took part in the Gimbel's Thanksgiving Day Parade, and we also traveled to Niagara Falls, Canada, for the Miss America Beauty Pageant and parade. After I graduated, the Charger Marching Band continued to spread music far and wide. They went to Disney World in Florida and to the Rose Bowl in California. In the last few years, they have competed nationally and have dominated the National High School marching band scene, being crowned UsBands Division IV Open National Champions in 2015, 2016, and 2019. I wonder how much the newest iteration of this organization knows about that fledgling group of kids and what they did in 1975. Some of their parents might not have even been born at the time.

To this day my eyes well up, a bit, when I think of being a part of that momentous achievement. More than twenty years later, when I visited the school, I went to the area of the building that housed the music room and the auditorium. Just outside the auditorium doors was a display case. It held the band's awards from Disney World, the Rose Bowl, and many others, but front and center, on the top shelf, was the plaque we took home from Washington, DC in 1975 (25 years after that, the single case had multiplied into four or more cases). What fun that was. I recently asked Tom Hessney what he considered to be the most special moment he and I had shared, and the memory of the 1975 Cherry Blossom Festival was his answer. Mine too, Tom… mine too.

In the aftermath of this obvious high point in my young life, my family reacted in similar ways but to different degrees. Dad had been working and was not one to join in gatherings such as the one that greeted our band upon our return. He offered subdued congratulations the next day. Mom was there when the buses arrived but offered even more subdued congratulations (she wanted me to grab my stuff and leave as quickly as possible—I wanted to linger). Chuckie and Faith were aware and were proud of me and happy for me. Lori decided that she now wanted to join the band, and Wendy had no clue what all the fuss was about. The only folks who really shared in the joy and elation I felt were my fellow band members. When I was among them there was a collective sense of accomplishment and an unspoken pride that we all felt for our joint efforts. I don't think my family really understood what this group of young people had accomplished together and how it made them feel so very special. Those members of my family had never taken part in anything like this, so there was no frame of reference... at least that's what I told myself.

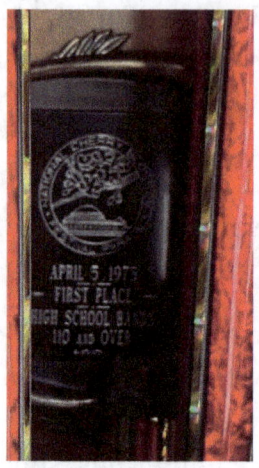

Although out of focus, this photo shows the plaque is still a part of the band's collection of trophies. It currently lives at the back of a cabinet – the pillars of another trophy can be seen framing that plaque we received all those years ago.

This photo does not capture all of the trophies the band has won since the Cherry Blossom Festival Parade in Washington DC on April 5, 1975, but gives some sense of how successful the program has been.

Seventeen

"Child abuse casts a shadow the length of a lifetime."

—*Herbert Ward*

Mom was used to getting her way. She ruled absolutely and with a proverbial iron fist. Beatings could be brutal. Until kindergarten, Mom had only used her hand to spank me. As I grew, she resorted increasingly to "The Strap." My siblings and I all lived in fear of this weapon. It was the non-buckle end of a leather belt just over an inch wide and fourteen to sixteen inches long, tapering to a rounded point. There were holes visible through which the prong had fit. I distinctly remember my first encounter with "The Strap." As before, I have no recollection of the offense for which this punishment was doled out, but I remember how surprised I was with the exponential intensity of the pain inflicted. If we cried early in the beating, she felt she had won. Faith and Lori even got to the point they preemptively cried, although neither faced Mom and "The Strap" as much as Chuckie and me. The two of us, who easily received the majority of these vicious attacks, had also taken the opposite tack in response:

holding out as long as the flesh was able. If she didn't get the desired response, however, the beating would intensify. If I did not cry after two or three licks, the ferocity and number of licks increased.

I remember the last strap beating I received: I was 14 years old. I had failed to do something, or Lori had told her I had done something (I likely hadn't done) in the half hour between breakfast and leaving the house for school. Mom ritualistically got the old metal highchair and placed it just inside the open bathroom door, facing to the left. This positioning was important for two reasons: it allowed Mom, who was right-handed, all the room the open door to her right afforded to swing the strap. It also provided the means by which my butt would have maximum exposure. Disgrace was a prime component in her "discipline" recipe. This chair was not a highchair like the one used by us as small children; there was no tray or means to secure one. This one was made of chromed steel tubes and had a red vinyl seat. There were steps that folded out, in the front, to make it useful as a step stool. In this case, the steps gave Mom a place to elevate one foot while she sat on the stool's seat. There was no question this mode of punishment was intended to humiliate. It was rehearsed, I think, from all the times she had previously handed down similar corporal punishment. Accordingly, I was required to retrieve the weapon from its storage spot in the drawer under the oven, report to the bathroom, hand her the strap, drop my pants and underwear and lay myself over her elevated leg—a kind of "assume the position" prelude, like a petty criminal well-known to local patrolmen.

She was possessed by her desire to inflict humiliation and pain. I suppose the dread of retrieving the instrument of my beating was expected to be a part of my punishment. Not this time. My pre-beating process was carried out as though I were an automaton. The bathroom door was left open, and my bottom was ritually exposed. She then began whipping me with the leather. With the first strike I winced. The pain was sharp and intense. I refused to feel the humiliation, though. I forced the thought from my mind the way one chooses to go ahead and swallow a nasty-tasting medicine. Sometimes, during these beatings, I would think about working on a car with Dad; sometimes I thought about going to school. I would think about anything except the leather striking my buttocks and upper thighs. Other times, instead of looking outside the situation for distraction, I would concentrate on the punishment itself. I would try to count each excruciating strike of the leather and try to guess when it would stop. Would she stop at ten? Fifteen? How many hits would be enough... for her?

I refused to even make a sound, although the sheer pain forced tears to form and fall. This beating began to take on a level of brutality I hadn't previously experienced. Partially due to my age, partially due to my refusal to cry out, and partially from her own self-feeding, violent, spanking frenzy, "The Strap" began to connect more frequently and with more violence in each stroke. Five... Six... Seven... she was obviously going beyond five. Nine... Ten... Eleven... she wasn't stopping at ten, either. She usually worked in multiples of five, so I figured it was to be fifteen. Fourteen... Fifteen... Sixteen... She hit me so many times I lost count. Still, she kept going. This beating was not about my failure to behave; this was about hate. This was malevolent, pent-up rage. She was a powder keg, and I had somehow, inadvertently lit the fuse. There was no goal other than to release her own, long-subdued disgust with the men in her life. I was in the sweet spot for her. I was nearly a man, but I could still be physically dominated and hurt by her. I was the perfect target. The perfect victim.

Lori had been peeking in from the kitchen side of the bathroom door—a combination of morbid curiosity and malevolent teasing. She relished the punishments I received in a sadistic and psychopathic way, a form of schadenfreude. In her book she made herself out to be the victim of one of these frenzied "Strap Attacks," but I rarely knew her to get strapped. She gave this away in her narrative when she spoke about checking to see if the holes in the leather left corresponding marks on the skin. She couldn't have checked that on herself, but it explained why she hovered so close to my beating. It also speaks to

Mom's focus and/or her bias that she either didn't notice Lori there or didn't care. Lori was probably the root cause of my punishment that morning, but now it didn't matter.

I then began to feel something that I'd felt just once before: the striking leather began cutting the young, soft skin already inflamed by the previous hits in the same area. I pushed it out of my mind. I was not going to give her the satisfaction of making me react anymore. When she finally exhausted herself, she shoved me off her lap and hissed, "Now get ready and go to school."

As she walked away, I silently pulled up my pants, got my stuff, and walked out the kitchen door, wiping tears away with my shirtsleeve. I walked to school, pain with every single step. I didn't know how I would hide that. My homeroom, that year, was in one of the science labs with stone tabletops. Our seats were metal stools. I dreaded the thought of sitting on one of those that morning. I was standing at the side of the room, not wanting to draw attention to myself. One of the other students said to me, "Hey, Francis, it looks like you sat in something, man."

I felt around my backside, and it felt damp. I asked to be excused and went to the boys' room.

Once inside a stall, I dropped my pants and underwear. The dampness on my backside was not due to me sitting in something. It was a somewhat unexpected result of the morning's beating. I hadn't felt the moisture because of all the inflamed tissue on my buttocks and thighs, but I had bled through my underwear and onto my pants (Lori's description also includes the bleeding welts which formed in a location not easily visible to the one on the receiving end of the punishment). I put a couple of paper towels inside my pants, between them and the blood-soaked whitey-tighties, then returned to homeroom and went about my morning classes with all the fortitude I could muster. I had difficulty sitting but managed to mostly hide my pain. I was very self-conscious—not only because of the wet pants, but also because of the crinkling paper towels—and tried to hide my backside throughout the morning. At lunchtime I hobbled home, changed my clothes, and went back to school. I had been careful to put the bloody pants and underwear in the dirty clothes hamper. Mom had not been home at the time and didn't know I had done this. When I got home after band rehearsal, however, she told me I needed to hand-wash my bloody underwear and pants because it was my fault that they were bloody, and she wasn't going to ruin other clothes with my blood.

Dad came home that evening and saw me in the bathroom, where I was hand-washing my whitey-tighties in the sink. He said, "What in the hell are you doing?"

I explained that I had to wash my underwear because of the blood.

"What blood?" he asked.

I was embarrassed, and he sensed this. His demeanor and his tone softened. His voice lowered, and mine, in barely a whisper, we discussed the beating I got with the strap before school that morning. I told him that I had to come home at lunch and change. I told him Mom insisted I hand-wash the bloody clothing. He said nothing but patted me on the shoulder and turned, walking toward the kitchen.

"What in the name of Jesus H. Christ did he do that deserved a bloody beating?" he yelled at Mom at the top of his voice.

She didn't miss a beat, "I'll not have you questioning my authority in front of..."

He didn't let her finish, and he had a big voice when he needed to be heard.

"He's fourteen goddamn years old! You made him bleed... for Christ's sake, Faith! What the hell is wrong with you?"

They went back and forth for a while after that. I tuned them out. I finished washing my clothes and took them to the basement to hang on the clotheslines down there. Then I sat down on the concrete floor. The coolness of the concrete eased the pain. I stayed down in the basement until I no longer heard the yelling.

It was not too long after this beating that I found a way to prevent her ever using "The Strap" again—on me or anyone else. Once a week, Dad would burn the household trash in a 55-gallon drum at the edge of the property. He used this time to sneak a cigarette when he was supposed to have quit. Knowing this was going to happen on a Saturday, I waited until late in the day and removed "The Strap" from under the oven and put it in the barrel. The fire burned, and the dreaded weapon was gone. No one else would ever feel that ripping and tearing of flesh from the leather in her hand.

But the result of my effort was mixed. Without her go-to weapon, Mom was forced to adapt. I'm sure she knew I was responsible for its disappearance, and I'm sure she wanted to punish me for it. If she acknowledged the sudden disappearance of "The Strap," though, it might somehow look bad for her. Narcissism had Mom in its grip, and she simply moved on, not ever mentioning "The Strap" again. If she didn't mention it, it was not a failure to have lost it.

Although the reign of terror related to "The Strap" was now over, Mom was still Mom. On some weekend family drive to either the White Mountains of New Hampshire or along the Mohawk Trail in northwestern Massachusetts, Mom had obtained what was supposed to be a visual souvenir. The item was made of wood and was about twenty inches in length and three inches in width. It was shaped like a narrow paddle. On the face of the souvenir paddle was a painted figure of a young deer looking over a shoulder at a bear cub with the scripted message: "For the Little Deer with the Bear Behind," all painted with red, white, and black enamel.

Mom now brought this out and hung it by the light switch in the kitchen. The message was received, loud and clear.

At first, she began with single blows and numerous semi-empty threats. I think she was feeling out the potential effectiveness of the new weapon. That thing, however, left a welt with a single blow. She hit me on the upper arm with it, and I made a point of ensuring the mark was visible. Dad saw it and asked what had happened. That discussion that followed was centered on her hitting me, not on anything I might have done to precipitate the violent punishment. He shook his head and, while I'm sure they spoke of it, I was not privy to that conversation.

For a while, it gathered dust on its perch. I wanted to think Dad had prevailed upon her not to use it. Then it happened again. This time, she avoided any spot that would normally be visible; she hit me across the lower back. The sting of the wood hitting me was felt even though there was a shirt between it and me. There was no way, though, that it hadn't left its mark. I checked in the bathroom mirror and there it was—hours after the initial blow—a dark red stripe with straight, well-defined edges.

Again, I showed Dad, and this time I overheard the argument. He told her she was going to cause a serious injury if she kept using it:

"...you could break a bone with that thing!"

She was undeterred.

I remember Lori had caught the paddle once and, instinctively, she had covered her head with her flailing, skinny arms. The next time it was her turn to face the paddle, Mom was ready. She faked a swing and up went Lori's arms.

"Don't you dare. I'll give you something to put those arms up for!"

And she swung—almost wildly—while Lori ran, screaming. Mom caught her, though. She really could have caused a severe injury this time because she was aiming for Lori's head. The wood struck Lori's elbow as she covered her head like a cornered boxer. There was an audible sound of wood splitting. This souvenir was not intended to be a practical weapon. It was made of cheap pine and could not hold up under these conditions. Lori got an extra hit because of the damage she had caused to the weapon.

Mom had been deprived of the use of "The Strap," and now her replacement weapon was damaged. Again, she was unwilling to accept any diminution in her ability to dole out her cruel punishments. The paddle, with a lengthwise split along the grain of the wood, was returned and remained in its place by the kitchen light switch. There must have been some processing and strategizing going on, but nothing replaced the paddle.

Then I did something to incite her wrath, and that brought back the frenzied style of vicious attack. She came after me with the paddle and hit me in the back. When she took a second swing, I was already turning and caught the splintered paddle on my forearm. This was different. This was very different.

I felt something new and very painful. The split wood, upon impact with unprotected skin, acted like a pair of scissors and cut me. It hurt badly, but I tried not to show it. I began bleeding almost immediately. She hit me a third time, but it was a glancing blow as I was moving away. She was caught off guard, I presume, by the sight of the quickly visible bleeding she had caused.

Not long after, my arm wound barely having time to heal, I was on the receiving end once more. Lori and I had been arguing over something and, to break up the sibling fight, Mom stepped in, shouting and swinging the paddle back and forth between us. It was like a sadistic form of pinball.

I was on the forehand swing and got first contact. I had long sleeves and was also able to deflect the blunt force (upper arm). Next, she caught Lori, who had her arms raised to protect her head. Mom went for her torso as she was turning (lower back). Then back to me (buttocks) before taking the final swing at Lori. As she connected with Lori's backside, the paddle had reached the end of its life and broke in two.

Mom slapped Lori with the back of her hand, then balled up a fist and caught me in the ear. Once again, it was our fault that her weapon was rendered useless, and the paddle was now kindling.

The paddle had a relatively short but consequential reign as the weapon of choice. From here on out, Mom's rage would usually result in improvised weapons being taken up. One such weapon was an old wooden textile bobbin/spindle.

Although not the first time she had used this on me (and I don't think I had actually done anything this time; she was just going to clobber me with it), one attack stands out: I caught sight of some motion in my peripheral vision and moved at what turned out to be the last minute. The force of her swing was so strong that, at the apex, the weighted end of the bobbin/spindle had enough centrifugal force that it flew from her hand. I remember it breaking something when it hit, but I don't remember what that was. If she had connected with that, I doubt human bone would have remained whole.

This type of bobbin/spindle was made of hard wood; some had a metal ring at the top. Dad had brought several of them home from the textile mill for us to play with.

Other weapons were whatever happened to be at hand: books, purse... anything to increase her ability to inflict pain. For a while, she had a large, leather, saddle bag–styled purse, and she carried books in it. It had a long strap handle and was used as a swinging weapon, like some demented version of a slingshot. I got knocked off my feet and had the wind knocked out of me when I caught that in the chest/stomach.

This happened in the high school parking lot one autumn night around 9:15 PM. Mom was attending night school classes offered at our school through Quinsigamond Community College. I had a stage band rehearsal that same night and was hoping to get a ride home, rather than having to walk home in the dark afterward.

The compressed sodium lights in the parking lot gave the whole area an eerie orange glow. I don't remember the exchange, but Mom turned her back to me while standing by the open driver's side door of the car. I thought she was just going to leave me there and said something to that effect. When she turned, the leather bag full of textbooks was already swinging at the full length of its strap handle.

Her aim was precise. It hit me mid-torso and sent me crashing into the rear fender of the car. I crumpled to the ground, gasping. She got in, started the car, and drove off... leaving me on the ground and struggling to catch my breath in the middle of the empty parking lot. I slowly got up and made my way home in the dark.

Chuckie had also been knocked to the ground by that thing. She was afraid of more violence, so she didn't complain about the headache and dizziness following that attack. I don't think the other three ever got hit with the saddlebag of books.

Dad would do anything and everything he could to bring money into the house. For a while, in 1968, he worked for a Singer sewing machine store in Woonsocket. He hauled away machines that had been traded to Singer for a new one but were considered beyond repair. He once brought home a pick-up truckload of these broken machines. I learned how sewing machines worked by taking them apart. I combined bits from all the different machines to make a couple of usable ones, and I scavenged motors and some other parts before the other pieces went to the scrapyard.

Among the other things he got from Singer, he brought home sewing cabinets and chairs. One example was an odd, futuristic-looking, plywood and tubular aluminum folding sewing table. There were three folding legs—the single one on the left end had a loop in the metal with a flat section that gave the table its stability. The tabletop was curved on all edges. There wasn't a straight edge on it.

There was a second tier with a fixed section at the rear (farthest from me as I sat in front of it), and that section had a hinged piece designed to come down around the body of the sewing machine. The plywood had a blonde finish. It must have been a display unit and so was barely used. I asked for it, and it at once became my desk (for my bedroom). Its design was the epitome of 1960s futurism.

To go with my new desk, I salvaged an old swiveling chair that was in another pile of stuff from Singer. It had four tubular steel legs with wheels and a very worn seat formed by stretching leather over horsehair and a set of springs. I used it as it was for over a year.

Then, when Dad was working for a textile mill, he obtained some garish gold-colored naugahyde. My mother wanted nothing to do with it, but I seized the opportunity and fabricated a number of things. My homemade hockey goalie glove featured this awful-looking stuff, but I also decided to reupholster my swivel chair. It was gloriously hideous, and I was quite proud of myself for figuring out how to recover the chair's seat and back. Now I had a set: a weird table/desk and a gaudy chair.

Eighteen

*"What puts someone on guard isn't necessarily
the fear of being found out."*

—*Terry Gross*

A single porcelain light fixture in the center of the ceiling illuminated my bedroom. I also had a high-intensity gooseneck lamp that split duties between my desk and my bedside table. I was fond of building models, and the illumination from that lamp, on my two-tiered desk, was more than adequate for the task. The desk was set almost as far away from the door to my bedroom as was possible. Just inside the door was where I kept my sports equipment.

One evening, I was listening to *Tchaikovsky's Greatest Hits* on my cheap old stereo and intently working on a model of a Fokker Tri-wing airplane (The Red Baron's plane). Thanks mostly to the positioning of that ceiling fixture, I happened to notice some movement. It may have been nothing more than a slight shifting of a shadow. Knowing its source needed to be behind me—and having the benefit of wheels on my chair—I pushed away from the desk just in time to see my mother swinging my baseball bat down from over her head. Before I could take in enough breath to say something, the bat made explosive contact. The record player skipped with the impact. My model was destroyed, and the plywood desk now had a splintered crack right in the middle of the working surface.

I shouted, "What was that for? Why? What did I do?"

I found myself stammering, trying to form other words or questions, but nothing else that would have been intelligible came out of my mouth. There was no response. The baseball bat was allowed to fall to the floor. The shark-like eyes stared at me for a minute with nothing but contempt shaping her countenance. She then silently turned and simply walked out of my room. Nothing was ever said about why she did this.

Had I not seen something—the flicker of a moving shadow—I shuddered. Was she expecting me to move? She had been, otherwise, so quiet... Would the bat's trajectory have been the same if I had not moved? I sat, alone and motionless, in my gaudy gold chair for several minutes, my head spinning and my chest heaving. I must have instinctively moved my hands to protect my head, and I found myself still holding them in that position minutes later. Had I just escaped death? I had questions, but there were no answers.

I picked up the broken pieces of the model that had been scattered all over that part of my room. For several weeks after, I continued to find an odd piece (most often when I stepped on it with a bare foot). I also made a very amateurish attempt to fix the desk. It eventually needed to be thrown out. It was too badly damaged. She didn't speak to me for more than a week.

After several attempts to learn why, and getting only silence in return, I tried to re-engage in some other ways, but it was a long time before we spoke civilly. If I tried to bring up the bat incident again, silence ensued. I learned this was not going to be discussed—as though it had never happened. I guessed that in her mind, it hadn't. In my mind, though, I felt as though I had escaped death, and I remained guarded for the rest of the time I lived under the same roof.

Dad wouldn't believe me when I first told him. I finally convinced him to come up to my room to see the desk. He just shook his head as he looked at the damage. There were no words. If her goal had been simply to scare me and put me on my guard, she had definitely succeeded. If the goal was, instead, to reign me in and make me more subservient, that had failed. I hadn't seriously thought about striking out on my own until this event had played out. From then until I finally left the house, my mind was never far from the shattered model and the broken desk that had remained in the path of the bat after I moved.

Suppertime was always a crapshoot. I couldn't tell, ahead of time, if it was going to be calm and congenial, ice-cold silence, or all-out screaming warfare. I didn't have a category for anything worse, but that was coming. The house had no formal dining room; instead, it had an eat-in kitchen. Mom would sit at the end of the table closest to the refrigerator. She thusly had ready access to the refrigerator, the stove, and the sink. Dad would sit to her right, with his back to the kitchen sink. I sat opposite Dad, Wendy would sit next to me, and Lori would sit to Dad's right, across from Wendy. This seating arrangement was of Mom's doing; Lori and I were too prone to fight, so we needed to be separated. I also deduced that Mom cared more about having me in close proximity so that I could be swatted when she felt like it.

One evening, at suppertime, Mom and Dad started having one of their increasingly frequent fights. It began before supper even started when Mom made some vague accusation of infidelity against Dad. She began listing women's names with whom she presumed he had affairs, and he would refute each in turn. His best argument was that he worked a lot, and when he wasn't at work, he was repairing cars in the backyard. She would know, by his paycheck, if he had not been there when he said he was. When he wasn't at work, he was home. There were no unaccounted-for times in his schedule. She didn't care for his logic and continued with more accusations.

During the meal, they took pot shots at one another; each snide comment leading to another snide retort. Lori and Wendy finished their meals and, after asking to be excused, had dashed off to the living room to watch TV before Wendy's bath time. I was finishing my dessert.

Mom was standing up, clearing the table, and was running water to wash the dishes in the sink. Right at that moment the argument escalated. I have no idea what it was all about, as I purposely ignored those tit-for-tat kinds of arguments. I finished my dessert and also asked to be excused. Mom turned from the sink, a fiery glare in her eyes, and yelled, "No—you may NOT be excused! You're the oldest one now, so you're going to sit and listen."

This made absolutely zero sense to me, but I knew better than to counter those kinds of orders. I'm sure my face was white and my eyes open wide as I returned to my chair. Dad looked at me, looked over his shoulder at Mom, then looked back my way and said something about there being no need for that, and then told me I could be excused, in direct defiance of Mom's orders. I started to get up again.

The next thing I knew, from behind Dad, Mom screamed, "SIT DOWN!"

I did as commanded. She then grabbed a handful of Dad's hair in her left hand, pulled his head back, and put a serrated steak knife to his exposed throat with her right. He was completely frozen in place but was not panicking. I was also frozen. They didn't get along, but I had never seen it escalate to a physical confrontation.

Mom glanced quickly at me and, seeing the terror I'm sure was easily read in my face, she let go of Dad and turned back to the sink. Dad motioned for me to go, and I did so without delay. I ran to the living room while they continued to argue. Dad said something to the effect of: "Nice. Letting the boy see that..." I tuned out from that point. I knew Dad was not the type to hurt Mom. Until now I had not thought she would hurt him, either. After what I had just seen, I wasn't so sure anymore. I think I knew, then, that she would eventually kill him. She had the anger, she showed she could catch him off guard, and she had just proven that she could summon the means.

I have often reflected on that incident. None of my siblings could corroborate what I had seen in the kitchen that evening. I was alone in the room with my parents. Mom was certainly the antagonist and the aggressor. Was she using me as a witness? Or was it more likely she was showing me that she could do harm to a fully grown man and so she would have no trouble with a scrawny teenaged boy? Was this the ultimate purpose of this show of power? Was this saber-rattling more for me than for Dad? Again, I had so many questions and no answers.

As a teenager, I had, of course, inserted myself into the dynamic. I included myself as a part of the tension in our home. Looking back, I can see why my thoughts had gone in that direction. Now I had just seen what she was capable of. Her recent history with the baseball bat and now this… I knew I needed to be even more vigilant and on guard than I already had been. I began to fear her in a whole new way. I feared the wrath of a tyrant who was only five feet tall.

The energy in that house was dark and powerful. Their situation was devolving into chaos, and tensions were escalating. I did my best to ignore or avoid their fights. Mom had brandished a deadly weapon against both Dad and me. I had an increased sense of danger, so I began to make myself scarce.

My involvement with both the stage band and the marching band allowed me an excuse to stay after school so I could avoid going home when Mom would be there without Dad present. Some of our rehearsals were at night. I'd get home in time to see Dad, get a bath or shower, maybe watch some TV, and then go to bed.

They also seemed to do their best to avoid each other. Dad worked in Fall River, so with that commute, he was gone for a good portion of the days. He didn't want us exposed to their quarrels; Mom didn't seem to care one way or the other.

During my entire existence on this planet, I had not seen them do anything but co-exist. I had never seen them kiss. I had never heard the words "I love you" spoken. In fact, I thought it would be totally weird to hear that—and even weirder to say it. It was not a happy, loving home by any metric.

Nineteen

"Divorce is probably as painful as death."

—*William Shatner*

In my sixteenth year, I endured a series of events that many people might think were contrived or at least exaggerated. They were neither. These kinds of events might contribute to a fanciful, dramatic, and far-fetched Hollywood or soap opera plot—experiences so outrageous they could easily be fiction. I only wish they were.

It began in January, when my mother finally decided she was going to divorce my dad. She announced this to me at breakfast, on the day before my sixteenth birthday. She insisted I keep her secret until Dad had been served with the official papers. It was 1976. The chances the Massachusetts courts might be kind to my father were next to nil. When I inquired whether I would be allowed to live with him, my mother's response was:

"I intend to have the house, the car, and the three of you at home—and to have him pay for it."

I asked, naively, where Dad would live. Her answer was terse:

"I don't care."

Although this day was so close to my birthday, it was still a school day. It would take a major catastrophe for me to miss a day of school. To that point—including kindergarten—I had missed a total of only six days, all due to extreme illness. (I think I missed a few of those days because I had contracted chickenpox in first grade.) That was the only reason my mother would allow us to miss school. Period. We often went to school so sick that we ended up going home early, but Mom nonetheless insisted we go.

I went to school that day emotionally sick. It was cruel of her to have done this. However, I knew her to be strict and without empathy. Although I was sixteen and now taller than her, I still feared that tiny tyrant's wrath and her not infrequent rages. As such, I made a conscious choice not to cross her or trespass on the promise she had imposed upon me. I had seen what she was capable of. I was scared and confused.

I kept her secret through the end of that school year—it was a long and emotionally difficult four months. As summer vacation arrived and I knew I'd be spending more time with Dad, I tried to ascertain whether he'd been served the divorce documents. I wanted to know if I could finally speak openly about the matter—the one I'd kept inside for so long. When I asked Mom, she went into a partially subdued rage. The papers had not been served, and she didn't know why.

Over the next couple of weeks, I struggled with the idea of keeping my promise to my mother or disclosing what I had been holding inside to my father... my hero... my best friend. That awful, awful secret—it was eating me up.

One Sunday afternoon we were working in our backyard shop, which we still affectionately called "The Shed." Knowing no delicate way, I blurted out:

"Mom's going to divorce you."

He said:

"I kind of figured that."

I asked him if he had received the papers. He had not. This confirmed what Mom had said. He then asked me how I knew. I told him of my morning encounter, the day before my birthday, and how she had extorted my promise not to tell him.

He yelled:

"JESUS H. CHRIST!"

(He often inserted the middle initial.) He was furious. He ranted on about how unfair it had been for her to tell me—and worse, that she made me promise to keep it secret. I think that aspect of it made him most angry. I emphatically begged him not to tell her I had divulged it. He assured me he would not let her know of my 'betrayal.'

Conversation then drifted into the possible reasons for Mom's actions. Dad was a big *All in the Family* fan. We had recently seen an episode— "Edith's Problem"—where Edith was "going through the change," and I asked if this was what he thought was going on with Mom. He laughed a little and complimented me on my ability to draw that conclusion. He tactfully avoided directly answering but alluded to it being possible. In hindsight, I doubt it was true. While her periods might have gotten worse, it's not likely she was going through menopause at 44 years old.

My negative feelings and emotions were legion. Perhaps some of it had to do with growing up in a home dominated by a Catholic matriarch and the guilt inherent in her preferred ideology. I felt remorse for having betrayed my mother's admonition. (I didn't count it as trust, since my compliance was involuntary.) At the same time, I felt as though a huge weight had been lifted from my chest, although I felt strangely bad for this selfish sentiment. I also felt as though I had somehow hastened the divorce process, which upset me.

Soon, the papers were duly served, and the reality of the split became more imminent. Dad kept his cool. In early July, they went to court for their first hearing. That afternoon, upon returning from the courthouse in Worcester, Mom stormed from the car into the house, and Dad casually walked down to the shed, lighting a cigarette on his way. I quickly followed him. I asked what had happened. He put a finger in front of his mouth, telling me to keep quiet. Then, after looking toward the back door and concluding no one was observing us, he motioned with his head, bidding me to follow him to the shed.

He prefaced his answer with an admonition: he believed I was old enough and smart enough to understand, but he absolutely forbade my talking about it to the other two. Wendy was too young to understand and would likely let a naïve question slip. Lori was just not trustworthy—she would certainly relay anything she heard if she thought someone else would suffer, or if she might somehow gain from it.

Dad described the courtroom setting and gave a basic synopsis of the hearing. I inquired about the grounds upon which Mom had sought divorce. The response was, I think, ironic: she accused him of "Extreme Cruelty." Dad explained that this stemmed from her assertion that she had to live and run a household with too little cash; that he was not providing appropriately, and this was causing her undue stress.

He then smiled—that slight sideward movement of his mouth, the blue eyes twinkling. My puzzled expression prompted him to explain something none of us could have guessed.

As far back as I could remember, Mom had been the financial manager for the household. Apparently, Dad's lawyer had discovered a *secret* bank account at the Woonsocket Institution for Savings & Trust into which Mom had been stashing a considerable amount of money. It was not a joint account; it was held in her name only. The likely—but incorrect—assumption was that this stash had been her money. However, she hadn't been employed for quite some time, and the deposits were regular and recent.

Why was this important? The judge had seen through her charade. It wasn't Dad who was failing to provide—it was Mom who had been skimming off the top of what he turned over to her every week. I doubt we'll ever really know why, but it stopped that day in July. The conjecture was that this was to be her nest egg—or insurance—once she was rid of him.

What the judge then ordered surprised me. I think it surprised Dad as well. The court issued temporary orders, which pretty much maintained the status quo. No one was to move out. The big change—the only change—was that control of household finances was transferred to Dad.

He was logical and reasonable, but I could not imagine him feeling comfortable with banking and paying bills. No wonder Mom was so angry when they got home. She had lost her secret source of income, lost control of the finances, and Dad was staying put.

Nonetheless, this ruling buoyed him, and he assured me he was up to the task. The court ordered a re-evaluation of the situation in mid-September. I was so happy my life wasn't going to be torn asunder early that summer. No decision would be made until autumn. My little world was, for the time, stable again.

It was, after all, all about me, right?

My father spent a lot of time that summer visiting my two older sisters, both of whom were married and living on their own. Chuckie and her husband Eddie had an infant son. Faith and her husband Dickie had two daughters and an infant son as well. As adults, both Faith and Chuckie lived within just a few miles of us.

Dad was under no delusions about the eventual outcome of the September hearing. In the intervening weeks, he began preparing me for the next phase of my life—living without him at home and stepping into my new role as 'man of the house.' One of those sessions began with the following preface:

"I'm going to get you a gun."

Here's the weirdest thing about that statement: during all the sixteen years I had known him, I had seen Dad with a gun just once. He had brought home a very old .22 caliber rifle that he called an M-1 (it wasn't—the M-1 was not a .22 caliber). I don't know for sure how old it really was. Dad had taken it out when we were having some problems with squirrels getting into our house. Without any target shooting or practice, he raised the gun and—POP! The squirrel, leaping between trees on the adjacent lot, dropped out of the sky. By his own admission, he hadn't handled a gun in nearly 30 years (since he had been in the Navy), and he had just killed a squirrel—in motion—on the very first shot he'd taken. Dad was such a soft touch, though, and couldn't stand that we had just witnessed him killing an animal. He got rid of that gun.

During my freshman year in high school, I studied human anatomy. I got home late from school one day and Dad was working on a car. I changed into my work clothes and went down to the backyard to see if I could help. In an honestly inquisitive manner, he asked me what I had learned that day. I began telling him about biology. He asked for more specifics. When I described the gastrointestinal system, I happened to mention the word *esophagus*. Having never heard that word, he asked me to repeat it. I complied. He laughed—and laughed a lot. It became not only a new vocabulary word for him, but since it tickled his funny bone so much, it also became a new pet name for me. Imagine being called "Esophagus"! For a long time afterward, he called me that. However, if he was frustrated or angry with me, I was also expected to answer to "Dammit Brian."

Dad went ahead with his hypothetical situation:

"Hey, Esophagus, let's suppose you have to protect your mother and sisters from someone?" My reply was quick and (I thought) self-evident.

"I'd shoot him."

Then came the follow-up question:

"I know, but where would you shoot him?"

It didn't take me very long to respond:

"In the head."

He looked truly puzzled and followed with:

"What about the heart?"

"I guess that would work, too," I responded.

At this point, he asked something I just did not expect. Placing his right hand over his left breast— almost into his armpit—just as he'd seen patriotic baseball fans do and as he would have done, himself, during the national anthem, he queried:

"Here?"

In typical sixteen-year-old, know-it-all fashion, without hiding my annoyance very well (and forgetting, for the moment, he hadn't had the benefit of high school biology), I quickly corrected his hand placement, moving that big, calloused paw more toward the center of his chest.

"Ah! Thanks, Esophagus."

That was it. We went on with what we were doing. That conversation came back to haunt me, though, and still does to this day.

Dad had only made it to the sixth grade. He lost his parents when he was quite young. Grandpa Jim died in 1936, and Mabel followed in 1942, before her fifty-fifth birthday (Dad was just fourteen). His mom's death certificate records the cause of her death as "La Grippe," and, according to Dad, she was quite sickly in her later years. The loss of both of his parents—especially his mother at her relatively young age—had a profound effect upon him. He often spoke of not wanting to live beyond his 50th birthday, which I presumed had to do with him not wishing for us to have to endure a parent's decline. When I pointed out that my high school graduation would occur past his 50th birthday, he would deftly change the subject.

Twenty

"What we have once enjoyed, we can never lose.
All that we love deeply becomes a part of us."

—*Helen Keller*

September in New England is magical, and it is my very favorite time of the year. The oak and maple leaves are wending their way toward the visible transformations in color for which New England is famous. The air becomes crisp but not cold. The sky is a miraculous shade of blue and often cloudless this time of year. The sun still shines during the day, but daytime becomes noticeably shorter. School shopping and mental preparation for the beginning of another nine months of incarceration—uh… public school—is occupying most kids' minds. School shopping and anticipation of time without kids underfoot occupy the minds of most parents.

Some of us looked forward, more than others, to seeing some school chums we hadn't seen during our vacation. We would, once again, establish the artificial barrier between 'school time' and 'after school time.' We anticipated the annual chore of raking leaves in the late September and early October afternoon hours, as those beautiful red and yellow leaves turned brown and fell from the trees; thus, most people greeted September with positive feelings. That September, by contrast, I felt trepidation, angst, and foreboding. I had no idea just how bad it was going to be... but I had guessed it was going to be very, very bad.

My sisters, Lori and Wendy, started the school year on Thursday, September 9th. By virtue of my status as a high school junior, my first day back was a day later: Friday the 10th. Usually, when we arose to prepare ourselves for school, Dad was already gone because of the distance he had to travel for work. His dedication and work ethic meant that he went to work in the rain, snow, or shine, and whether or not he was sick. I couldn't recall a time when he hadn't gone to work... until Friday, September 10th, 1976.

When I came downstairs for breakfast that Friday morning, the first thing I noticed was the green and white Guimond Bros. Farms' utility truck Dad drove. It was still parked in the yard next to the family car. I asked my mother where Dad was, and she gestured—with a sour face and a thumb over her shoulder—toward the closed bedroom door down the hall behind her. His work boots were visible in the corner, sitting on folded newspaper just outside the bedroom door. They had shared that bedroom until the previous winter (when she had begun sleeping on the sofa). Something really didn't feel right. When I asked, "Is Dad sick?" my mother dismissed the question and urged us to finish our breakfast and get off to school. This was definitely not okay. I felt something was really wrong. I couldn't place a finger on exactly what was so wrong, and that bothered me terribly. I finished my breakfast, brushed my teeth, grabbed my stuff, and headed out on my half-mile walk to school for my first day of the 1976–1977 school year.

The first days of the school year were usually tedious and awkward. This one was no different—at least when it came to those things associated exclusively with school. My uneasiness about the seemingly hopeless nature of my parents' domestic situation, alone, was not terribly overbearing. They were scheduled for their return to court the following week. What was making me feel so uneasy? It was Dad's truck sitting in our yard instead of being in Fall River, at the dairy. Some people describe the feeling, I think, as 'butterflies in [their] stomach.' Whatever it was, I was thinking of home and the odd sensation in my gut instead of my English class orientation.

When that 55-minute period ended, I moved like a zombie toward the boys' locker room where I was to experience the sheer pleasure of orientation to Mr. Robliss's physical education class... for the fifth time in six years. The school administration attempted to alternate students between the two physical education teachers—Mr. Michael Drake and

Mr. Emil Robliss. Due to the shutting down of one of the Catholic schools in town and the resulting influx of students into the public-school system, our class was sent to the new Junior-Senior High School for our sixth-grade year. It was a stop-gap measure, and it was never repeated. What this meant for me, however, was that I had the pleasure of being in Mr. Robliss's class in that sixth-grade year… and for seventh grade, ninth grade, tenth grade, and now, in eleventh grade, as well (eventually, I would have the pleasure of being in his class all but one year between sixth and twelfth grade, with the sole exception being my eighth-grade year with Mr. Drake. To my knowledge, I was one of the only students to have Mr. Robliss as my physical education teacher for six years).

Every year, the little banty rooster went through the very same routine. By this time, I knew it so well I could have done it for him. Mr. Robliss was droning on, in his harsh New England accent, as he was wont to do:

"We'll be studying weight training. There are two reasons to train with weights: one is to build endurance, the other is to build muscle mass. Like the guy on the beach who, when asked which way the bus went, replies…"

(at this point he demonstrates for us by flexing both arms to show off his biceps, then turning one wrist with an extended forefinger outward and turning his head in the same direction)

"… it went… that way"

(eliciting laughs from those unfamiliar with the routine).

This speech had comical elements but was already a tired trope for me. It had usually gone off without a hitch, but this time his rhythm was interrupted in a way I had not previously experienced; nor was it expected. At about 9:30 AM, the door to the boys' locker room suddenly swung open and standing there was a woman. Not just any woman… she was the school nurse.

Mrs. Zekanowski was a warm and friendly person, and everyone I knew loved her. She wore a cardigan over her white nursing uniform and usually had a smile on her face as she peered over her reading glasses. This time, though, she had a noticeably grim visage, and it spoke volumes. It was Mr. Robliss's expression, however, that stole the scene. This was his 'man sanctuary,' a 'no female zone.' 'How dare a woman come in here?' His thoughts were patently obvious by simply looking at his face. The blue eyes were stabbing the air and the face was reddened.

"I need to see Brian Francis," came Mrs. Zekanowski's request.

Mr. Robliss, perturbed, asked, "Will he be returning?"

This was the point where all of those things I was thinking and feeling came rushing back, crashing over and suffocating me.

"No," came the nurse's response.

I swallowed hard, to suppress the nausea.

Mrs. Zekanowski then led me, in total and uncomfortable silence, to the principal's office. (In five years in this school, I had never been in his office.) Mr. Neri was a man of small stature, said to have been a retired boxer. Simply looking at his nose, one could easily believe this unconfirmed rumor. He was quiet and pleasant, though. He bid me take a seat opposite his desk, which I did without question. Mrs. Zekanowski left. I was afraid. I didn't even know what I was afraid of. I ventured to ask what this was about. Mr. Neri said (without looking at me): "Your uncle is coming to get you."

My uncle? Which uncle? Why would any uncle be coming for me?

A few moments later, my sister Lori—two years behind me, but in the same school building— was also led to Mr. Neri's office by Mrs. Zekanowski. We were not there more than a couple of minutes, but it felt like an eternity. It was as if the second hand on the clock was counting drips of water from a slowly leaking faucet; each second stretching to five or six.

We were sitting in the seats opposite the principal's desk—seats usually reserved for the bad kids. Neither of us were real troublemakers. None of this made any sense. During this encounter, he didn't lift his eyes, and he said nothing. He knew something we did not.

Uncle Rene was my mother's younger brother. He was the exception in his family—the only surviving male sibling—and, if I didn't know him, I would have taken him to be quite rakish. He was just shy of six feet tall, and in the 1960s, he had worn his dark hair in a pompadour. He liked his beer, but I'd never seen him lose control. He and my father had mutual admiration for each other. We were frequent guests in his home, and vice versa.

Usually quite jovial and very outgoing, he was a different person on that Friday. Lori bounded into the passenger seat of his car, and I got into the back seat behind her, so I had a clear view of Uncle Rene. Lori was bouncing on the seat, seeming blissfully unaware of the gravity of any situation that would have caused Uncle Rene to remove us from school. She was simply happy to be out of the school environment. He had put the car in gear and slowly headed down the school's drive when I asked him what was going on. He stopped the car. With one of the most haggard, grief-stricken, and traumatized looks I'd seen on anyone's face—ever—he looked over his shoulder... our eyes locked and he said in a voice that matched his visage:

"There's been an accident; your mother is in the hospital and… your father's dead."

"Accident? What kind of accident? How?" I shouted.

He made the universal sign for a handgun and said:

"…he shot her… then killed himself," pointing his finger at his own temple and moving his thumb, like the falling hammer of a gun.

Lori acted as though this was a melodrama; suddenly shifting from the fourteen-year-old happy to be getting out of school to an obviously forced scream and crocodile tears. The conversation was beyond her, as Uncle Rene and I continued. I asked where we were going. He told us we still had to pick up my youngest sister Wendy (she was 9 years old and attended fourth-grade classes at the Augustine F. Maloney School, the old high school, which was in a different part of town) and then head over to the hospital in Woonsocket. Details were so sketchy that they were mostly absent, but Uncle Rene's demeanor, that September morning, told me a lot.

Twenty-One

*"You think you know who you are.
What's to come. You haven't even begun."*

—*Tara Maclay*

To this day, Wendy's recollections of those events seem vague, at best. She claims that she barely remembers Dad. That may be a weird advantage, for her, if it is true. To me, it seems a conscious choice. When the four of us arrived at the hospital, we were led to a waiting area near the intensive care unit. My older sisters, one of my brothers-in-law, Memere, and several of my mother's siblings were already there. Initially, we were told my mother was still in surgery. We were informed that a bullet fragment was lodged in her pericardial sac, the fluid-filled membrane surrounding the heart. They were not going to try to remove it, as she was very weak and had already lost a lot of blood.

While we waited, a couple of my aunts were encouraging Wendy to do something she had not yet done—they were trying to get her to cry. She showed no emotion. All the armchair psychiatrists were diagnosing her as being in shock. They may have been right, but I thought it was at least possible that she hadn't really grasped the situation yet. Some of her behavior in later years could be construed as reflecting the trauma, but she has often made a show of being a strong woman. Perhaps she was just making a show of being a strong nine-year-old girl? Or was it more simply the behavior of a sociopath, unable to display emotion? To this day, I cannot fathom how she remained so emotionless.

The other pseudo-psychiatric diagnosis, which poked its nose into those waiting room conversations, had to do with my dad.

"He must've snapped," Aunt Mary said.

Aunt Dotty and Aunt Shirley agreed. Aunt Rose and Uncle Rene abstained. Shortly after we received word that she was in recovery, someone mentioned that my mother did not yet know my dad was dead. Now the conversation switched to speculation as to what she might think. Would she think he was on the run? Would she think he was in custody? Then, to my amazement, surprise, and shock—and without any input whatsoever from me— it was decided that I should be the one to tell her of his death. After all, wasn't I now the oldest one still at home? Wasn't I now the "man of the house"? I really despised that phrase, but I especially despised it at that moment and under those conditions. I didn't feel like a man. I felt like a little lost boy and just wanted someone to take care of me. Didn't they realize this?

Just a few hours prior, my dad was alive. I knew as much as most and, as time would tell, not as much as some. I was sixteen years old! I was NOT "the man of the house," but apparently it wasn't up to me.

When Mom was finally awake, I was directed to go into her room and did so… alone. She had tubes coming out of her and wires attached everywhere. She was not quite five feet tall, but I had always seen her in her domineering function—someone I needed to look up at. Right now, she looked so very small in that hospital bed. I was looking down at her for essentially the first time in my memory. She appeared very weak, and the doctors had said as much— however, I was not really prepared for the exchange which followed:

"Hi Mom. How are you feeling?"

"…mmmmm…"

"Do you feel weak?"

"…uh-huh…"

"Does it hurt?"

"Yes, Brian. I hurt everywhere."

"Uh, Mom, the family thought you should know that Dad's dead."

"Good enough for him!" she spat.

I was already overwhelmed by the whole situation and frustrated that I hadn't any input in the decision about telling her. I was completely thrown by this response and could say no more. I simply had no more words. I kissed her cheek, turned, and left the room. She did not look at me. Not once. No eye contact at all. After I left the room, other family members filtered in and out. There were a few more details emerging: Dad had not used a handgun. He had bought a .22 caliber, single-shot, bolt-action rifle through a neighbor who held a Massachusetts Firearm Identification Card. Massachusetts was an early bastion of gun control legislation, and there was no way Dad could have obtained the card required to buy this gun—or any gun—in the short amount of time between June and now.

His first shot had missed her and pierced the aluminum screen door leading out of the kitchen where she had escaped. It was the only damage to the house that was ever visible. As she ran down the steps and onto the sidewalk, along the side of the house, he quickly reloaded, stepped outside, and fired again. This one found its mark, but just barely. It shattered one of her ribs and the bullet fragmented, sending a piece into her right upper arm. He ran after her, quickly reloading. He stopped in the front yard, aimed the gun, and got a third shot off as she ran across the lawn. Our neighbor, Mr. Robinson, was out in his yard and had seen Dad firing the shot that hit her in the shoulder blade. He later recounted this to the police and news reporters. That third shot had bowled her over, but Mom came right back up on her feet, adrenaline coursing through her veins. She made it to the Robinsons' house and rang the doorbell. When Mrs. Robinson answered the door, Mom simply said:

"Charlie just shot me."

And then she collapsed, bleeding heavily. Mr. Robinson and another neighbor, Mrs. Salome, picked her up, wrapped her in a blanket, put her in the back seat of Mr. Robinson's car, and the two of them rushed her to the hospital. Mrs. Robinson called the police. The fire and police chiefs later said that the quick action on the parts of Mr. Robinson and Mrs. Salome "...probably saved [Mom's] life." This was the second time Mr. Robinson had personally rushed a member of my family to the hospital.

Dad retreated into the house, thinking he had done to her what he had set out to do. He loaded the fourth bullet into the gun, placed the muzzle over the center of his chest, raised the butt, and with his thumb, pushed the trigger back. The bullet passed through his heart, but he was still conscious. He turned the gun around, loaded the fifth shell into this weapon, and repeated. He collapsed after the second shot in the hallway outside the bathroom near the foot of the stairs. He fell forward, well into the bedroom he and Mom had shared. He had taken his life at a location in the house where no one would have seen him from an outside window. The local newspaper reporter/photographer was among the first on the scene. The ambulance personnel indicated they had a weak pulse when they arrived. He died moments later, though, due to a massive loss of blood.

The newspaper journalist's photo, which I'm sure he and his superiors were amazed to have obtained, was printed on the front page of the paper that evening. There it was for all to see: a picture of Dad, wearing his work clothes and house slippers, lying in spattered blood. His Timex wristwatch was visible on his left wrist, resting palm up by his side, and his right arm bent at the elbow against the bedroom door. The printing of this appallingly thoughtless photo on the front page of the newspaper had a couple of secondary effects: a large number of subscribers to *The Woonsocket Call* canceled their subscriptions at once, calling it tasteless, insensitive, and cruel. It was all of that and more. What really hurt, though, was the reaction of my five-year-old niece to this bit of photojournalism. Jenny had called him "Baba" since she began speaking. When she saw the paper that evening, she asked:

"Why is my Baba in the paper? What's wrong with my Baba?"

Her naïve little statement hit us all like a ton of bricks.

My first "man of the house" job was done, and I felt awful—both because he was dead and because I had to be the one to tell her he was dead. I was certainly feeling the fatigue of the day and was thinking about my bed at home. Until just then, I hadn't given a thought to the fact that neither of my parents would be home that night. This was further complicated by something I had not actually considered. Apparently, no one had been inside the house since the authorities were there in the morning. There was no telling what might be found. Additionally, no one had been inside to clean up the blood. This all translated to the three of us having to spend the night elsewhere. Faith had three little ones at home and I had done some babysitting for them. My familiarity with that household, plus the lack of adequate space elsewhere, made it easier to decide I would go with the Trudels. Lori and Wendy went with Dotty, Mom's older sister.

My world had crashed in around me with all the force of an atomic bomb and, as I was to learn in the coming weeks, I had just passed from adolescence into the responsibilities of full-blown adulthood— without any of the benefits. There was to be no going back.

Twenty-Two

"Now I know why you always told me to be strong. You knew that one day I would need the strength to bear your loss."

—Anonymous

Saturdays usually meant relaxation and fun. It might have meant sleeping an extra half hour (all Mom would allow). It might also have meant going to a friend's house, riding our bikes, playing baseball, football, or hockey (depending on the time of year). It might also have meant working in the backyard or even watching cartoons if the weather was bad or there were none of the other things going on... but not on this Saturday. September 11th began, for most people, as another beautiful New England Saturday morning. The sun was shining, the sky was crystal clear, and it was just cold enough to require a light jacket. Under other circumstances, it would have been a picture-perfect morning. It was not a perfect morning for me.

Minute details were beginning to make the very muddy picture ever so slightly clearer. For instance: Dad had left a note—of sorts. It was not a suicide note, giving reasons for his actions. Instead, it was an informal last will and testament. Handwritten in blue ink on white lined paper, it was found in the living room, along with all the cash he had on his person when he came out of the bedroom Friday morning. It had been found on the table, in the living room, next to his chair.

As everyone expected, he asked that his CB radio be given to Lori (who had been fascinated with talking to complete strangers on that device) and all his tools to me. He had taken the precaution of moving them out of the shed and into the home of Al Guilbeault (a trusted neighbor), across the street. (Incidentally, it was Al's son who had made the weapon purchase for my dad.) I haven't ever figured out why he moved them. Maybe it was his preparation for not having access to them, should he lose his nerve, and the court remove him from the home. Maybe it was insurance in the event Mom survived. I know he had wanted me to have the tools. If Mom had these without his wishes being known, she might have sold them or, in some other way, divested herself of things that had a decided value to Lori and to me. These processes were not, in my opinion, the results of the thinking of someone who had snapped. This had been thought out. It was planned.

We learned that Dad also seemed to have planned extensively for this change in all our lives. He had taken my mother off his medical insurance.

He did not expect her to need it, so why keep paying for insurance? He also took the precaution of changing the home's mortgage insurance beneficiary from my mother to my two older sisters. When my sisters and I started comparing notes afterward, more twists became known.

In retrospect, and in my naïveté, I believed he would not have shot himself through the heart had he not verified its physiological position in the chest with his sixteen-year-old anatomy student. He would have, however, endured excruciating pain if he didn't immediately die of his injuries—and although prolonged, he would likely have kept trying (or maybe he would have changed the target to his head). In Dad's frequent visits to both of my older sisters' homes, he had repeatedly sought their absolute assurance regarding the fate of my younger sisters and me. He would say:

"If something were to happen to both your mother and me, who will look after the three younger ones?"

He was repeatedly guaranteed that we would be looked after. What was interesting was that he asked Faith and Chuckie independently of each other and asked them not to divulge the nature of those discussions to anyone.

I was beginning to see a more complete picture. From all of this I deduced he had not snapped at all. He was not insane. This was very carefully calculated, and it very nearly worked—just as he had planned. The only part that did not go according to his plan was that Mom survived.

Here's what I did and do believe:

1. Dad knew he was going to be removed from the family home because in those days, regardless of the reason(s), if a woman asked for a divorce, she got it. She would also get the house, the car, the kids, and money from her ex-husband. There was no denying this part.

2. Mom had a violent streak in her and could become extremely angry with little or no provocation. There was the occasion where I went to school with bleeding welts on my backside. Chuckie once had a perfect (red) imprint of Mom's hand on her face. No split lips, bloody noses, or black eyes for the world to see, but we sometimes had difficulty sitting.

3. Dad would intervene when he was there. If he were permanently out of the house, he couldn't protect us.

4. If all he had succeeded in doing was to remove the cause of the abuse (Mom), he would go to jail.

5. He was 48 years old. He was nearly to his self-imposed age limit of 50. He had gotten the assurances he wanted regarding his kids. He

knew we would be cared for by the family he trusted. He needed to provide for our care, and he'd done that through the insurance policy changes.

It was a near-perfect plan, and he had executed it over the course of nearly three months. No. He did not snap.

Now we really faced a dilemma: Mom was in the hospital, recovering from multiple gunshot wounds. She had surgery and was in intensive care for the first 24 hours following that surgery. The costs would have been astronomical if we had to pay privately—and because of Dad's planning, Mom no longer had insurance. Dad's life insurance had a clause prohibiting payment if the cause of death was suicide. We were up a creek unless we could convince the insurance companies that things were other than what they appeared to me, at least. We all knew—or I thought we all had agreed—that Dad was sane. His reasons for doing what he did were manifestly clear (to me, anyway). This now became an ethical issue, or maybe it only really seemed so for me. Do I cause undue suffering for the family by insisting he was sane and justified? Or do I betray that image of Dad as savior in order to salvage my mom's and the rest of the surviving family's financial well-being?

Faith and I set out early Monday morning. This was the first time I had missed a day of school in years. Weirdly enough, I felt guilty about that. There were things to be taken care of that were more pressing and of (supposedly) higher import. Faith made it plain I was not going to school that day—I was going to go with her. She was not usually this assertive, so I listened... and obeyed.

Our first stop was to be the Metropolitan Life insurance office in Milford. Faith was incredibly careful to admonish me about the need for us to play the game. Dad was gone and these people did not know him or care about how or what we thought about him. We had to do what we could to get Mom through this. That meant I had to support a description of my dad which I knew to be untrue. We had to make it appear, to these businesspeople, as though he was mentally ill or unstable. They had to believe he was chronically depressed and had snapped under the pressure of the impending divorce. We pleaded with them, mentioning our mom who lay in a hospital bed in intensive care and the three of us, aged sixteen, fourteen, and nine, who suddenly found ourselves without our dad. This was a sob story and, fortunately, they bought it. They would authorize payment under his life insurance policy. It is interesting—and although I don't think anyone thought of this connection at the time—Faith's husband Dickie had once worked for Metropolitan Life and had sold that life insurance policy.

We headed out of the Metropolitan Life office and were on our way to the next business affecting the money. In the car, I asked Faith if she believed what we had just told these people. She caught me totally off guard: she was a little ambiguous in her response, but hinted that Dad probably was insane. I did not hide my shock, because I expected everyone to have thought as I did. Did she really think he 'snapped'? I found it hard to believe she could consider that paradigm but, apparently, she did... and she considered it a foregone conclusion. I did not.

After our morning missions, which I believe were successful, we headed to the hospital. Mom was doing much better and there was talk of her being discharged in a day or two. It was now that I became aware of a thought, which until then had been buried deep in my subconscious. It was not a nice thought, either. In later years I was asked, more than once, if there was a part of me that wished it were my mother who had died and my dad who had survived. This day, in the hospital waiting area, that thought was there. I repeatedly pushed the thought back to the recesses of my awareness, but it was there. In exploring the thought, I became aware that it had morphed into its final iteration from hearing the doctor's pronouncement that she would be well enough to leave the hospital in just a few days. She was going to get better. My mother, the violent abuser, was going to live.

Since she was now more alert, Mom began to describe some more of what had happened the day of the tragedy (as it was now being described by family). Once all the kids had left the house, Dad emerged from the bedroom dressed in his dark green Dickies work clothes and carrying the .22 caliber rifle over his bent arm. He told her:

"We need to talk."

He laid his handwritten note on the living room end table and then emptied his pockets of all the cash he had, which was less than $50. (Although the newspaper reported a sum of $400, Mom said it was closer to $40. In Lori's account—and ever prone to exaggeration—she said it was $500. Dad would not have had access to that kind of money in 1976.) Appropriately, at this point, Mom began to fear for her life and took off running. He took his first shot at her from within the house, as previously described, and followed her out the door. The rest we had already pieced together.

Faith and I both went into her hospital room and discussed what we had done that morning with the insurance. Mom was blatantly bitter. I guess that she was justified in her feelings from her perspective. She made no pretense to hide her abject hatred for Dad. In some ways, I can understand her having felt that way, too. A part of me felt, though, that she should have considered us. She should have considered that our perspective was probably different from hers. She really should have known my perspective was different... I know it was a lot to ask, given her place in all of this. Even if she despised him on a personal level, though, we still loved him, and he was our dad. Her disparaging and sometimes vitriolic comments were definitely not something we wanted or needed to hear—even from her, especially now. Hearing her talk about him in this fashion right after he had died both reinforced and brought to the fore my thoughts about whom I wished had died and whom I wished had survived. My reaction was also natural and expected... just not in my mother's mind.

About suppertime that evening, my brothers-in-law arrived at the hospital. There was discussion between them and my older sisters about cleaning up the house in the aftermath of the shooting. I volunteered, and a near argument ensued. Dickie (Faith's husband) and Eddie (Chuckie's) were planning to do this cleanup. Dickie and Eddie were both veterans, were both older, and were somehow supposed to be more hardened to this type of situation. I know for certain Dickie had dealt with others' deaths. These two men were not going to allow their wives (my sisters) or any of the younger kids to be exposed to the scene. Even though they were family members and adults, neither Chuckie nor Faith were going to be allowed to be exposed, so there was no way the guys would let me, as a mere teenager, in there. No one who had just lost their father would be going into that house to clean up his blood. I argued and argued for my right to be a part of that, but to no avail. The discussion was over. The decision was made. Dickie and Eddie would clean up, and I would not.

Lori claimed, in her book, that she was in the house to get her suitcase (she didn't have a suitcase) and that Faith was there as well (she was at her house, with me). She described seeing blood splatter, etc.—a scene which she obviously pieced together from newspaper reports and other sources, but one she did not experience firsthand. Not surprisingly, she also described damage to a window frame or a windowsill from a bullet that didn't hit anything like that. She remembered the trauma, put together some descriptions from the newspaper, and filled in with details that only existed in her imagination.

The mood was somber for the seemingly endless drive to Faith's house in Bellingham that night. I felt empty and comforted myself by imagining my father speaking to me from beyond. That voice I conjured told me to go on with my life and not to dwell on the past. I was counseling myself. So be it.

Twenty-Three

*"Remember me and smile, for it's better to forget
than to remember me and cry."*

—Dr. Seuss

The next morning, the guys went over to the house to clean. We kids were still to be scattered because we were going to be without Mom for at least this week, as she would not be home from the hospital. A plan was needed, however, for our eventual return home. My family also had to begin planning our final goodbye to Dad. I do not remember going back to the hospital during that weekend, but I'm sure we did. It was during this weekend that I learned that Memere had expressed sentiments about the tragedy, which surprised some people.

Memere had really liked Dad. It was understood. They joked with each other at family gatherings, and he called her by a nickname, "Maxi," that was based upon her first given name, Maximillienne. She defended him whenever my mother and Aunt Mary would begin picking on him. I did not realize just how much she had liked him until after his death. It was her opinion that *the tragedy* was—in all likelihood—my mother's fault. She felt that whatever Dad may have done, Mom drove him to it, and she deserved much—if not all—of the blame. This, again, brought that troubling thought out of its hiding place in the recesses of my mind. Her own mother thought she was the cause.

Once the house was ready for our return, Chuckie came to stay with us to provide an adult presence. It was the best arrangement the adults had come up with. Faith and Dickie needed to stay with their three kids; Eddie could watch his and Chuckie's little boy. What I remember about arriving back home was pulling into the driveway after dark. Chuckie and my younger sisters were already there, and lights were burning. I could tell the TV was on from the play of light on the drawn curtains, but I don't recall what show or who (if anyone) was watching.

Lori and Wendy were either watching TV or had gone to bed. They were not present. Faith and Dickie stayed a while and talked with Chuckie and me at the kitchen table. There was a lot of discussion about the varying thoughts regarding Dad's remains. He had been quite adamant that he be cremated. We were all in agreement on that. Dad had expressed to me, on many occasions, that he did not want a gravestone, and he did not want a funeral. He wanted us to remember him as he was when he was alive. There was profound wisdom in this request. In his mind, if you see someone dead, you will remember that image of them. If you know there's a body in a box under the dirt and with a piece of granite or marble to mark it, you think of that body... that lifeless body. It was a matter of separating life from death and going with life, instead. Faith agreed with me. Chuckie was not in total agreement. Notably, Dad's older sisters, Ruth and Helen, wanted a service and were prepared to buy a cemetery plot and headstone. We obviously differed about the idea of a service. A compromise had to be reached. I was not happy.

What the adults present decided was that there would, indeed, be a service. It would be just for our immediate and extended family, with one exception. George Schram, one of Dad's best friends, would be invited to his service. It was not going to be called a funeral; it was to be a *service*. This was a semantic change only and was a concession made mostly for my benefit, I think. It was also decided that the casket would remain closed. Chuckie, in absolute defiance of both Dad's wishes and against the opinions of the rest of us, pushed for her right to gaze upon Dad's face one last time. We agreed (quite reluctantly, on my part) that she could do so but only before the service. The casket would remain closed for the rest of us.

Ruth and Helen could not be dissuaded from their plan to buy a plot and headstone for their brother. In one aspect of all this, we were unanimous:

we all agreed we would not bury him. Dad would be cremated. (Still, Ruth and Helen went ahead with their plan, and to this day, there is a plot and a headstone with his name on it in a cemetery somewhere. Aside from his name on a headstone, no part of him is there.) What to do with his ashes? Besides his kids and tinkering with cars, he had only one other pleasure: he used to enjoy saltwater surf casting (ocean fishing from the shore). He would sometimes go out in a boat with a family friend—our adopted uncle, Roland Larsh—near the Quincy Light in Boston Harbor. We agreed that's where Dad's ashes would be spread. What I didn't realize at the time was that nothing had been said about how that would happen or who would do it. I acquiesced to most of these conditions but vigorously challenged Chuckie to reconsider her desire to view Dad's body. It was Dad's specific wish that we would not see him dead. I was sixteen years old. I was very frustrated as I realized other people were overruling me because they were adults and I was not; that my best friend, who had expressed his wishes to me as his only son and primary confidant, was not getting what he had wished for. I was powerless to stop the juggernaut of my sisters and one of their husbands. I knew Mom would not be an arbiter for any disagreement, and though I opposed their decisions, I specifically wanted Chuckie to know how I felt. I thought she, more than anyone else, would have respected Dad's wishes. My efforts were in vain—in her defense, however, she had often been deprived of normal adult interactions with Dad due to the frequent bouts of stubbornness surrounding hers and Mom's squabbles.

Things had to move quickly. I was not invited to go to the funeral home for the planning of the service. My Aunt Mary and Chuckie made those arrangements, as Faith would have no part of it. I thought this was a bit weird. However, the night before Dad died, he had an altercation with Faith. While he worked at Guimond Bros. Farms, Dad had brought home items that were not shipped out that day. His bounty often included milk in varying forms, yogurt, and other dairy products. Mom got first choice, then Faith and Chuckie got stuff for their families. On that Thursday night, Dad had gone to Faith's house to offer what he had to her family. Mom had previously divulged something to Faith, and she had obviously taken a side—Mom's side—of whatever the issue was, and when she met him at the door that night, she told Dad to leave, that she never wanted to see him again. He asked, but she would not even let him see his grandkids (I'm sure he was thinking about seeing them one more time). She closed the door in his face. He was hurt deeply but did not seem to be too surprised by this turn of events. Reflecting on that interaction, I wondered how she felt the next day. Knowing all of this and reflecting on the days immediately following his death, Faith's comments, responses to my questions, and general demeanor made a lot more sense. That was the definitive end of the relationship between Faith and Dad. She chose to end it. In the years since his death, she has occasionally made comments about missing him. I have questioned her sincerity, and I wish I had not.

I remember discussions over the ridiculous restriction on the casket. A straight cremation required only a simple box. Because he was to be viewed by at least one family member, he had to be in a proper casket—however, it seemed that in order for him to be cremated we had to buy a very expensive casket, made of wood with no metal sheathing. When I heard this, two things happened:

I tried to remake my case for a simple process of having no service and no one viewing his dead body (as Dad had wished), and...

I knew from this moment forward, that I would build my own pine box. My family would not be burdened by overpaying for something that amounted to firewood.

I was, of course, shut down on my wish to change the plans. It was already done. Well, no, it wasn't. He hadn't been put in the coffin, and it wasn't burned yet. Again, I wasted my breath. This part of the whole process was so frustrating. I was being included because of my close relationship with him and because I was the oldest of the three siblings still at home, yet I did not really have a say because I was too young.

Some of what happened in those few days has become a blur with the passage of time. The service was to be held on Wednesday. We went to the funeral home in the morning; Lori had decided to join Chuckie in viewing Dad's body before they closed the casket, although nearly everyone questioned her motivation. Later, Lori denied doing so and, when confronted with the truth, made up some elaborate story about it. Chuckie said of her viewing that she hadn't seen him look that peaceful in a very long time. (With my mother's passing in 2017, Chuckie became the only one of the five of us to have viewed both parents' bodies after their demise.)

When I saw the coffin, draped with an American flag, I had a very hard time containing my emotions—but I did… for a while. I don't have any recollection of anything that was said by any officiant. What I do remember was a woman I did not at once recognize (later identified as Aunt Helen) wailing and bawling in the back of the room. She cried out:

"What have you done to my baby brother?"

It was precisely at that moment that I lost the battle of self-control. I had held it together for the last six days, but with that outburst, I could no longer hold back the tears. My brothers-in-law were somehow right there at my side and escorted me out of the funeral home. I was grateful to have that part of this whole affair behind me. The flag that had draped his coffin was folded into the traditional triangle and was presented to me. I kept it in a dry-cleaning bag for a few years and then got a mahogany and glass case for it. It continues to live in my home.

Memere's comments in the hospital and Aunt Helen's comments during Dad's service both pointed to an adult opinion that Dad was the victim. I understand that—in a literal sense—he physically perpetrated the violence that wounded Mom and took his life. I totally accept that. Especially while writing these accounts, though, I have had the opportunity to relive and rehash the events of 1976. There is no way to isolate or to definitively determine causality, and there is no one left to punish for what occurred. No degree of punishment could ever bring back my dad.

Twenty-Four

"Challenges are gifts that force us to search for a new center of gravity."

—*Oprah Winfrey*

Although I was sixteen, my mother still imposed a strict bedtime for me. While Chuckie was staying with us, she had not enforced our bedtimes. After the service, though, I was emotionally spent. I'd been running on adrenaline for several days. I went to bed at about 9 or 9:30 that night. Again, I conjured up the voice of my father telling me it was okay to let go. I was exhausted and quickly fell into a very deep sleep. Somewhere around one in the morning, Chuckie shook me awake. I thought something was seriously wrong.

"There's a huge spider in the living room—I can't sleep in there!"

Groggy and with vision blurred from sleep, I made my way downstairs.

"Where?" I asked.

She pointed to a tiny speck where the wall met the ceiling on the opposite side of the room.

"You're joking, right?" She wasn't.

A bit of toilet paper and a small amount of pressure, and the spider was no more. I went back to bed. I doubt she slept, despite my effort.

The next day was nothing… quite literally, nothing. We didn't go anywhere or do anything. We sat in the house. Mom wasn't quite ready to come home. I was bored. I told Chuckie I was going back to school on Friday. She told me I didn't need to… that I could stay home as long as I thought I needed. I told her there was nothing more for me to do, and I didn't want to just sit around. The boredom invited problems with feeling sorry for myself, and I needed to get on with life. Lori wanted to capitalize on the situation and said that she wasn't going back to school this week—or next week (I believe she was overruled, though, and went back the following week. The same with Wendy).

I didn't know, at the time, when Dad's ashes were scattered or by whom. When I asked Chuckie, she didn't know either. I recently confirmed it was Faith and Dickie who did it. In retrospect, they may have taken it upon themselves to spare me the anguish. Since I had been such a staunch advocate for remembering him as he was when he was alive, maybe they thought it would be best not to involve me. Chuckie and Lori had looked upon his body as it lay in the coffin. If Faith had taken part in the scattering of his ashes, it could be construed as having dealt with Dad in a death state, which was, technically, against his wishes. That means that Wendy and I were the only ones left who had kept the separation between his life and his death—and only one of us had done so of our own volition. To this day, I have no vision of him after death, save for that which was involuntarily thrust upon me by the photographer from *The Woonsocket Call*. I don't know where the plot and headstone, purchased by my aunts, is located. My last memory of his face comes from when he was still among the living. I will cherish that memory, too.

Twenty-Five

"Tis better to have loved and lost than never to have loved at all."

—*Alfred, Lord Tennyson*

I missed most of the school day on the previous Friday and all the next week. Friday, the day of 'the tragedy,' hadn't counted against me because I had been there to start the day. The other four days represented nearly half of the days of school I had missed since kindergarten—ten days in eleven years. It was quite out of the ordinary for me to miss school. Going back that Friday morning made me feel a little like Rosa Parks might have felt on the bus. Every single eye was on me. I felt a weird cross between shame and anger. People didn't know what to think, let alone how to act or interact with me. People pointed and spoke to each other with hushed voices while looking at me. Normal conversation stopped as I drew near. I was alone in a building with seven hundred other kids and forty or so teachers. The adults were no better with the awkwardness than were the kids. There were neither grief counselors nor anyone else to help people deal with such a tragedy. Granted, only one person had died, but ours was a regional school representing two small towns. There might have been 10,000 people combined between them. It really was a small and relatively tight-knit community. What had happened had affected everyone.

A good friend of mine saw me at my locker and came up to express his condolences. Dave Gauthier came from a big family in Millville. He and every single one of his siblings were extremely good-looking, extremely well-mannered, talented athletes and musicians, and were all very intelligent. It felt as if he had stepped in to prove I wasn't poisonous, because once he broke that ice, others seemed to understand it was okay to speak to me. Throughout the day, I received awkward comments meant to resemble condolences from classmates and awkward comments from teachers, as well.

For most of those teachers (and for me, as well), it was essentially my first day of the school year. Many classes were well underway, and this placed me behind from the start. A couple of teachers seemed to overcompensate and relieved me of an assignment already handed out. Others felt I would do well to just step right into the waters. In other words, I was a week behind and still needed to get the assignment in. No pity.

In the days and weeks that followed 'the tragedy,' I had returned to my school routine. Shortly after my return to school, Mr. Hessney approached me and offered his sympathies. He told me that if I needed anything, I should not hesitate to let him know. I don't think either of us knew where that would take us in the year ahead. For those of us in the music department, there was a lot of practice both during and after school hours. The September weather in New England was generally quite nice. We practiced outdoors at every opportunity, preparing for the Gimbels Thanksgiving Day Parade in Philadelphia. It is the oldest Thanksgiving Day parade in the U.S., and we were invited as a result of our showing in Washington, D.C., the previous spring.

One day, when rehearsal was over and we headed back into the building, I was approached by Phoebe Collins, a fellow clarinetist who was a year ahead of me in school. She had previously made me aware that she was (romantically?) interested in me. She was nice enough and pleasant looking, but I was turned off by her smoking habit. Because we played in the same section of the band, we were usually near each other. As we approached the door to the school, she said she was "really sorry about what had happened." My awkward response was:

"Don't worry about it."

Her reply was sarcastic, though I don't think she meant it to be mean-spirited. She said something like:

"I'm not worried about it. Get over it."

And she walked away. I was trying to get over it, but what I'd just been through was not something you just get over.

On the home front, Mom was released from the hospital and was recovering from her physical wounds. I was trying to be 'the man of the house' and had offered to repair things when needed. The fan in the range hood stopped working. When I offered to try and fix it, my mother exploded. I had seen her explode before. This common occurrence was likely linked to her intermittent explosive disorder. She would fly into a rage with little (and sometimes no) provocation. This was one of those times. When I spoke with Faith and Chuckie about it, they explained that maybe I reminded Mom a little too much of my dad already, and by offering to do something he would have done, it was too much for her. That's possible, but there was no way I could know for sure, and as a teenager, that made no sense. So, what if I looked like him? I wasn't Dad. She didn't mention him, except to denigrate or otherwise insult him and his memory.

Regardless of the reason behind it, I was seeing a decided trend, and the 'anti-me' activity seemed to be steadily increasing. I already thought she hated me. As the tension became progressively worse between Mom and me, my time with—and the counsel of—my friends grew to be more important. I wasn't always able to visit other homes (hiding from my mother might have been a better description than to "visit" someone else), so the telephone became somewhat important. I didn't dare speak of what was going on for fear of being overheard. That meant that most conversations with most friends needed to be succinct and consisted mostly of small talk. The exception to this was Clark. He and I applied a system he and another friend, Mike Suss, had developed. Clark would ask pointed questions that allowed me to answer simply "Yes" or "No." He would then pose follow-up questions or would posit a couple of likely but different situations. To these I could answer "the former" or "the latter"; thus, he could ascertain what was going on without me actually saying anything. It was clever, kept me from going insane due to solitude, and my mother didn't know what was being said.

My friend Clark was not typical in any way. He was a bright guy, a phenomenal cartoonist/caricaturist, and a hell of a musician. We had met, initially, when we were both about ten years old and he had come into our classroom to showcase his saxophone. Thin, sinewy, and just over six feet tall, he had dark, straight hair and feet that appeared as though he wouldn't ever grow into them. He was one of the best friends I had. We liked a lot of the same things, and we hung out more and more with each other as time wore on. Clark's mother thought Suss was a bad influence on him, and my mother thought Clark was a bad influence on me. Most people, including our mothers, considered us weird. Clark's mother was tough; however, he said that I was the only person he knew whose mother was worse than his.

Over the course of several years, we built our own way of communication, which no one else ever really figured out. We took words whose pronunciations were already mangled by the local accent and dialect and often mangled them a bit further before spelling that bizarrely pronounced word phonetically. We knew what each other was saying, but no one else did. This was especially effective in a written format. Often, using onomatopoeia, we'd create a word for a sound or action that didn't have a word (and probably didn't need one). Clark would look at me and say:

"Spell that."

I'd add silent letters and parentheses in the spelling, and we'd fall on the floor laughing. We enjoyed *Monty Python* and *MAD Magazine*; we built (and destroyed) models; we created a myth about our hatred of cats and were so convincing that people believed we were guilty of some heinous things. We even adopted a cat named Peef that Clark kept with him until the cat died. He had Peef cremated and hand-carved a box for his ashes, which I believe he still has.

While the Gimbels Thanksgiving Day Parade was still ahead of us, we did almost nothing but marching band practice; however, after Thanksgiving, we began rehearsing, in earnest, for the winter concert. Most of those rehearsals took place on the stage in the high school auditorium. It was a really nice and well-equipped stage, capable of hosting traveling shows or major theater productions. It had a fly gallery and an oak hardwood deck. Lori had had no real interest in the band. When I began playing, I got a refurbished student model clarinet. My mother was very hesitant to invest in it. I was thrilled to have any instrument. With our recent Cherry Blossom triumph, Lori, along with a lot of other kids, thought the band would be a good thing to be a part of. She decided the flute would be a good instrument. My mother literally ran out and bought her a brand-new, advanced student model silver flute. She likely paid twice or thrice the investment made in my clarinet. Lori gave it up less than six months later. Still, Lori wanted to belong to the program. She signed up as part of the color guard and began training to manipulate a flag on an aluminum pole. She was a clumsy girl with a very short attention span and somehow managed to stab herself (not deeply) in the palm of her hand with the finial at the top of her flagpole. Her association with the marching band fizzled to nothing. I was still playing the cheap student horn.

When flutes play in a marching band, it's often difficult to hear them above the thumping of the drums and the blaring of the brass instruments. Mr. Hessney had asked me to take up an E-flat clarinet and to double the flute line to help them be heard. The instrument was a recent acquisition for the school, so when the new concert season began, the scores Mr. Hessney bought often included a part for E-flat clarinet. In addition to my regular clarinet, I usually also carried the school's instrument. During band rehearsals, I sat next to two really sweet young women. I had a crush on Susan, and Karen had a crush on me. We often joked and goofed off together, and we were part of a larger, but fairly well-defined, group of friends.

I came into rehearsal, on the stage, one day carrying both the E-flat and my regular clarinet. I had a folder for my music clamped between my teeth. I leaned over the music stand in front of my chair and dropped the folder onto it. I then sat down... or at least that's what I meant to do and what would have happened, if the chair had remained where I saw it just seconds before. Karen had decided to pull one of the oldest pranks known to kids. I hit the deck and, because I had an expensive instrument in each hand, I could not break my fall. Crack! Even in all the years since, I cannot recall ever being in that much pain. I suffered through the rest of band rehearsal and put my instruments away. Then, instead of going to lunch, I hobbled my way upstairs (excruciating!) to the nurse's office.

Mrs. Zekanowski looked over her reading glasses and, seeing the anguish on my face, she simply asked:

"What happened?"

I explained that someone (I didn't name names) had pulled a chair out from under me and I landed on the stage floor. She made me lie on my stomach and placed an ice pack on my backside. Then she went next door to her office and called my mother.

"...Mrs. Francis? Hi. This is Mrs. Zekanowski, the school nurse. Yes. Seems Brian had an accident during band. I think he needs to go to the hospital for x-rays... Mrs. Francis, I can assure you he is not faking it, he's in a lot of pain... Mrs. Francis, if you won't come and get him, I'm prepared to call the police. [long pause] ...Thank you, Mrs. Francis."

Mrs. Zekanowski then came back into the little room in which I was resting and told me my mom was coming to get me. I don't think she understood that I had heard the entire telephone conversation—at least her side of it. Mom did come to the school, and the nurse walked me out to the car. I had great difficulty getting into the passenger seat, and my mother made no attempt to hide her disgust and disdain at having to come and get me.

On the positive side, it was a short ride. On the negative side, it was a short ride—because she took me home, not to any hospital. On the way home, I was told that maybe I had them snowed, but I wasn't fooling her. I was allowed to lie down on the sofa, but there was to be no TV. I lay there, in deafening silence, for more than an hour. The pain was like nothing I'd ever felt. I began feeling nauseous. I had had no food since breakfast, so I didn't think I would vomit, but I did. I was then accused of forcing myself to be sick.

There was nothing I could say to defend myself that wasn't turned right around and used against me. After my younger sisters got home from school and after they got their homework done, my mother announced supper was ready. I replied that I wasn't hungry. The three of them ate while I silently lay on the sofa. After the meal, my mother came into the living room and informed me that since I insisted on this charade, I needed to get up and she would take me to the emergency room. It was a cold announcement. There was absolutely no empathy. No sympathy. No understanding, on her part. I understood, unequivocally, that I was disrupting her evening.

After a stone-cold silent ride to the hospital, I was brought into an exam room. The nurse asked my mom a bunch of questions and then left. When she returned, she looked at me and asked if I had ever had an enema.

"A what?"

She described what it was and why it was needed. Did I really need that? The answer was "yes." I was told to hold it in, as long as I was able. The idea was to clear my bowel enough to allow an unobstructed path for the x-ray to view my lower spine. I did as I was told. I held and held. It was terribly uncomfortable. My bowel began spasming and cramping. Sitting down on the toilet was awfully painful. Tears were streaming down my face as I relaxed my sphincter... *sploosh*. I came out of the bathroom and announced what I thought was success.

"Okay. Now please follow me."

Into the x-ray room we went. This was also my first experience with a "Johnny," as the open-back hospital gowns were colloquially known. No underwear... not a thing between my butt and the air.

"Please get up here," said the technician.

The table was cold, and the pain exquisite until... the two women pushed down on my pelvis to force my butt onto the cold table.

"Hold, please."

I had thought the pain was bad before. Nothing did, or ever has, compared. Apparently, I didn't do as they asked. I was supporting the middle section of my body with my hands, which meant my butt was not down on the table. They came at me again and forced the issue. I could not hold back the tears.

A few minutes later I was seated next to my mother and the nurse came up to us…

"Uh… we're going to need to give you another enema…"

I didn't hear the rest of what she said. If I didn't actually pass out, I certainly checked out. What followed was another enema and another battle with the x-ray ladies and another bit of time with my annoyed mother. Then the word came:

"You can get dressed; the doctor will be in to see you shortly."

I wasn't quite finished dressing when he came in.

"Brian? Mrs. Francis? Hi. I looked at the x-rays; how did this happen?"

I explained the chair incident. He shook his head.

"Well, Brian has a very clear break in his sacrum."

The words were barely past his lips, and my question as to what a *sacrum* was had formed and was on my lips, but my mother's question made it out first:

"Are you sure?" she spat.

This was both an insult to the doctor's training and ability and was a reinforcement of her disbelief in the legitimacy of my complaint. She couldn't believe I wasn't faking or lying. The doctor was quite appropriate and assured in his response:

"Yes, I'm quite sure."

He looked at me with a half-smile as if to say "Sorry, kid," and then proceeded to tell us there was, essentially, nothing they could do except to give me something for the pain. I had to ride it out.

I was given a prescription for Percocet, instructions to use a rolled towel to keep weight off the bottom of my spine when I sat, and I was sent home. It was well after dark when we got there. About a half-hour later, the phone rang. Lori answered and handed it to me. Karen was almost too cute for words. Dark eyes and dark, straight hair and bangs cut straight across her forehead and a splash of freckles across her face. She tended to wear a little too much perfume—Avon's *Sweet Honesty* was her preferred scent—but this was usually tolerable. When I picked up the phone, she was crying, and her words were mostly unintelligible. After a while, her friend

Emily got on the phone. Emily explained that Karen was mortified when she realized that I had been seriously hurt because of her playful little stunt. For years after, she felt guilt and was remorseful. She couldn't understand how or why I would forgive her (which I did right away). I knew there wasn't a malicious bone in her body. She was cute and sweet, and I simply was not interested in her in the manner I think she had hoped I was. The object of my affection was Susan.

The next morning, I was hoping to just rest. Apparently, this was not an option. Mom woke me up at the usual time. I skipped breakfast for two reasons: 1) I wasn't really hungry, and 2) after a request for a ride (denied), I realized I was being forced to walk to school. I wasn't moving too quickly, and I calculated it would take me longer than usual. The usual fifteen-minute walk took me over twenty-five minutes. I had taken a pain pill before leaving the house. It had a double effect: the pain began drifting into the realm of "I don't care," and my stomach began churning. In the middle of second period, I had to make an emergency dash for the boys' room. I was done for the day, and Mrs. Zekanowski had to call my mother for the second day in a row. Needless to say, Mom was not amused.

I was back into the swing of day-to-day existence and the trials and tribulations of attending public high school. Life at home was tedious. I was constantly walking on eggshells around my mother. I spent time down in the shed. I visited my older sisters. I practiced my music. I did enough schoolwork to keep my grades around a 'B'. I listened to the old Philco AM radio Memere had given me at night… trying to keep up with the Boston Bruins or the Boston Celtics. I thought I was living. In retrospect, I was barely existing. The Christmas season was soon upon us. I didn't really know what to expect for my first Christmas without Dad.

Twenty-Six

"But I've strayed so far from normal now, I'll never find my way back. And the truth is, I no longer want to."

— Alyson Noel, *Saving Zoë*

Christmas morning arrived. I went downstairs with the two younger girls. Wendy was 9 and maybe still believed in the myth of Santa Claus, so Lori and I played along. Lori, endlessly greedy, began tearing her way through the presents placed under the tree. She was specifically looking for those intended for her. She found several for Wendy and herself. When she happened upon a stout and heavy package addressed to her, she stopped handing out presents and began ripping paper and tearing at tape. Inside, she discovered a Singer sewing machine. She also had several other packages. I had one. I opened it to find two pairs of pants – corduroy – one a dark brown and the other a burnt orange color. That was it. My birthday, the following month, yielded even less from my mother.

There was something else brewing, though again, I couldn't put my finger on it. Knowing you're not welcome in your parent's home is an awkward and simultaneously disheartening feeling. 1976 had been the year from hell… what was in store for 1977?

Material things like the flute and the sewing machine were hard to ignore, but there was also an air of favoritism that apparently only Lori didn't perceive. She was fond of invading my space – my bedroom – and rifling through my things. I felt violated every time, and my mother refused to do anything beyond an occasional and extremely mild admonishment. I discovered Lori leaving my room on one occasion and questioned her about it. Her response was to throw a freshly toasted English muffin (with hot peanut butter) at me. It glanced off me and stuck on the door to my room, damaging a cherished souvenir mask I had purchased on a school trip. I had had enough. I pushed her out of the way and punched her in the shoulder as I went past her.

The histrionics went into 'turbo-charged' mode. My mother would not hear my entreaties for fairness. If I touched Lori again,

"…a complaint of assault and battery will be filed with the police."

She was going to call the police on me!

Twenty-Seven

*"In healthy families, we encourage children to be loving
and close to each other.
In narcissistic families, children are pitted against each other
and taught competition."*

—Dr. Karyl McBride

I had been taking Driver's Education classes in school. Had I already completed the course, I could have taken the test for licensure at sixteen and a half years of age. Even though the course I took was not quite over, with my 17th birthday approaching, I could get my license with or without the course. I made my appointment for Friday, the eleventh of February, to take my driving test. My mother agreed to take me to the nearest licensing office for the test.

As was typical of New England in January, there was snow on the ground. We had had quite a bit. The morning of the eleventh dawned white and cold, but with a beautiful blue sky. This was going to be a great day for me! I was very excited as I ran down the stairs, ate my breakfast, and got ready for school. I had walked out the door and was halfway down the sidewalk when Mom poked her head out of the door and called after me. As I turned toward her, she said (quite matter-of-factly):

"I'm not taking you to get your license, today."

Her words stopped me in my tracks. She then closed the door, leaving me standing in the crisp winter air in a state of bewilderment and pain. I was close to tears—not from sadness, but from frustration. I followed her back inside.

"How? Why? What have I done to deserve this?"

She would give no answers, just a cold reminder to get myself to school. She had casually gone back inside, sat down, and continued drinking her coffee. She was hurting me. I didn't understand any of this. It felt so mean-spirited... so deliberate. I was determined she would not win this one.

I went to school and spoke to some of my friends and the Driver's Ed teacher, Mr. Larsen. The gist of what they all said was this: I didn't need a parent to do this. If I could find someone who was at least eighteen, had their own car and insurance, they could take me for my driving exam. I knew it was a stretch, but I started asking everyone I knew for help. Once again, being involved in the music department paid off. Tim McQuade, the clarinetist I sat next to in band, had recently turned eighteen and had his own car. I asked, fully expecting him to decline. Instead, he said:

"Sure, Fran, I can do it."

I didn't know what kind of car he had—let alone ever having driven it. Although I knew how to drive a manual, I was grateful this unfamiliar car had an automatic transmission. That's where the conveniences ended, though. It was a beast—a 1966 Chevrolet Impala four-door without power brakes or power steering. Anyone who's ever seen or driven one of those cars knows they're just a few inches shorter than a football field. Add in the lack of power steering, and one might as well be driving a locomotive through the city. Still, it was a car, and I was going to take my test that afternoon, despite my mother's antics.

In Massachusetts, the State Police administered driving tests (back then, at least—I don't know if they still do so). I will never forget that encounter. This guy was huge! His pant legs were tucked into his lace-up, spit-shined boots. Tim was asked if this was his car and was asked to show proof of insurance, which he did. He was then invited to take a seat in the rear. The "Statey" took his seat on the passenger side of the yawning front bench in the Impala. He was obviously scripted, but was nonetheless quite intimidating. What came next made such a lasting impression that I remember it verbatim to this day:

"I'm going to place my foot on the hump. If, for any reason—accident or near accident—I have to get to the brake, I will do so even if I have to go through your foot."

I was duly impressed.

The route we took included several small side streets where the snowplows had left artificial banks of dirty, white, icy snow close to ten feet high on both sides of the roads. He had me stop and directed me to perform a three-point turn. The car was too long, the steering too tough, and the snowbanks encroached too much on the roadway. The physics of the situation did not allow a three-point turn. I managed to get turned around by performing a five-point turn. I was then directed to pull up behind the building where I had started and parallel park the car. I did so. We then proceeded to the parking lot, and I was instructed to place the vehicle in Park and shut off the ignition. The "Statey" was silent as he made his notes. At least, I thought what he was doing was making notes. What he was really doing was giving me my temporary license. I had passed. The only thing for which he had deducted points was parallel parking too far from the curb. My five-point turn was apparently okay.

Tim allowed me to drive his car to my house. I thanked him profusely. To this day I feel as though I owe him something. He wouldn't accept anything then, but I've felt I owed him more than just "Thanks." Upon entering the house through the kitchen door, I placed my temporary license on the table and "forgot" to pick it back up as I went to my room upstairs. This was a major moment for me, as I'd just proven to her — and, more importantly, to myself—that she did not have the absolute ability to negatively impact my life that she was attempting to exert. I could move forward from here.

I was a licensed driver, but I had no car. It turns out the vehicle Dad was repairing for me didn't belong to him. He had it on credit from his friend, George. George ran a used car lot and, over the years, had worked many deals with my dad. Dad would repair vehicles and George would sell them. If Dad wanted a car painted, George would allow him to use his garage after hours. It was a win-win, symbiotic relationship. This time, as usual, Dad had gotten the vehicle without paying for it. George was out $300, and even though Dad had gotten it running, George needed to recoup what he had into it. I begged Mom for the money, to no avail; therefore, that car was no longer a possibility. I had no job, so I had no money of my own. I couldn't get to a job without a car, and I couldn't buy a car without a job. I started looking for some other way to make money.

Twenty-Eight

"Make the most of yourself, for that is all there is of you."

—*Ralph Waldo Emerson*

In the early spring of 1977, I had wired in a telephone extension in my bedroom and kept it hidden. The bedroom was, if we all interpreted correctly, designed to be the master bedroom, so the telephone wiring was already there. I needed only to find an outlet. Dad was fond of collecting things that might be useful someday, and there was a telephone outlet among those things. Lori found my connection and made a great show of telling Mom, who then proceeded to literally rip the phone out of its place. She broke the wire that connected it to the wall. I searched for the phone for over a week and, by process of elimination, figured out that the only place in the house it could be hiding was in a chest freezer in the basement.

Here's how far my mother would go to thwart me: the freezer was locked. One afternoon, I found myself alone in the house and went to the basement to see if I could open the freezer. I was successful. There, inside and covered with frost, was the old black telephone Dad had appropriated and that I had used as an extension in my bedroom. I took it, made sure the freezer was once again locked, and returned the phone to my room. I waited several days before reconnecting it. Lori found out, once again, that the phone was there. I challenged her to come up with a manner in which that discovery could have been made without her having gone into my room. Outmaneuvered, she offered a deal: she wouldn't tell Mom as long as I let her use it. Against my better judgment, I acquiesced. The phone was simply an extension of the main line and Lori was not careful. My mother picked up the living room phone to make a call and discovered Lori talking with a friend on the extension. Gone again.

Home was not a happy place. To me, it felt not only hostile but dangerous. Always on the lookout for more excuses to stay away from home, I auditioned for the high school musical production of *West Side Story*. I had begun to explore making music with my voice once it had finally changed. This was my first foray into musical theater. I did well enough to be cast as Riff—a major supporting role. Many rehearsals were held during the daily time slot reserved for chorus, but as we approached the time for the show to go up, we had some after-school and evening rehearsals, as well as set-building and painting sessions. I admit that I lied a few times—claiming to need to stay for rehearsal when there was none. I would hang out in the music room for a couple hours after school. Sometimes there was someone else to keep me company—other times I was alone. I'd practice on my clarinet, finish homework, or I'd read. Whatever it took to pass the time.

Faith and Dickie were both employed and were working different shifts. After school, I'd bicycle across town to their apartment and babysit their three little ones between the time Faith left for work and the time Dickie came home from his job. They couldn't really afford to pay me. They were also getting ready to buy a new home in the next town, so money was tight. Sometimes I would visit Chuckie at her apartment in Woonsocket. I'd eat at my sisters' homes as often as I could.

I went home one evening during spring break not because I wanted to, but because I had nothing else to do. There hadn't been any conversation that day between my mother and me, so I wasn't on alert. I entered the house, as usual, through the kitchen door. Lori made an off-color remark toward me, and I gave an equally snide response. I continued through the kitchen toward the bathroom to wash up before supper. I thought nothing of the exchange as it was par for the course. As I was returning to the kitchen, I saw only Lori and Wendy sitting at the table and could not see my mother. However, their glancing eyes gave her away—as I rounded the corner from the hall, I saw the cast iron skillet descending quickly toward my head. I ducked and dodged to my left. The skillet caught me on the right shoulder. The blow knocked me to the floor. The pain in my shoulder was intense.

I had taught myself to be as stoic as possible whenever Mom attacked me. From the floor where I had landed, I asked why she had hit me with the skillet. No answer. She just turned around and went back to the stove as if nothing had happened. This kind of attack could not have been merited by my lack of respect or any degree of sarcasm toward my sister. The physical abuse had become *de rigueur*—it didn't need a reason.

I felt pain in my shoulder and was having many other thoughts in the moment—but being a teenaged male, my hunger overrode everything else. I got up and surveyed the food situation. Mom had her back to me in the corner between the sink and the stove. As I looked at the table, it became obvious that it had not been anything I said or did. There were three place settings only—one for Mom and one each for the girls. There was no place set for me. Lori was sitting in my usual spot and Wendy was seated across from her. It became obvious that the attack had not resulted from anything I said or did. In a moment of sickening clarity, I realized Mom's attack on me was premeditated.

I silently took a seat at the table next to Wendy. Mom then made it patently clear that I was not welcome for that evening's meal. I asked why. She gave no answer. I asked if there was something I could take and eat on my own. She said, "No." The physical pain in my shoulder was really beginning to register... it began throbbing, as did my head. I was injured, both physically and emotionally. I was furious and very confused. I said, "Fine," got up, turned, and walked right out the kitchen door. This whole episode lasted no more than seven or eight minutes. I was hungry—I had no money and was at a total loss as to what to do. What I did know was that I was unwelcome and potentially in grave danger being in that house. I had to leave.

The weather was still cold, and I did not trust my bike in the dark without a light, so I started walking. I walked to Woonsocket and showed up at Chuckie's door. She asked me what I was doing, and I explained what little I knew of what had just transpired an hour and a half before. Of course, she invited me in and fed me. She said I could stay the night, but that she was not going to get between Mom and me. I slept on her sofa that night. In the morning, I set out for home, not really knowing what I was going to do. No one was at the house when I arrived. I had a key, so I went inside and found something to eat. I felt as though I was in that house illegally. My own home, and it felt wrong to be there. I grabbed a change of underwear and socks and ensured the door was locked again as I exited.

I went down to the shed and got my bicycle. I pedaled around, not really knowing where I was going, and ended up over at Faith and Dickie's new house. They welcomed me, and after telling them what had happened, they told me I could stay. By the weekend, though, they were feeling uncomfortable. Dickie called Mom and spoke with her for some time. After which, he told me to gather my things. I was going back. As we drove in the direction of the house, Dickie gave me quite a lecture about diplomacy. I tried to tell him again that I had done nothing to provoke her. He said that when he spoke with her, she agreed to let it go if I would. That was *so* weird. She attacked me with a potentially lethal weapon, and she was "willing to let it go"? He told me I should be the bigger person and apologize. Again, I pointed out that I had done nothing which could remotely require anything resembling an apology and that I did not have anything to "let go," except that I had been physically attacked. He stopped by a florist and bought a small bouquet, which I was to give her as a peace offering. I really liked Dickie, but at that moment, I really felt betrayed by him. Though, as I had no alternatives, I had to go along with his plan.

When we got to the house, you could have "cut the tension with a knife," as they say. I gave her the flowers and dutifully recited the scripted apology Dickie had suggested. Her attitude and her appearance could not have been described as anything but contentious. I felt like I was walking into a doctor's office knowing that his specialty was involuntary lobotomies. In the back of my mind, I was also thinking about some of the horror movies I'd seen where the victim decides to "check out" the home of the killer despite all common sense. I felt scared. After the initial encounter, I retreated to my room. For the next few months, I tolerated the living situation by staying away from the house as much as possible—even more than I had before.

One distraction I had was in preparation for the school's annual talent show. My friend Clark was going to graduate at the end of May, so he wanted to do something as a kind of "gift" from him to the school. His idea was to recreate the Mel Brooks / Carl Reiner sketch, *The 2000-Year-Old Man*. Clark had an LP of the sketch that we listened to over and over again. We painstakingly transcribed every word they said. We then developed costumes and rehearsed the thing *ad nauseam*. The faculty advisor for the talent show, Mr. Ethier, held auditions, but basically, anyone who tried got in. We had him in stitches. Many of the acts were either singing or dancing and required musical accompaniment. Ronny Stockard (Clark affectionately called him "Bullwinkle" due to his long face) was a particularly gifted young pianist and had agreed to play for all those who needed musical accompaniment. Everyone involved agreed our act was one of the most polished and certainly the funniest in the show. After a dress rehearsal on May ninth, we were scheduled to open the next night and run for two nights of performances.

May tenth came, and with it came a freak New England ice storm. Branches soft with new growth snapped under the ice and power lines came down. Electrical power was interrupted for most of the area. Clark and I paid no attention to the weather and reported to the school to begin putting on our makeup and costumes. We were in the boys' restroom between the cafeteria and the auditorium, and who should walk in but the notoriously dour vice principal, Mr. Powers. His first reaction was something neither of us had ever seen: he laughed. He then told us the show was cancelled that night due to the weather. To have said we were disappointed would have been an understatement.

The next night we were back, and the show began on time. We were slated to be the last act in the first half of the show, just before intermission. Our position on the stage was slightly stage right and seated in a couple of chairs in front of the main curtain. I knew it was static, but this was an interview. It was a satirical look at typical interviews from television, such as one would see with Merv Griffin, David Frost, or William F. Buckley. I was wearing a ridiculously loud and ill-fitting suit. Clark had a bald cap, white beard/eyebrows, and a toga. Our routine was performed flawlessly. We could see people in the front rows bent over with laughter.

Anyone familiar with Mel Brooks knows he sometimes got a bit raunchy. We did not really alter or censor the skit—we didn't think we needed to. We were wrong.

At the very moment we were performing *The 2000-Year-Old Man*, the school board was meeting in another part of the building. Unbeknownst to us, a cast member's dad had burst in upon the school board and demanded they "...do something about the filth in that show" or he would pull his child out of it.

We learned of Mr. Scott's demands at intermission when we were summoned to Mr. Neri's office. This was the second time this school year I had the privilege of a private audience with the principal. He apologized because his office was unavailable and led us, instead, into Mrs. Zekanowski's health office. He then asked us to perform our routine... a private showing. Curious but compliant, we did the whole thing with an audience of one. He had to exert considerable effort to keep from laughing out loud throughout the routine. When the private performance for Mr. Neri was done, he suggested we return to the auditorium.

Before we left that night, Mr. Ethier came to us in a very agitated state. It seems we were being cut from the show. Why? Mr. Scott (and our piano player's mom) had an objection to a reference in the routine to breast-feeding. Clark, as Brooks's character, attributed part of his long life to having

"…breast fed for two hundred years… I used to con a lot of ladies into doing it… they took pity on me!"

Either we were cut, or the musical accompanist for several acts as well as a lighting guy would be pulled, and the whole show would suffer. Mr. Ethier was even more upset than we were, and he told the powers-that-be this would be the last year he'd be the advisor for the talent show. To my knowledge, he made good on that vow. Several newspapers, including the *Providence Journal*, ran stories the next day in which they charged the school and the school board with censorship. What was particularly disappointing, for us, was that we could not see the howling, raucous laughter we had witnessed the night before. We also felt badly for Mr. Ethier, who had poured his soul into this talent show year after year. I felt particularly badly for Ronny Stockard and the Scott kid, as they bore the brunt of this narrow-minded extortion. Many students were upset. They had planned to return to see us and to bring family and friends. It was good while it lasted, and we had a lot of fun with it. Thank you, Mel and Carl.

Twenty-Nine

"The worst thing about being left out is knowing you weren't even a simple thought in any of their minds."

—*Anonymous*

That summer was a tumultuous one. In late July, I got an unexpected call from Clark.

"Hey Fran... can I borrow your black monkey suit?"

For a concert in the last school year, I got an all-black suit. It was very much like a tuxedo with its satin-like lapels, but it had no coordinating stripe down the pant legs. I had worn the suit when I had my senior portrait done. The key element was that it was black. My head was spinning. Why would gangly Clark want to borrow my suit? Then it dawned on me. It was black.

"Oh no!" I said. "Who?"

His voice was solemn but not overtly emotional.

"The old man (meaning his grandfather) walked into the store yesterday, looking like shit. I took him to the hospital. He had a burst aorta. He was gone in an instant—there was nothing they could do."

This was a devastating thing to have happened to Clark. The old man was the only father figure he had ever known. My suit didn't really fit him. It looked too small, but he was dressed nicely and in black. We spoke about how both of us had lost the father figures in our lives and how it seemed there were many parallels. We really did have many things in common.

During the latter part of spring and into that summer, I had been seeing a young woman from Millville. Of course, being without a car made the whole dating thing quite awkward and very near impossible (I was so very self-conscious of this). Very shortly after the school year was finished, I went to see her on a Thursday evening. I left her house at about 8:30 so I could make it back home by my 9 PM curfew. I found it extremely odd and embarrassing that a seventeen-year-old would have a curfew of 9 PM during summer vacation. But it was Mom's house and her rule. She had imparted some of her vitriolic opinion upon me:

"I don't know why you're bothering. No one is going to seek you out as a husband. You shouldn't expect to marry anyone beautiful, talented, or rich because they're all going to be out of your league. You should accept whoever comes along and this girl won't stick with you when she finds out who you really are."

She didn't even know the young lady. It wasn't about her—it was about me and how awful I was as a person.

I got back to our driveway at precisely 9 PM. There were no lights on whatsoever—none inside and certainly none outside. The only visible light came from the streetlight opposite our house. I walked the bicycle down to the shed, rather than try to ride in the dark. By the time I had put the bike away and walked back up to the house and got to the kitchen door, it must have been about 9:05. I opened the screen door and found the inside door locked. I got my key out of my pocket and turned it in the lock. When I tried to open the door, it wouldn't budge. I was quite puzzled. After a moment, my mind racing, I decided to try the front door. The locks on both front and back doors were opened by the same key, so my key fit both. Walking up the concrete stairs and grasping the latch, I found the screen door locked. This wasn't unusual. We didn't use that door, so having it locked made sense.

Ever resourceful and under the meagre illumination of the streetlight, I slowly and carefully pulled back the spline holding the screen to the frame. With a corner of the screen pulled back, I was able to manipulate the lock and opened that door. Then, after replacing the screen and spline, I put my key in the front door lock and opened it. I stepped into the dark living room, and I quietly closed the door behind me.

I was startled by my mother's voice behind me:

"Very clever. Tomorrow there'll be a bolt on that door, too."

She had totally spooked me. Upon hearing her voice in the dark, I felt adrenaline flooding my bloodstream, which made the hair on my neck and arms stand on end. She then got up from the sofa, upon which she had been sitting in the dark, and silently walked into her bedroom, closing the door behind her. I went upstairs to bed. Sleep did not come easily.

That next morning, when I got up and went to leave the house, I saw what had prevented me from opening the kitchen door: a skilled carpenter had carefully installed a very stout, brass-toned sliding steel bolt on the kitchen door. It had not been there the day before.

When I returned home that night (I made sure it was well before 9 PM), the same type of bolt had been installed on the front door—and just as carefully. I had to be sure I either followed the rules to the letter or that I had another way into the house.

When no one else was home on Saturday, I went around and tried the basement windows. She must have guessed I would try that route, as I found both of them nailed shut. Going back inside and up to my room, I sat and brainstormed. I wasn't sure of anything. I was in survival mode. I was also feeling very competitive, and I did not believe this was a game in which my mother was a truly suitable opponent. I could figure out anything she could conjure up—and I could find a way around it.

Saturday evening, I was back on my bike in Millville. Not being a disruptive kind of kid, I decided to head home so there would be no question about curfew time. This time I got home at 8:30. All lights were out and both doors were bolted again. In the backyard, my dad had kept an old oak extension ladder. It was extremely heavy. In order to get it to a window in my room, I had to carry it around the corner of the house occupied by my mother's bedroom. The ladder weighed almost as much as I did. I thought I was very careful and oh-so-quiet. The moon provided plenty of light for my activities. I put the ladder in place, climbed up and, half expecting her to have guessed I'd do this, tried my window. Apparently, she had not predicted this approach so, to my pleasant surprise, my window had remained unlatched. I pushed it up, climbed through, and went to bed. After my mother left for church in the morning, I got up, restored the ladder to its place in the backyard, and left the house for the day.

Sunday was an aimless waste of time, for the most part. I rode my bike nearly all day and really did nothing except a lot of thought and contemplation. That night, I returned home at 8 PM and found the same dark house to which I'd been coming home for the previous three nights, with doors locked and bolted (again). I went to the backyard... no ladder. It was gone. Where?

I walked the couple hundred feet from the house down to the shed and looked all around, inside and out. Not there. The only place I could think it might be was the basement. I went back and circled the house—wracking my brain—I could not think of a way into the house.

I went back down to the shed and set up my dad's hammock on the concrete driveway we had built to get in and out of the shed. I also helped him to bring electricity from the house down to the shed. It originated with a plug inserted into a 220-volt electric dryer outlet in the basement of the house. I turned on the lights in the shed and turned on a radio.

Ten minutes later, the radio went silent, and the lights went off. Mom had gone to the basement and unplugged the feed to the shed. This was a very petty move on her part, which left me wondering: *"What next?"*

I gathered some wood scraps and some twigs. I had a square, aluminum case from some electronic equipment I had previously disassembled. I put that out on the shed's driveway and built a fire in it.

My mother yelled from the house that she was going to call the fire department if I didn't put the fire out. I yelled back, *"What do you think they're going to say when I tell them why I'm out here?"*

She didn't reply, but I heard the door close.

I threw some more wood on the fire and tried to relax. Even though it was summertime, it was not really warm at night, and I was dressed only for daytime temperatures. The weather being cool, I kept the fire going most of the night. Although no firemen showed up, sleep was not something I experienced that night.

As my vigilance relaxed, I became aware of my hunger. I hadn't eaten for more than 24 hours. I was fatigued and hungry, but I was stubborn (I wonder where I learned that?). I was determined not to let her get the best of me.

I started formulating a new plan.

In the morning, I was up and away from the house just after dawn. In lieu of a shower, I washed my face and hands at the outside hose bib and then got on my bicycle and rode to nowhere in particular. I had no money and no food. I knew she had to go to work, so I waited until well past the time she needed to leave, and I went back to the house. I don't remember where Lori and Wendy went every day, but they went with Mom each morning. I knew she would be unable to bolt the doors from the outside, so

I knew I could make my way into the house—which I did. Having not eaten for some time, I was very hungry. I found something to eat, took a shower, and changed my clothes.

I called Clark to relate what had transpired over the previous three or four days and to see what he thought. He said, "Get your ass out of there!"

His mother and mine behaved similarly, though he frequently reminded me that mine was more prone to physical violence. I think this was his way of expressing his affection for me because I do believe he was concerned for my safety. I asked where he thought I might be able to go. He didn't have an answer.

After that phone call, I went to the basement and plugged in the power line to the shed. Not surprisingly, the big oak ladder was there. I unlocked the bulkhead door (access to the basement) in case I needed to try and get inside later, then I went back upstairs. I grabbed some more food, tried to make the house look as though I hadn't been there, and went out, locking the door behind me.

I was a stranger in the only home I had. I was breaking in for basic needs and felt as though I was doing something illegal. Even if it wasn't technically illegal, I was sure she could make it look that way to law enforcement. Adrenaline was again coursing through my veins. The house was silent except for my own pulse beating like a bass drum in my head.

In an attempt to ensure I didn't have to interact with my mother, I went into the house for what I needed, but then I didn't stick around. I roamed around the empty school grounds; I went to the downtown area... anywhere but home.

When I got home that evening, I went directly to the shed. I pulled the hammock out and put my bicycle inside. I then tested to see if the power was on. It was. She hadn't discovered that. I kept the lights off so as not to tip her off. I then turned the radio on (keeping the volume low), built my fire, and settled in. This time I had some warmer clothes and was somewhat more comfortable, so sleep found me. My rest may have been initially uneasy, but eventually, I slept "the sleep of the dead." I'd had no real sleep in two days... this felt good.

In the morning, I put the hammock away and walked my bike up to the house. Planning on repeating the prior morning's routine, I went to the kitchen door, put my key in the lock and... it wouldn't turn. She'd had the lock changed. I went around to the front door and found the same. Obviously, my attempts to obscure my presence in the house had not been sufficient.

What now? I remembered the basement bulkhead. She hadn't found it and I was in, once more. After my shower, I went to get some food. She had emptied the refrigerator! I could not believe she was going to all these elaborate means to do... what? Was this her way of pushing me out of the nest? I believed there was a legal requirement to care for a minor. I was still just seventeen. I had no idea what was going through her mind. I was simply trying my best to survive. A thousand thoughts were racing through my head.

I figured she could and probably would find the bulkhead unlocked and I would have no access. I went to the basement to look around. I had an epiphany: I went to the shed and got some tools. Returning to the basement, I worked for close to an hour to remove the nails on one of the basement windows without leaving evidence of having done so. I carefully cut the nails so that they didn't protrude enough to secure the window to the sash and appeared to be in place. I then put the tools away and searched the house for something to eat.

I found some Ritz crackers and a can of Spam. For a moment I considered being a total jerk and engaging the bolt before I exited through the basement. I thought better of it and left.

Crackers and Spam went only so far. I was hungry by the time I returned to the house that night. The bike went in and the hammock came out, as usual. I lay there, thinking about how hungry I was when I felt the first few drops of rain. Great. I pulled the hammock to a spot just inside the roll-up door and then used a tool to slide my firebox as close as I dared. When I settled again, my thoughts at once returned to my stomach.

Sometime after midnight, the rain stopped. I got up from the hammock and wandered up to the garden my mother had cultivated. Looking through the plantings, I spied a small bell pepper. I grabbed that and ate it on the spot. There wasn't much more.

I started walking down the street because I knew of a neighbor, a couple of houses down, who usually kept a garden. I walked that way and stood in the street contemplating the trespass and possible larceny I was about to commit. Finally satisfied no one was awake and no cars were coming, I walked into their backyard.

Their garden also had bell peppers. There were a few tomatoes and something else I don't quite remember taking, but I took food from their garden to stave off my hunger. I went back to the hammock.

In the morning, I heard Mom and the girls come out of the house, which meant I had fallen asleep and slept beyond my normal time to rise. After they left, I went up to the bulkhead and pulled. She'd found it and relocked it. It was time to implement Plan B.

I went to the basement window where I had removed the nails and discovered my work had not been noticed. I swung it open (it was hinged at the top) and began to squirm through. The last time I'd been through one of these basement windows, I was considerably younger and smaller. Getting through the window this time was difficult and I ended up scraping my back and my abdomen.

I was shocked, though, when I looked for food. What were they eating? There was nothing! I found a quart of frozen yogurt in the chest freezer in the basement and took a spoon with which to eat it. Not wanting to keep the spoon, I had to make plans to return it. I also didn't want to be caught inside the house, so I took everything outside, sat on the ground next to the chimney, and ate the entire quart.

I returned inside, washed, dried, and returned the spoon to the silverware drawer. I left via the kitchen door and made sure it was locked so my trespass into my own home would (hopefully) go unnoticed — including the now missing frozen yogurt.

My existence during this week was making me more and more depressed. It was time to do something else, but what?

Thirty

"A distracted existence leads us to no goal."

—*Johanne Wolfgang von Goethe*

I rode my bike down into Woonsocket and went to the Navy recruiting office. I spoke to the first-class petty officer that ran this office. I began by inquiring as to what was involved in 'signing up'. He explained many things and asked if I had time to take a quick test. He explained that there was no commitment in doing so, that it just helped him guide me in choosing the right program. I agreed. It was not lengthy, perhaps only thirty or thirty-five questions, and they were oddly simplistic—or so I thought. When I had completed it and handed him the test, he sat down and graded it. He turned to me and said:

"The real test is called the ASVAB* and you'll still have to take that, but based on your score on my little test, you could go into any program the Navy offers."

I was pleased. I liked doing well on tests, and I had apparently done so here. I asked what the next step would be. He said, "Since you're seventeen and you haven't graduated high school, we need two things: first, we need your parents' permission and…"

I stopped him. I began to explain my situation – that I had been locked out of the family home and was starving. He offered to call my mother and have her come to his office to sign the requisite form. I replied that he could do that but entreated him not to put me in a position in which I would need to deal with her.

"Once we have your mother's permission, we'll schedule you to take the ASVAB. If all of that goes well – and I expect it will – we'll then set you up to get your GED." Back then I hadn't a clue what a GED was, but he explained that the Navy required a high school diploma or its equivalent, the GED (General Educational Development).

(*ASVAB was an acronym for the Armed Services Vocational Aptitude Battery)

The recruiter asked me to come back on Wednesday evening, as he hosted a gathering of guys who were in various stages of recruitment through his office, and then bid me adieu. As I left his office, the recruiter called after me, "Hey… here's five dollars. Get yourself something to eat."

I think I was expecting to walk in there and get shipped out to boot camp the same day (I had watched too many WWII movies). I found myself still stuck in limbo. I was disappointed and wished I didn't have to go back to Mom's house. Almost immediately next door to the recruiter's office was a Chinese restaurant called *House of Chan*. I went in and found a way to eat for under five dollars. It was lunchtime, and the specials were cheap enough to allow this. From there, I wandered through downtown Woonsocket for a while. I was lonely and feeling a bit sorry for myself. I started walking my bike and making my way toward Chuckie's apartment.

I arrived at her apartment and knocked on the door. Upon opening it, she took one look at me and asked what was going on. I told her what led me to living on a hammock in the backyard. I did not tell her about stealing food from the neighbors or about the visit to the Navy recruiter. She asked if I was hungry, to which I answered an emphatic "YES!". She asked me when I had showered last (I probably didn't smell too good). I told her it had been two days, but that I had not had clean clothes in a while because I didn't want to alert Mom that I had been in the house. She gave me a towel and something to cover myself afterward. She said, "Go into the bathroom, take off those yucky clothes and hand them out the door to me."

I took a nice, leisurely hot shower. For the first time in over a week, I wasn't frightened of being found out. I could have fallen asleep in that shower. I felt safe. It was an unusual sensation, given what I had been through recently. It was weird realizing that feeling safe was the exception.

Chuckie washed my clothes while we ate supper. I asked if I could stay the night. She acquiesced but reiterated what she had said during my spring break episode, "You can't make a habit of this."

After supper, Chuckie, her husband, her son "Little Man" and I sat down and watched TV. I hadn't realized just how much of normal life I was missing by living out in the backyard. As banal and mindless as TV was, it represented something of which I had been deprived. Chuckie had been my favorite sibling, and I felt almost betrayed by her refusal to step between Mom and me. Realizing I was being somewhat selfish, I had still expected her—of all my siblings—to help me out. After these conversations, and realizing I wasn't getting her help, I felt truly alone in the world.

In the morning, I had breakfast and hung around for a while. My clothes were clean and dry and I felt a whole bunch better – in a physical sense. I knew I wasn't staying there another night, but I really had nothing else to do and nowhere to go. A little before lunchtime I said goodbye to Chuckie and Little Man (Eddie had already left for work) and got on my bike. I was just riding and thinking. I ended up crossing over the state line at the east end of Blackstone. This area put me near Bellingham and although I hadn't consciously planned it this way, I was headed toward Faith's house. There were just three places I could go: Faith's house in Bellingham, Chuckie's apartment in Woonsocket, or my mother's house. This time, I had left Mom's for Chuckie's, and I guess I subconsciously just headed toward Faith's. "Why not?" I said to myself. It was a bit of a ride, but I now made that my destination. I didn't know what else to do.

At this point, following Chuckie's refusal of asylum, I didn't have much hope. I had never been as close to Faith as I was to Chuckie. I started a debate with myself as to how much I should tell her. Dickie had been medically retired from the Marine Corps following his time in Vietnam and the loss of his fingers. He was a neat character, and the whole family liked him. My father had really liked him and all of my siblings found him charming and entertaining. He was good to my sister and that meant a lot to all of us. Maybe I needed to talk to him. He might understand, and he might be proud of me for trying to join the Navy.

I got to their house around 6 PM. There were no lights on and no one was home. Was this to be a recurring theme in my life? Was there really something wrong with me? Did I have bad breath? Body odor? As silly as these thoughts were, my life had been reduced to trying to figure this out, and I went overboard. I just didn't know. I headed back to

Blackstone. At least I'd had a few decent meals over the past couple of days.

Once again, it was dark when I arrived at the Blackstone Street house. However, this time the interior lights were on. I stood straddling my bike at the edge of the road, feeling like a Dickens character while watching the shadows playing against the curtains as my mother and sisters went about watching TV and readying themselves for bed. It was as if I had been surgically excised from the family — like I no longer existed. Was this what she was doing? Erasing me? I couldn't understand what this was about. My dad was no longer a part of her life. Was I really that much like him, or that much of a threat to her sanity that she couldn't handle me being there? Was that it? Was it her? Or was it really me? I still wondered.

I quietly retired to the shed. The power was still on (I guess Mom hadn't thought to look at that again), so I tuned the radio to WCRB, a Boston classical music station, and settled into my hammock. There was no fire this night. After all the miles I had put on my bike over the last couple of days, I was physically exhausted and quickly drifted off to sleep.

In the morning, I was up with the dawn, but as my situational depression increased its grip on me, I really didn't have the desire to go out and about. There really wasn't anything for me to do, anyway. I quietly closed the rolling garage door and stayed inside. It occurred to me that I hadn't been there the night before, and my arrival last night likely went unnoticed. Not having lit a fire also played into this scenario. Maybe I could keep this charade going and maybe she would think I had found somewhere else to go. It was quite likely she didn't even know I was there.

As I heard Mom and the girls coming out of the house in the morning and getting into the car, I peeked through the window of the roll-up door. My guess was pretty much confirmed. They didn't appear to know I was there.

After a while, I decided to try and see my friend, Clark. He lived in the "High Rocks" section of town, not nearly as far away as either of my sisters. When I got to his house, his mother answered the door. She called out his given name, "Stephen... Brian's here."

Clark had just graduated from high school. He was only eight weeks older than I, but because we were born on opposite sides of New Year's Day, he got to start school a year before I did. Clark distrusted his mother, but he nonetheless invited me into the apartment the two of them shared. After I began telling him about the life I'd been leading for the last week, he signaled for me to be quiet and to follow him. We headed out the door and walked up the street toward his grandparents' house.

On the way, he explained that he was sure his mother had been listening to us, and since she knew my mother, he thought it best not to let her hear any more about my dealings with Mom. As I described the whole series of events, he said:

"Jesus Christ, Fran! You need to get the fuck outta there!"

He was being emphatic and made me think my life might actually be in danger. Rather sullenly, I replied,

"I know."

And I did... I just didn't know how, what I could do, or where I could go.

Thirty-One

"Perhaps love is like a resting place, a shelter from the storm.
It exists to give you comfort,
It is there to keep you warm and in those times of trouble when you are
most alone, The memory of love will bring you home."

—*John Denver*

Clark's grandmother was a sweet old Polish woman. We weren't in the door two minutes before she was listing off all the different foods available for us to eat. We got some sustenance and headed upstairs to his music room. His grandparents had been more like parents to him than his own mother. They had purchased a nice stereo system for him, and he kept it at their house—maybe so his mother couldn't pawn it for beer money. Given that scenario, I would likely have chosen to do the same thing.

It was stiflingly hot in that upstairs room. We took off our shirts and draped wet towels over our heads and shoulders to try staying cool. We mostly just listened to music and talked. I ate there that day, but I could not stay. As I got on my bike to go, I remembered that this was the night I was supposed to go to the recruiter's office for that social "thing." I had discussed it all with Clark. Although his grandfather had been in the Navy (he had, in fact, retired from the service after more than 20 years), Clark was against me joining. I explained that I had no car and no job—I was essentially homeless. He still didn't like the idea and told me so, but he acknowledged my situation was dire and admitted he didn't really have a viable alternative.

I got to the recruiter's office around 7 PM. There were snacks and soda pop on a table and a number of young men seated in a couple of rows. Apparently, I was the last expected guest to arrive. After a little chatter, the recruiter announced he had an exercise for us. He asked us to take the next five minutes and get to know some basics about at least three other guys there. I started moving around the room, introducing myself and trying to remember names. When the five minutes were up, he asked us to grab some food and take a seat. He then began questioning each of us about the other men we'd met. Every single other young man had gotten to know three others and no more. I was able to give six names and some minor details about each. The recruiter pointed this out, and I was embarrassed. The lesson was something about exceeding expectations versus meeting minimum standards.

The evening's event was over by about 8:00, and a small group of guys surrounded the recruiter. The chatter and their attitudes were lively. Most new recruits had some delay between when they initially volunteered and when they were due to report. This group had been waiting the longest to report and had developed quite the rapport with this Navy man. As I said good night to him, he stopped me.

"Brian... Your mom came by and signed the document. How do you feel about taking the ASVAB on Friday?"

I indicated this would be fine and asked if she had given him any grief. He showed me what she had written:

"Although I believe this is not in Brian's best interest, I reluctantly give my permission."

I could not understand why she seemed to want to continue to torture me. Was she trying to break me? If so, to what end? I wasn't allowed in the home, I wasn't being fed, and now she was reluctant to let me go into the service as an alternative? I just could not get my head around it. What horrible crime had I committed to deserve this treatment at seventeen years of age? I wasn't a bad kid, but she had me second-guessing myself. These thoughts spiraled around in my head as I rode back to Blackstone that night.

I had several more nights in the shed similar to my first few. It got a bit monotonous—sleeping on the hammock in the same clothes night after night. I ranged further and further in my food forays in the wee hours. Strawberries were beginning to come into season. I added them to the other fruits and vegetables I collected. Mostly, my diet consisted of stolen produce and occasional bits of rolls or bread. I no longer tried to get into the house. I washed with the garden hose and found places in the forested lot next to us to use as a latrine. I was tired, though. Tired of living like this. It had only been a couple of weeks, and yet I knew, deep inside, that this was not right. Something had to change. I was hopeful the Navy might be that change—but when?

Friday came, and I got to the recruiter's office early in the morning. Two other potential recruits were going to be testing that day. The recruiter drove us down to Providence for the test. The subject matter was quite varied, and the test was separated into five sections, if I remember correctly. It was all multiple-choice, and each section was timed. When we were done, the four of us headed back to the recruiter's office in Woonsocket. He asked us to stick around until he got the results. Some of his other recruits were there when we got back. The phone call came within about twenty minutes. When he got off the phone, he told the other recruits around him, "Pay up! I told you so."

He turned to me and explained that a 100% on the ASVAB was not a mathematical possibility—99% was the best possible score. He then said, "You, my young friend, have just made me $60! I told them you'd ace it, and you did."

"How could you possibly have bet on me doing that?" I asked.

He said, "Simple... you aced the practice test I gave you when you first came in here."

I had done well on the test—now I was to learn about what that actually meant for me.

The recruiter told me that, as he had suggested on my first visit, I could have my choice of ANY training program the Navy offered. He suggested the nuclear power program. Massachusetts and the East Coast, in general, were politically left-leaning at the time as well as environmentally sensitive. The initial construction of the Seabrook (Nuclear) Power Station in New Hampshire had been the subject of huge protests the year prior. It was still quite fresh in everyone's mind. I was definitely a product of that local attitude. Nuclear anything rubbed me the wrong way, and I balked. He continued to try to sell me on that program (for which, I later learned, recruiters earned extra points for placing new recruits). He finally gave up on that and focused, instead, on the Advanced Electronics Program. (He would get the same recruitment bonus as if I had opted for the nuclear power program.) I had taken electricity and electronics in high school and quite enjoyed it. My interest was piqued.

According to the Navy, the training for this program was worth the equivalent of a $17,000 civilian education (a figure I later learned was grossly exaggerated). I also learned that every enlistment was for six years, not four, as I had thought. Most involved four years active duty and two years inactive reserve time. They were just beginning to utilize the new "three by three" enlistments, offering three years active duty, one-year active reserves, and then two years inactive reserves. However, both Nuclear Power and Advanced Electronics required a full six-year active-duty commitment. In exchange, the new recruit (me) would enter as an E-3 with an automatic ("Push-Button") advancement to E-4 upon completion of A school. The added money right up front sounded pretty good to me. I needed to know more.

"What can I do with this? What kind of job would I be doing?" I asked.

The recruiter started listing all the jobs available in this program. We soon zoned in on Aviation Electronics Technician—likely to station me on an aircraft carrier. I signed the papers that day, but I wasn't scheduled to report for basic training until October 8th. That was more than two months away—a long time to be living in a shed and stealing food. The recruiter scheduled me for my GED test. Even though that seemed quite some time away, I was disappointed that things couldn't move more quickly. But happy there would eventually be some resolution to my predicament, I resumed my strange, semi-homeless lifestyle.

I wasn't aware of it right away, but my reduced calorie intake and increased activity (bicycling everywhere) were causing me to lose weight. At the end of the school year, I weighed between 150 and 160 lbs. By mid-July, I weighed just 129 lbs. I was taller than 5'10" by now, so I must have been looking pretty skinny. My appetite decreased because I was getting less to eat. I had been supplementing what I could bum from friends and my sisters with stolen food from people's gardens and, on occasion, I would also steal from a supermarket. I'd walk into the store and, when I found something I could eat (that didn't require cooking), I'd eat it right there in the store. Fruit was the easiest. A few veggies, crackers, and bread were my other mainstays. I was on my own. I didn't bother trying to go into my mother's house and no longer cared if she knew I was sleeping in the shed. I wasn't building fires or in other ways making my presence known, but I just didn't care if she was aware. There were no interactions between us, and that was the best I could hope for.

I hadn't seen Faith in several weeks, and Dickie's birthday was coming up at the end of July. I didn't have anything for him, nor did I have any way of getting something for a gift. I rode over to their house to see if there was some way I could do something or be a part of his birthday celebration. When she saw me, she immediately noticed that I was dirty and thin. I told her most of what had been going on. She had talked to Mom recently (on the phone), and Mom had said nothing. Nothing about locking me out of the house, nothing about removing food from the house so I could not eat, and nothing about having signed for me to join the Navy. Faith was both shocked and incredulous at first, but the more I explained and described my world, the more she started seeing (and believing) what was going on.

Dickie got home from work a little after 5 PM. He, Faith, and I sat down at the trestle-style table he had custom-built, and we talked well into the night. I got the impression he believed I was exaggerating and maybe even fabricating most of what I told them. It was suggested that I might have been belligerent or that I was much later getting home after curfew. They thought I was staying outside of my own volition and that I could return to the house any time I wished — that I was being stubborn and imagining things. They assured me I could sleep on their sofa and that they would do what they could to help me.

The next day was Saturday, so neither Faith nor Dickie had to go to work. He called my mother, thinking he could broker another treaty like he did the last time. When he got off the phone, he was visibly shaken and red-faced with anger. He said to me, "I'm sorry, Brian. I thought you were making this stuff up. There's something very wrong with her. You're not going back there. You're staying here. We'll figure something out."

I couldn't hear what she said on her end, and I don't remember what else Dickie may have said about that conversation. I was experiencing a strange combination of relief and feeling justified. Apparently, she went off on him and Faith for taking me in, saying they were interfering in business that was not theirs. What I do know is that Dickie, who had a notoriously short fuse, was furious. Faith chimed in, apologizing for there being no more than a sofa for me to sleep on. I don't think she realized I hadn't slept in a bed in quite a long time, and the sofa was quite inviting. They both asked if I thought Lori or Wendy were in any danger. I honestly did not think they were and said so, although I hadn't seen either one of them for some time and really couldn't confirm it. It seemed to me as though their lives were just going forward as usual. I said as much. Faith turned away. I think she was probably crying. I had no more tears.

Dickie had an old high school friend, Howie McGouty, who had become a Blackstone police officer. Dickie called him, gave a brief description of the situation, and asked for his help. Sunday evening, right around suppertime, Dickie and I went to my mother's house (it was no longer my home, in my mind). He brought with him a few things he had borrowed from my mother and wanted to return. Among them was a pair of garden shears. As we approached the house, I remember Dickie—the Vietnam veteran—looking concerned as he handled the shears, then saying something like, "In her current state of mind, I'm not going to give her anything she might use as a weapon."

He ended up putting the shears and the other items behind the house and out of sight before we went up to the door.

Howie met us there in his police car. We approached the kitchen door, and the policeman rang the doorbell. My mother got up from the dinner table where she, Lori, and Wendy were eating and answered the door. Before anyone else could say anything, she sternly looked Howie right in the eye and asked, "Is this a police escort by request?"

The indignation and arrogance she embodied was hilarious. Here was a middle-aged woman who stretched truth to claim to be five feet tall, attempting to stare down a six-foot officer in uniform and armed with a gun. He played his part perfectly and simply replied to her, "The boy's just here to get his things, ma'am."

She reluctantly stepped aside, avoiding eye contact with me, and we went in. Lori and Wendy remained at the table. Now that all those years have passed, I can only imagine what she was thinking about Dickie and that police officer. In the moment, though, I needed to have this all behind me. I thought of little else.

Dickie helped me gather some clothes and a few other personal items. I got my clarinet, my cheap stereo, and my chord organ (the one Lori used to reach in and interfere with). Most of my belongings were upstairs in my room, including a number of things Dad had given me that I would be forced to leave behind. Among those things was a beautiful oak and glass case containing a set of scales and including the brass weights used to measure the weight of small items. I also left behind his *Bluejackets Manual* and his honorable discharge from the Navy. Dickie had warned me that I might not be able to fit everything in the car and to try to prioritize. I was carrying things down the stairs, out the front door, across the front yard to Dickie's big old Dodge Polara at the curb. My adrenaline must have been at a peak! I was carrying things with one hand that I later needed help lifting when it came time to unload them from the trunk of the car. It was very tense, and I was shaking all the way back to their house. I couldn't speak. I had just wanted to get out of there and ended up leaving many precious things and many mementos behind. I never saw those things—or the inside of that house—again.

Shortly after we got back to Faith and Dickie's house, the phone rang. Dickie answered. Faith and I could tell by the look on his face that it was Mom. At first, she demanded to talk to Faith, but Dickie said that anything she felt she needed to say to Faith, she could say to him. She chewed him up one side and down the other. He was shaken again following that call. My mother had disowned them for protecting me. If they were going to step in and prevent her from performing her "parenting duties" with me, then she wanted nothing to do with them. At one point, Dickie said, "But you're NOT parenting him! You've abandoned him, and you're grossly neglecting him!"

I could hear her raised voice over the phone from across the room. He hung up while she was mid-rant. She called back. He told her not to call again.

Happy Birthday, Dickie.

I felt only slightly bad about them incurring my mother's wrath because of me. The problem was: I was numb. I had just endured several weeks of being essentially homeless. I was still at a loss as to why she wanted so badly to stop me from basically living. This was not what I had expected from my teen years. I had no inkling that parents could be capable of such cruelty—like the way my mother had treated me. I was also surprised that Faith had helped where Chuckie had not. I was grateful but confused, and I don't think the enormity of this most recent change had fully sunk in.

Thirty-Two

"Always, after a defeat and a respite,
the shadow takes another shape and grows again."

—*JRR Tolkien*

Over the next few weeks, some of the shock from the change wore off. I slept on the Trudels' sofa because there was no extra bed. They began using me as a built-in babysitter, which I certainly didn't mind. I needed to contribute. When I went into Woonsocket for my GED testing, Dickie told me I still needed to get my high school diploma. A GED was fine, but I needed to graduate from high school. This was not a request. He asked if I still wanted to go into the Navy, because he thought I might be able to get out of the enlistment due to extenuating circumstances. I was not prepared to go to college, so my options were somewhat limited. I told Dickie I felt the Navy was my best bet at that point. He wasn't totally sold on it but accepted my position. He said the service had been a good thing for him and that he was proud to have served. The problem, of course, was that October eighth reporting date. I was contractually bound, and that date was not compatible with finishing my senior year of high school. He said he'd go down to the recruiter's office and convince them to change the date.

Dickie was as good as his word. He used his status and experience as a retired Marine Sergeant to push his point. I was still going in, but my reporting date had been changed to June 3rd, 1978—the following year. My graduation from high school was to be May 28th. I was going to graduate. Now a new issue came to the fore: Faith and Dickie lived in Bellingham. Not only were they in a different school district and a different county, but they were also quite a long distance from my high school. It was probably only seven or eight miles, but it required driving first into Rhode Island and then back into Massachusetts. It was typically a half hour or more, depending on traffic. While the weather remained decent, I could ride my bike to school. But what could I do when the rain and snows of winter came upon us? Dickie offered to drive me to school, but that was going to be difficult and costly. He worked in Sharon, Massachusetts, which was in the opposite direction. Faith, too, considered transporting me, but she worked nights. She would have had to drive home in the morning to get me and bring me to school, and then drive back home so she could sleep. No real solution jumped out at us. They were also feeding a teenage male. That alone took a lot of money, and they had already been barely getting by. Adding the extra costs for gas to transport me—it was not looking good. Faith took me shopping for school but was only able to afford a couple of pairs of cheap jeans. I expressed my thanks, but it could not be enough. Money was obviously becoming an issue.

The first day of school arrived. This was my senior year. Wow! I was a senior. Faith drove me in that morning, but we still didn't know how we were going to make the round-trip transportation work. During band, I got the chance to speak with Mr. Hessney one-on-one. He asked how things were going. I gave him the condensed version. He couldn't believe what had happened. Adding to his conflicted sense of things was my mother's contribution to the band boosters group (the group of parents that helped with fundraising for our burgeoning marching band). He had gotten to know her and liked her. Of course, she had a very different public persona than what I had lived with. I'm sure he was having difficulty reconciling what I was telling him about her with her diminutive size and appearance. He tried to understand and was apologetic but let me know in no uncertain terms that he was having a problem believing my version, having had interactions with my mom. I told him of my change in living situations. He offered to give me a ride in both directions every day. Since he now lived in Bellingham as well, it wouldn't be a problem. The only restriction was that he had to stay at the school for an hour after I did each day. I could handle that. This arrangement saved Faith and Dickie a lot of headaches (and money). So began an even better relationship with my music teacher than I'd already had. I was able to confide in him, and he offered advice when I asked.

I spoke to Faith and Dickie that night. Although they were elated with my news, they had some difficult thoughts to share with me. They had discussed the situation both with each other and with some other folks. My mother was receiving veteran's survivor benefits and social security benefits to help care for three minor children. When Faith and Dickie approached her for some financial assistance, Mom refused. They had decided to take her to court to obtain child support and let me know of the plan. This was already quite stressful, but there were other factors to be taken into account. For one thing, Dickie was not a blood relative, and there was something related to this preventing him from taking custody of me. It had to be Faith who was suing for custody. For another, they wanted me to go to the hearing as well. Poor Faith—she was already the meekest and most conformist of my siblings. Now she was faced with a very uncomfortable and contentious hearing with my mother on the other side of the courtroom. This was so far out of her comfort zone—but she took a deep breath, swallowed hard, and took on this task. I loved my sister, but this seemed so far out—especially for her—I really felt the force of my imposition on her.

I asked her how she felt about meeting Mom in court, and she said she was scared but that she knew she had to do it. What Mom had done to me was unforgivable, in Faith's eyes. It was the first time I had ever known Faith to really take a stand. Then Dickie and Faith told me something that perhaps spoke to my mother's mental state. The dollar amount of the government benefits she was receiving was the same for three children as it was for two. They had asked her simply to sign over responsibility for me. This would have given them the benefits needed to help support me and would not have decreased the benefits she was receiving for Lori and Wendy at all. Because she refused to do this, she would be giving up money she hadn't needed to give up if the court ruled against her.

Mrs. Suzanne Mahoney had been the chorus teacher and the director for the two high school musicals in which I performed. She was a generous and loving individual who grasped the value of the arts in my life. She treated everyone with the same lovely tenderness with which she treated me. I was not anyone special—but she made me feel as though I was. Here was another example of love and attention emanating from an adult in my life that gave me hope. Both Mr. Hessney and Mrs. Mahoney gave me encouragement. With the loss of my father, Mr. Hessney had stepped in and shown me love and given me guidance. Was he a father figure? I would say he was. Mrs. Mahoney (as well as the nurse Mrs. Zekanowski and a few other female teachers) had shown me that it was possible to be an adult female who showed tenderness, concern, and even love to a young male. The contrast between them and my mother was stark.

Although my two older sisters had played amazing roles in my young life, and they were now grown and had families of their own, I still thought of them as siblings. I knew they were adults, but I categorized their places in my world on a different plane. Chuckie and Faith had shown me familial love when my mother had not. When I felt most alone in the world, they let me know I was not. Still, they weren't the same as the teachers. Maybe it had something to do with them being blood relations. Robert Frost said:

"Home is the place where, when you have to go there, they have to take you in."

Mr. Hessney and Mrs. Mahoney did not have to take me in. That was a huge difference in the relationships between them and me. They did not have to, but they nonetheless took me in through their love, their caring, and their recognition that we had a common passion.

The day arrived for the hearing, and I accompanied Faith to the courthouse. In my memory, it seemed to be a very dark courtroom. When it was our turn, the judge basically read statements aloud and then stated:

"Mrs. Francis, you will pay Mrs. Trudel for the support of the minor child, Brian Francis. Any questions?"

Mom started off on some tangential rant and the judge stopped her. He restated his order and asked if she had any questions specifically about that. She said "no." That was that. Mom would have to pay Faith to support me. My thoughts returned to the day before my sixteenth birthday, when Mom said she was going to have Dad pay to support us. Now it was she who would be paying to support me. There was a bit of irony and some poetic justice in all of this. The payments became a sort of windfall for Faith and Dickie. I soon got a few more clothes and Dickie started building a bedroom for me in the basement of their home.

The bedroom was being designed as we went, but I'd like to think the design leaned partly toward my tastes. I had long been enamored with the sea and sailing ships, especially those of the 18th and early 19th century. I had a full-size brass porthole mirror that I had previously received as a gift from Faith and Dickie. It opened and had screw clamps to "batten it down." Dickie installed this by cutting a hole in the hollow-core door to allow a full view from the bedroom to the hall outside through the open porthole. The bed was quite unique—at least on land. It consisted of a wooden frame with one side attached to the wall with hinges. The mattress was supported by a grid of hemp rope. The novelty of this nautical room was not its sole appeal—there was also the benefit of peace and quiet. Privacy was not assured, though.

I now had a place for all the stuff that had been relegated to a pile in another corner of the basement. I brought out my many completed models—there was a Ford Model A, a Duesenberg touring car, and a 1932 Chevy with a rumble seat. All three of those were made of metal and were beautiful. However, the prizes of my collection were the four tractor-trailers I had built. They were made of plastic and were more fragile. Some of my meagre belongings—of which I was most proud—now had a home. Faith had been fond of a 1975 song called *Convoy*, which featured descriptions of several trucks. Her favorite had been the "cab-over Pete with a refer on." While I had brought several complete specimens from my mother's house when I evacuated, I had also built several more during the time I lived with the Trudels. One that I built while there was a cab-over Peterbilt, and I hooked it up to a refrigerator trailer. I made sure she saw both my progress and the finished model. I had painstakingly rendered intricate detail on these models—especially the trucks. Speedometers and other dashboard gauges with discernible needles, radio dials, door handles and locks, engine components, and other such details made them very special to me.

Faith was not a disciplinarian, and all three of her children behaved in ways that would drive my mother crazy. When I babysat for them and the kids acted up, I would separate them and make them stay seated in a chair. That was sheer torture for all three children. Jason was the youngest and, aside from his gender, had quite a different demeanor than his two sisters. He found my model trucks and thought they were play toys. His mother did nothing when she saw him playing with them. Even when the fragile models started falling apart or breaking, she thought nothing of it. When I discovered and complained, Faith's response was:

"He didn't know any better."

I responded that even if he didn't know better, she did. All that work was now trashcan fodder.

For the many months I had slept on the Trudels' sofa, their oldest daughter, Jenny, had been allowed to watch the television whenever she wanted. Faith and Dickie figured this would allow them the luxury of sleeping in if they so desired. Over several years Jenny had gotten into the habit of rising earlier and earlier. With the TV and the sofa both being in the living room, there was going to be a conflict— which I lost. Jenny was not to be dissuaded, nor was her TV time to be curtailed. The only concession made was that she was directed to keep the volume down. After living in my mother's house and outdoors, I had learned to be vigilant, which meant I had become a very light sleeper, so I lost sleep. Just a month before I went off to boot camp, I moved into that downstairs room. That month gave me the best sleep I had had since my dad died—as well as for a long time thereafter.

I helped as much as I was able and chipped in whenever I could. At times, I got the distinct impression of being a "third wheel." I was also aware that there were limits to what I could ask of them. I wasn't bringing money into the home (except the stipend they received from my mother), and I was a teenager with a voracious appetite. To be honest—I doubt their increased food bill exceeded what they got from Mom. The difference probably helped offset any increase in their utility bills and added a little bit to some rare treats for me. On the other hand, Faith and Dickie were truly generous in their treatment of me—this is especially clear to me in hindsight. They were my saviors, and I appreciated them opening their home to me.

I had my driver's license but had next to no experience on the road. Dickie would take me out driving in their big old 1970 Dodge Polara. That thing was a beast! They later traded it for a 1977 Chevy Nova. During that winter, he took me to a supermarket parking lot that was just down the street from their house. In Massachusetts in the 1970s, supermarkets were closed on Sundays, so we had use of the whole lot. We'd go down there during—or right after—a snowstorm, and I would learn how to handle a sliding or skidding car in the snow. For me, it was just playing, and it was fun—but I soon learned the importance of these skills. One storm came upon us while Dickie and I were out running an errand. We were heading home and almost hit a semi-truck because the snow was falling so heavily. We could not see him until we were only a few feet from his rear bumper. I watched as Dickie skillfully avoided an accident.

Early that February, during a full moon, Massachusetts, Rhode Island, and Connecticut were hit with a powerful confluence of an Atlantic hurricane and an Arctic cold air mass. It was a full-blown blizzard! Over the thirty-six-hour course of that storm, Boston's official snowfall was measured around 27 inches. Where Faith and Dickie lived, we had between 36 and 40 inches—and still, it felt like a lot more. The winds ranged anywhere from about 80 mph to more than 100 mph for the duration of the storm. Logan International Airport had trouble keeping runways clear for the National Guard troops who were being flown in to help with clean-up. People died in their cars. Snowplows had a tough time getting through all the abandoned cars, and even when they could get through, the snow piling up on the sides of the roads was prohibiting further plowing. It was a mess.

We heard that the primary way people in need were being reached was almost solely by snowmobile. People with four-wheel-drive vehicles were called upon to help, as they were among the few who could move. The morning after the storm dawned cold but bright with cloudless blue skies. The Trudels' house was a split-level ranch. The front door could not be used because of the snow that had blown against it. When we opened it, there was nothing to see but the perfect imprint of the entire paneled door in the cold white stuff. Likewise, the garage door could not be used. This left the back door, which opened onto a deck some ten or twelve feet above the ground. However, that morning the snow brought the apparent ground level considerably higher. Since my sister was about 5'2" and her husband about 5'6", they volunteered the 5'11" teenager who lived with them to go out into the arctic wasteland. As I descended the stairs from the deck, I found that I was not able to reach the ground at what should have been ground level. I got stuck in the cold white powder several times and ended up rolling across the surface of the snow in order to get to the front of the house. I had a snow shovel with me, and my first job was to open a passage to the front door. Once that was done, Dickie was able to join me, and we set about clearing off the car and working on a way to get out of the driveway.

We shoveled snow from between the car and the garage door. Then we were able to open the garage and go through it and into the house for breaks from shoveling. Morning turned into afternoon, and still we shoveled. We lived on a state highway, and after the county-owned snowplows had hit their limit, we started seeing National Guard equipment clearing the road. Big, olive drab front-end loaders were heaving snow onto already gargantuan piles at the side of the road. There was a mountain of snow scrapings at the end of our drive that easily reached eleven or twelve feet in height. It was so dense and so tall that we feared not being able to get out. Using our snow shovels, we ended up cutting a tunnel into the banked snow. It was nearly dark when we had cleared enough of this frozen mess to get the car out. Dickie and I rewarded ourselves by doing just that. We took a brief spin around the block. We saw an occasional four-wheel-drive vehicle or a snowmobile, but no other traffic. We didn't linger but returned the car to the driveway.

The next morning was another crystal-clear New England winter day. I decided to go exploring. I walked down the street to the supermarket where Dickie had taken me to practice driving. I got to where the entry to their parking lot should have been and stared in awe. I had never seen that much snow. Not only was the parking lot inaccessible, but the supermarket building itself could not be seen! The snow had piled up and drifted in such a manner that the entire building was engulfed. It was as if it were wiped off the face of the planet. There were no footprints at all. Nothing. It took several days for the people of that area to dig out after the blizzard. It will eventually be forgotten, I'm sure… but not by me.

It was "The Blizzard of '78!"

Thirty-Three

"Music has healing power.
It has the ability to take people out of themselves for a little while."

—*Elton John*

I was a senior in high school. At the end of my junior year, having completed all credits needed for graduation (so I thought), I asked to graduate early. This would have resolved my reporting date for the Navy. The request had been denied because I was technically one-quarter credit short. Physical education provided one quarter of a credit for each year of high school. That quarter credit for my senior year had held up my request. To make matters worse, for the sixth time in seven years, I had managed to be assigned to Mr. Robliss's physical education class. To my knowledge, no one in the history of that school had been assigned the same Phys-Ed teacher six times. The silver lining was that, aside from Phys-Ed, I had no academic requirements for my senior year. I chose to fill the rest of my schedule with band, chorus, music theory, and study hall. I was in the music department most of every day.

Early in the school year, our little community earned a dubious distinction.

Although I held a lofty opinion of my band mates, not everyone in the music program could be considered an angel, and it was the dawn of a new era in street drugs. The hallucinogen phencyclidine—known on the street as PCP or "angel dust"—made its Massachusetts public-school debut in our little town when three band members decided to smoke some pot laced with this drug at lunchtime. The concentration of the drug they ingested must have been high. After lunch, all three of them began to display seizure-like symptoms during band rehearsal. They didn't lose consciousness but seemed to lose control of their bodies. At least two of the three ended up on the floor. However, they did not lose the ability to speak and began shouting obscenities—often targeting Mr. Hessney. Emergency services were dispatched to transport the boys to the hospital, further disrupting our band rehearsal.

I had begun to immerse myself in music. I auditioned for and was cast as the lead in the high school musical *My Fair Lady*. I also planned on participating in the various festival events in music during that year, as in years past. There was the local one, the Blackstone Valley Music Festival, which encompassed several local school districts. I'd auditioned for the Blackstone Valley band for many years and was always selected for the festival. The next step up was the Central District Festival. A musician had to do well in the Blackstone Valley auditions in order to get the coveted "Central District recommendation," without which one could not audition at the Central District level. I had reached that level a couple of times. However, I hadn't done quite well enough to earn the very prestigious recommendation to audition for the "All-State" band.

After my voice had finally changed in my tenth-grade year, I had started singing in the chorus. I enjoyed success with *West Side Story* in my junior year, so I decided, as a senior, to audition for the Blackstone Valley Festival's chorus instead of the band. I did very well and garnered the recommendation for the Central District chorus. I went to those auditions and received, for the first time in my entire involvement with high school music, a recommendation to audition for the All-State Music Festival.

The All-State auditions came in early January, if I remember correctly. I was selected to sing in the bass section of the 250-voice choir. The choral conductor was Dr. Lloyd Pfautsch, who was Professor of Sacred Music and Director of Choral Activities at Southern Methodist University. One of the pieces we would be performing was one of his original works. What an opportunity! When we had been selected to participate in one of the lesser festivals, we would go to rehearsals—usually at some other school in the area—for a few hours on each of the three or four days preceding the planned concert, then perform. We were home every night. The All-State Festival was different. The University of Massachusetts at Amherst hosted the All-State Festival in 1978. All those high school musicians from all over the state descended upon the western Massachusetts town of Amherst, where we would stay for five days. Several local families had offered to put us up.

Over two years of summer music camp on the campus of the University of Rhode Island, my adventures had left me with a limited idea regarding college campuses. I had only that one campus to compare with the place I now found myself. URI was a lovely university campus, but the UMass campus was huge! Nestled against the backdrop of the Berkshire Mountains in the Connecticut River Valley, the area was incredibly picturesque. UMass's student body was also about double the size of URI's. It was enticing and a little bittersweet for me. I felt surprisingly at home and at peace in this academic atmosphere, but I knew when the school year was done, I was headed into the Navy.

My friends and I went exploring every afternoon following rehearsal and before heading to our host homes for the night. The theater building was a draw, as most of us in the chorus had been involved in theater as well. I remember climbing a spiral stair up to the catwalks above the stage. It must have been four stories high! We found the library and went inside for a peek. For the most part, it was overwhelming. At the perimeter of the building, there was an enclosed but external stairway. Every part of that building was concrete, and those smooth and unsupervised stairway walls had invited numerous profoundly philosophical monographs. Sometimes the graffiti was obscure and meant nothing to us. Some things were blatant and crystal clear. One statement had unfortunate but very funny relevance to our little group, which included a sweet young woman and gifted soprano named Rose Nobel. She had been cursed through an unfortunate genetic inheritance with a disproportionately oversized nose.

She was a very good sport about it and even joined in the jokes about her poor nose, signing notes "Rose Nose," among other things. Looking back, we had been horribly cruel, and I have many regrets for the part I played in her torment. There were five or six of us in the stairwell when someone stopped and guffawed—there, on the wall in front of us and painted quite legibly, was the phrase "Nasal Sex." For a moment, the rest of us held our breath, but when Rose burst out laughing, the rest of us followed. No one needed to elaborate or to say anything at all. It became a running joke amongst us until the end of the school year, when we parted ways the night of our high school graduation.

Our concert was presented April first. Here was yet another example of the loneliness and isolation I'd experienced over the previous twenty-six months—it seemed to me that all those other high school musicians had someone there to witness their triumph. They all had family present—either parents or siblings, extended families, friends, or all of the above. Faith and Dickie had three little kids and jobs to tend to. No one outside my immediate circle of high school "All-State" music chums was anywhere near Amherst, Massachusetts. I loved music and loved singing, but no one I was related to was there to hear my performance.

The chorus had been combined with the orchestra for one of the Coronation Anthems of Georg Frederick Handel. Unfortunately, the chorus had completely overpowered and outclassed the orchestra. It was stunning to hear 250 voices come in at once singing, "Zadok the priest and Nathan the prophet anointed Solomon King." I got chills every time I heard it. We were able to order a recording of that concert, and it would be mailed to us at a later date. Fortunately, Faith and Dickie had given me the money to purchase the LP of that concert. I still have that two-record set and still get chills whenever I listen to that choral entrance.

I don't remember how I managed to get home from that event. I probably got a ride with the parents of a friend. It could have even been Rose Nose's family. I was coming down off another one of the decidedly high points of my young life. I later tried to share the experience with others by playing the recording, but it was not really the same.

As amateurish as the performance might have been, it was and has been for me a cherished memory. Three years prior, about 100 of us had returned— triumphant—from Washington, D.C. Now, in 1978, seven of us were returning from Amherst. It wasn't quite the same, but I felt the same degree of accomplishment. I realized something else: while I was on the UMass campus and engrossed in my music, I didn't think about all the problems I'd experienced at home—not once. I was with musician friends, and we were having the time of our young lives.

Nothing any of us had previously experienced in sleepy Blackstone could compare with this. Now that it was over and things were returning to normal—or what was "normal" for me—thoughts about the past and future started creeping into my consciousness. It was the beginning of April, and I was going to boot camp in two months. Maybe I would finally be able to leave all the mess behind.

Thirty-Four

*"Promise me you'll never forget me because if
I thought you would I'd never leave."*

—*Winnie the Pooh*

Soon there came that time of year when we seniors got our high school yearbooks and the exchanging and signing began. Once again, Faith had come through for me. She found a way to give me enough money to buy the yearbook. Sometimes people sign a yearbook without either of you really knowing each other. It would be passed around and anyone who got it signed it. That accounted for at least a few of the notes in my copy. Some of the other signatories revealed things I was either too insecure or too shy to notice. In an odd, passive-aggressive manner that seems peculiarly unique to high school yearbook signing, I learned (for the first time) about girls who liked me. I was not, in any way, a ladies' man. I was quite shy around girls. As I read comments written by many of these young ladies, I was in shock. For instance, my friend Tim (who had taken me to get my driver's license) had a younger sister, Christine. Seems she had a considerable crush on me. I wish I'd been more perceptive. I thought she was simply trying to be a part of the smaller circle of musicians with whom I hung out. I would have liked to have gotten to know her better. I didn't have the social tools to handle that and did the only thing I knew—I ignored her playful advances and even said some things that were less than kind. I effectively pushed her away. I came to regret my behavior. She was a sweet young woman and didn't deserve my reaction to her. Christine, if you read this, please accept my apologies.

As the weather got better, more and more outdoor activities were planned. A friend of mine from the chorus hosted a 'get-together'. Rolly (short for Roland) was someone I'd known for a long time. He was a really humble guy, and he seemed as though he was desperate for guy friends. His folks had a really nice home with an in-ground swimming pool, and they had approved his plan for a pizza/pool party. All we had to do was show up with our swimsuits. In his attempts to get me to accept the invitation, he mentioned all the friends from the music department he had invited, including another girl who had apparently expressed interest in me. Her name was Annette Duffy. She was a sophomore and an oboe player. Like her sister Cynthia, she was very tall and very pretty. Cynthia was in Clark's class and had graduated the year before. I can remember admiring her, but I had hardly even known of Annette's existence. Now my interest in Rolly's party was definitely piqued.

With my departure for boot camp looming and with my natural shyness around members of the opposite sex, I wasn't really primed for a relationship of any magnitude. However, she was quite cute and unabashed with her feelings toward me. We danced and snuggled most of that night, but that was as far as it went. We smiled and flirted with each other over the next few weeks. She also signed my yearbook, but nothing more ever developed. I would have liked to have known her better, too. *C'est la vie!*

On another night, many of the friends with whom I had attended the All-State festival, as well as a couple of others, got together for some fun. We were out and about, but without a car. Surprisingly, this really was good, wholesome fun. There was no alcohol and no drugs of any kind involved. Several members of our little posse wanted to swim across the lake. It wasn't a big lake... it was more like a big pond, but I was not up for a late-night swim. I had been out with some other friends the night before and had not slept in over twenty-four hours. I was quite tired. Overruling my objections, the rest of them decided to go swimming. With their encouragement, I went along. We were fully clothed when we walked into the water. I still don't know what I was thinking. I wasn't a particularly strong swimmer, and together with my now wet and heavy clothes and my level of fatigue, I tired in the water very quickly. It was near midnight when we started, and I began to falter when we were only halfway across. As I fell further behind,

I was grateful for the conditioning and faithfulness of this group. Without their awareness and their help, I would not have made it out of the lake. They pulled me for quite a while. I swam the final hundred feet or so to the other shore. I was exhausted. Of course, I was also the butt of several jokes about this event, but I was alive. I thank my friends Dave and Rose Nose for my life. A little embarrassment was a small price to pay to avoid the alternative.

Dan Mumford was a jock and a particularly good-looking young man. He bore a striking resemblance to the guy on the Brawny paper towel wrapper. He had no shortage of girls to go out with. He was also quite fond of cannabis. During this high school twilight, I hung out with him on one occasion that I'd not soon forget. I don't know how he heard about it, but there was to be a great party in the woods. He had an old Chevy Vega (it was actually his dad's) and had picked me up for this Friday night party. We met up with a bunch of other vehicles in a parking lot (I think it was associated with a funeral home). We waited and waited. I didn't know what was going on. Then a white van pulled into the lot and all the waiting cars started their engines and turned their headlights on. I asked, "What? Where are we going?"

He said: "You'll see!"

The van drove through the parking lot to the far corner, then slowly negotiated its way over the edge of the pavement and into the woods. We found ourselves part of a line of some twenty cars and pickup trucks that followed the van. We were deep in the woods when we came upon a huge, raging bonfire. The van parked near the fire and opened the side doors. Inside were two kegs of beer! For a $5 donation, we could drink as much of the kegs as we wished.

It was a cool setting and there were a lot of people partying. Dan wandered off for a few minutes and returned beaming. He held a couple of joints in his hand. That was the night I was introduced to marijuana. It was also the last time I used it. After we had smoked both joints, Dan's eyes were bloodshot, and he was obviously intoxicated. He asked me what I thought. I honestly was not feeling a whole lot from either the beer or the pot. I was then informed that this particular sample of weed was laced with 'Angel Dust'. I had seen the effects of PCP on my fellow band members and was not happy that Dan waited until afterward to inform me of that adulteration. After a few more beers, we left the party in the woods. While I didn't feel high, I did feel incredibly hungry. We headed to a McDonald's and ordered enough food for eight guys… and the two of us ate it all.

Another incident from that spring (one of which I'm not too proud) occurred while I was out with Dan again. He had arranged a double date for us. The girl he set me up with was a cute little blonde from Warwick, Rhode Island (he had quite a network). Because there were to be four of us, we eschewed his little Vega. Instead, Dickie agreed to loan us his much roomier 1977 Chevy Nova. Dan and his date were in the back seat, while Diedre and I were in the front. This young lady was not shy and was snuggled against my side as we drove into Providence. We had purchased a six-pack of beer that was on the floorboards in the back-seat area. None of it was opened. Sensing her 'willingness', I put my arm around her shoulders, and she snuggled in even closer. She was guiding my hand down her partially unbuttoned blouse when my cuff button got caught up and tangled with her necklace. In attempting to disentangle us, I took my eyes off the road for just a moment and... BAM! We hit a tree. The front right side of the Nova was a mess, but no one was hurt. Dan got out of the back seat and angrily slammed the entire, unopened six-pack onto the ground, breaking all the bottles.

We headed home in disgust and disgrace. I got back to Faith's house in the wee hours and went to bed. In the morning, I explained to Dickie what had happened before he saw the car. He was upset about it, but not angry with me. When he took the car in for an estimate, the shop told him I should not have been able to drive it from Providence to Bellingham because of the extent of the damage, but that's precisely what occurred. Many months later, Lori told Dickie that Dan and I had been drinking beer when it happened. This was a lie intended to cause discord. Dickie was upset with me until I reminded him that Lori had not been a witness and that I had been honest and had told him about the unopened six-pack the very next morning. I withheld nothing. My relationship with Dickie was fraternal, and I told him why I had taken my eyes off the road. He accepted my defense after considering the source. I realized that somehow, I was still defending against Lori's fabrications, after years of doing so.

It became clear that my impending departure for boot camp was probably a good thing for all concerned. I knew Faith and Dickie both loved me, but our time living together needed to end. I was a burden, and I was extremely aware of that. During my time living with the Trudels, I had endured indignities and affronts. I was not in a position to request special treatment or accommodation, and I learned that by trial and error. We all knew the time was growing short, and I think we consciously made the effort to make it work for what time was left.

I think they were glad to see the end of May approaching. I know I was. There was one final musical event for this school year. Those of us who sang in the All-State chorus were to sing at some school-connected but extra-curricular nighttime event. I don't remember what the event was, exactly. What I do remember was being unexpectedly singled out by Mrs. Mahoney, our chorus teacher. She described to the audience all I had done that year. She then announced that I would be leaving soon to join the United States Navy. I was surprised by this and learned that my fellow chorus members were in on the surprise. They had all taken one step backward, like that comic gag where a leader asks for volunteers and the only guy not paying attention gets selected. I felt like that fool, and I was embarrassed, but my embarrassment faded as we sang. I think we got to eat for free that night, too.

High school graduation was nearly upon us. We began rehearsing so we would know when to walk, how to get from the floor to the stage, and how long it should take. We were assigned seats. There were risers placed on the stage so that families in the audience would have a clear view of their new high school graduate. I was disappointed to learn about the National Honor Society even though I was graduating with Honors. I didn't get to wear the collar. Turns out I hadn't maintained honors-level grades long enough. So be it, I still managed to be on the honor roll for my senior year as a whole.

I was surprised at my classmates who didn't see the simplicity of the instruction requested by the organizers. I realized, though, that most of the class of '78 had not been in the marching band, chorus, or theater where we had order, discipline, and followed direction. Of course, a certain percentage of the class really didn't care. There were the druggies, slugs, and other dregs that are an element of American society. These people were overwhelmingly male (although some in my class were female) and only cared that they had met minimal requirements for graduation and would be free of the prison we had known as school. Somewhat surprisingly, many from this group had turned themselves around by the time we saw each other again twenty years later.

The day approached. May 28th, 1978, was that special date that many of us both looked forward to and remembered forever—one of American teenagers' rites of passage. Later, I learned that the school sent out invitations to all parents. I had invited Faith and Dickie, and the school invited my mother. I hadn't expected her to show up, but she did. I didn't even know she had been there until afterward. Dickie told me he saw her in the auditorium that night. I guess some maternal heartstring had been plucked. I don't know. There was no interaction, and I was glad for that. I had learned to hold a grudge, and I'd learned from someone who was a world champion— my mother. It was sad, though, to think of her attending this momentous occasion on her own and for the child she had abused and ostracized. I prefer to think of her attendance as an act of remorse.

There was still a modicum of self-respect and some sense of decorum, which influenced people to dress nicely. Even the worst slugs in my class wore ties and decent shoes. Not one of my classmates dressed inappropriately. I was proud of that. The band was there to play the Elgar *Pomp and Circumstance* march. Speeches were made by the Superintendent of schools (a tall, awkward man with a heavy New England accent), by the diminutive Principal, and by the Valedictorian and Salutatorian of our class—both of whom were young women. Years later, I heard a sad rumor that the Valedictorian had flunked out of college. Having been released from the constant oversight of her parents, she had found boys, drugs, alcohol, and freedom.

After the graduation ceremony, my sister and her husband admonished me and entreated me to be responsible that night. They accepted that high school graduation was a rite of passage and that most new grads celebrated, but they reminded me that it was one of the most likely situations contributing to an early demise, and they implored me to call them if I needed a ride. I loved Faith and Dickie. I hoped I didn't disappoint them that night.

I was invited to a party at the home of a friend that was about the same distance from my mother's house as it was from the school. The party was mostly outdoors. Penny had a big yard, and the weather was balmy. There were a lot of people there and a considerable amount of booze was flowing. For some reason, the only things I could remember drinking that night were Sloe Gin Fizzes (yuck!). They were way too sweet, but alcohol was alcohol, and since I was getting something for free, it would have been rude of me not to accept. Our host had been a chorus member and a cast member in both of the high school musicals in which I had a part. Penny was short but busty, reminding me of a stout Sophia Loren. She had been after a band member whom just about everyone except Penny presumed was gay. We had tried to warn her, but lust was blind. That night she came up to me with tears in her eyes. When I asked her what was wrong, she described offering him oral sex and him turning her down. He told her, that night, that he was gay. She was devastated.

I'm sure the rest of my evening would be considered boring by most accounts. I was home by one o'clock and in bed by one-thirty. I just didn't find the idea of drinking until I puked or passed out very enticing, and no one I knew was doing much of anything besides drinking. I had somewhat inadvertently followed my sister's warning.

I had five days until I reported for boot camp. Even at this late date, I was still unsure of what was to happen. In the meantime, I was in touch with a couple of close friends. We planned an outing. My friend David, his younger brother Bryan, and a common friend whose name was also David planned to have a night of fun. Both Davids had unique nicknames. David Gauthier's was 'Gauch' and the other David was 'Bush'. Bryan was often referred to as 'Little Gauch' (although he eventually ended up being taller than David). We went out to a freshwater-swimming pond, where there was a floating diving platform. This was the first time any of the rest of us learned that Bush couldn't swim. We were out there near sundown. I don't remember why, but we were the only people there. Four teenaged boys, unsupervised and in a place like this had to mean trouble, but we were fairly well-behaved. While Gauch, his brother, and I were out near the diving platform, Bush was getting frustrated and bored, having been left on the shore alone. He started innocently throwing rocks in our general direction. In a totally unfortunate series of events, I returned to the surface after diving and as I was climbing up onto the platform, one of Bush's projectiles caught me right on my forehead at the hairline. I saw stars! He was apologetic, and I knew there was nothing malicious about it, but the brothers certainly gave him a razzing.

When we were done swimming, we started wandering aimlessly around rural Millville. We should have stopped right there, but we didn't. As we wandered down back roads in the wee hours, mischief was sure to result, and it did. We began daring each other to do stupid things. When it came to my turn, I was dared to do something with a mailbox we happened upon. I went up to the mailbox and, finding it to be very loosely secured to its post, just picked it up. Apparently, all the giggling aroused the owner of the mailbox, who proceeded to yell at us from his doorway. We took off running, but I had forgotten to drop the mailbox! We were a quarter mile away before I realized I still had it under my arm. I dropped it, and we ran on, leaving the scene of the crime. I'm not particularly proud of that shenanigan. Decades later, when I spoke of this with David Gauthier, his response was:

"That mailbox was due for replacement anyway."

It was a night for blowing off steam.

I took the next couple of days and just organized my things. I packed up most of my belongings at the Trudel's house. I took this time to visit the recruiter, who gave me the instructions to be followed on the 3rd of June. Of the three possible destinations for me, Orlando was easily my first choice. San Diego was a distant second choice, and Great Lakes, Illinois was my least favored. Earlier, I had requested that I be sent to Orlando for boot camp. The recruiter had assured me that my request would be honored. When I went down to his office on June first, I asked again about Orlando. I was once again assured this would be no problem. I was now looking forward to sunny Florida. Faith and Dickie agreed to drive me to Boston on the 3rd, where I was to receive my entrance physical. Once that was done, I'd board a plane at Logan International Airport and be bound for Orlando. I was ready.

Thirty-Five

"It takes courage to grow up and become who you really are."

—*E.E. Cummings*

I experienced my first disappointment with the Navy on that very first day. I did not go to Orlando, but to Great Lakes — strike one for the Navy. However, bootcamp gave me the opportunity to convince myself that I could live without the oversight of someone related to me. I recall that weird sensation of becoming a real adult. Not a kid forced into growing up at sixteen, but a young man that actually made it at a somewhat normal pace. I was eighteen years old and on my own — I had found a way to put a roof over my head, collect a paycheck, and I could vote. I didn't feel truly autonomous, though — there was a lot of structure within which I needed to work. I had no trouble adapting to the rigid parameters of the military operations. In fact, I thrived. Could my mother's strictness have prepared me for this next chapter? Possibly. However, there was not the constant threat of violence hanging over everything I thought or did. I finished at the top of my bootcamp company and earned the designation "Honorman." There was not a whole lot that went with that, but I did get an extra night off upon graduation.

From bootcamp I went to submarine training school in Groton, Connecticut. I got past the weeding-out process, and I learned enough that I was then ready to be trained for a job on submarines. From Connecticut, I went to San Diego to learn about sonar — in particular, how to operate the sonar equipment on a Fleet Ballistic Missile (FBM) submarine. During my first month in San Diego, Memere succumbed to pancreatic cancer. I was not allowed to go back east to attend her funeral. Strike two for the Navy. However, I was able to go back to New England for Thanksgiving that year. I spent the holiday with the Trudels, and afterward, I returned to school in San Diego. I remember walking onto the San Diego tarmac on December first and thinking the weather was mild enough that I felt comfortable wearing a T-shirt with no jacket. Southern California was a lot warmer than Massachusetts.

During my enlistment I was attached to three different nuclear-powered Fleet Ballistic Missile submarines: USS *Ulysses S. Grant*, SSBN 631 (Blue), USS *Benjamin Franklin*, SSBN 640 (Blue), and USS *James K. Polk*, SSBN 645 (Gold). All three ships had undergone major shipyard overhauls, and I was assigned to each of them as they made their way back into active service. During two separate school assignments in San Diego, I was trained to operate and repair submarine sonar equipment. I also underwent extensive training to be a sonar supervisor. I completed the rigorous requirements of qualifying in submarines. This process is intended to ensure that all crew members know enough about the submarine to lead or support damage control efforts in all areas and with all systems throughout the ship. Completing this kind of qualification took approximately a year. Upon completion, it allowed the sailor to wear the coveted Dolphins insignia.

My realization in bootcamp that I had grown into adulthood was a part of the maturing process. This continued in subsequent years on board those three submarines. I had not consciously remembered my mother's admonition that I was nothing special and that I should, essentially, marry the first woman who would have me. But suggestions heard and carried in the subconscious have their own way of making it back to the surface. While attached to a school command between submarines, my sister Lori fixed me up with one of her friends. I married Cheryl in 1981 when I was just twenty-one years old. She and I were going to try living together to see if we were compatible, but her parents insisted we get married instead. That was a red flag, but I tried to see past it. Cheryl had been raised in a Catholic household and had some strongly held beliefs — even as a young woman. She followed her mother's example and used violence to emphasize her opinion, and she was emotionally abusive. I didn't see the correlation at first, but I had subconsciously and inadvertently married someone with behaviors similar to my mother.

Despite the behavioral issues, we tried to make it work. She followed me to Charleston when I was stationed there on board the *Franklin*. While there, our apartment was broken into twice, and the second break-in occurred while Cheryl was home alone. Although she claimed otherwise at the time, I believe she had been sexually assaulted during that break-in. She left me in Charleston and returned to her parents' home in Massachusetts. I attributed this setback to a failure on the Navy's part. I was thinking too broadly and idealistically. I linked the available housing to high-crime areas and, since the Navy's housing allowance was so low, we could only afford to live in poorer neighborhoods. Of course, the Navy was not really to blame. Cheryl was not in the Navy — I was. Still, I looked at this and called "Strike Three" on the Navy. I tried to get transferred closer to her. After exploring several different options and being persistent, I was finally transferred to the *Polk*, which was undergoing a major overhaul at the Portsmouth Naval Shipyard in Kittery, Maine.

As had been the case with both the *Grant* and the *Franklin*, the *Polk* was a ballistic missile submarine — a mobile launch platform. The Navy had forty-one of these submarines in service at the time — the "41 for Freedom" — each equipped with sixteen ballistic missiles. Each of those missiles carried multiple re-entry vehicles (MRVs), with which nuclear warheads could be carried to their target. These missiles were on lease from the manufacturer (at the time I think it was Raytheon Corp.) until they were used. Like all things military and mechanical, the entire system for their use had to be periodically tested. The best time to do so was during a post-overhaul Demonstration And Shakedown Operation (DASO), which for East Coast submarines was typically conducted in the Caribbean. While there were two crews for each submarine, only one would test-launch a missile during DASO.

I was a part of the crew scheduled to conduct the *Polk's* missile test. These test missiles did not, we were assured, have actual warheads. Instead, they were loaded with guidance and telemetry equipment that could be monitored from a land-based facility as well as from the launching submarine. The launch went off just fine, but just a few minutes into the flight, the missile veered off course and was on a new trajectory that would have sent it somewhere in Florida. It had to be destroyed just a few minutes after launch, and although it landed in the ocean — miles away from the submarine — the concussion generated by the destruction of the missile felt as though it had come back and landed on the ship. That was a scary moment!

This whole affair was very disturbing to me. What if we did not have all that telemetry equipment in place of the warheads on that missile? Would we even know it was veering off course, and could we destroy it mid-flight if it was? Or would a wayward missile turn the wrong town into another Nagasaki or Hiroshima? These nukes were a lot more powerful than *Fat Boy* or *Little Man*. What if the Navy's party-line propaganda — that we were so accurate we could hit a pack of cigarettes from space — was just so many words? This test seemed to confirm my worst fears about nuclear weapons. They don't need to be "accurate," but the vehicles carrying them to a destination must be. The potential was real for a disastrous "friendly fire" incident. They were supposedly a deterrent to the Soviets, and most submarine-launched missile tests were reported to be "successful." The only one I personally witnessed was not. All it would take... is that one.

Following Cheryl's harrowing experience and after consideration of all that was going on around me, I came to realize just how much of a pacifist I had become. Pacifism and the military don't go well together, and I began having a lot of anxiety and inner turmoil over this schism. I decided I needed to be designated a conscientious objector and asked for that to happen. I was willing to remain in the Navy — just not as a part of something capable of such death and destruction (intentional or accidental). I just didn't know how to do this. It was not a common occurrence, and while I'm sure there were rules regarding the process, I could not find them anywhere. I wrote a letter, expressing my views and making the request.

Although enacted too late to help me, the following is taken from Wikipedia and supports my argument:

On March 8, 1995, the United Nations Commission on Human Rights resolution 1995/83 stated that "persons performing military service should not be excluded from the right to have conscientious objections to military service." This was re-affirmed on April 22, 1998, when resolution 1998/77 recognized that "persons [already] performing military service may develop conscientious objections."

All Navy commands have a Commanding Officer (CO) and an Executive Officer (XO). As it turned out, my attempt to gain conscientious objector status was somewhat ham-fisted on my part, but it was not approached in a disrespectful way. The *Polk's* XO took it upon himself to deal with me (and what he perceived to be my problem). As a dedicated military man, who was also deeply religious, this XO put a lot of thought into making my life a living hell. Although he was in the service of the secular government of the United States, he nonetheless suggested I needed to pray for guidance, and he asked me, point blank, if I believed in Jesus Christ. I told him I was, and had been, an atheist my entire life. He berated my atheism and went on a tirade about how I needed Jesus Christ in my heart and, without that, I would never amount to anything. Without the Lord, I would burn in hell and would

"...fail at absolutely everything" I might attempt.

He asked me who had put me "up to this" and told me I would definitely not be granted conscientious objector status if he had anything to do with it. He added that my only hope was to find a way to be discharged.

I was sent to the base medical clinic to be evaluated by a Navy psychiatrist. I was asked why I had an aversion to guns. I explained what had happened with my parents, including how my dad had died. I also related accounts of some of the abuse I suffered at my mother's hands after my father's death. The psychiatrist told me she didn't believe me and said, "Even if that's all true, why would you even join the military?"

I told her that, due to my mother's abuses, I had found myself essentially homeless at the time and without resources. She responded, "Well, whose fault was that?"

I pointed out how, since joining the Navy, I had attempted to be the best I could, and I described my many accomplishments over the past five years.

She decided I was self-pitying and without the requisite intelligence to try to obtain conscientious objector status on my own. She asked me a question the XO had asked (almost verbatim):

"Who put you up to this?"

I responded, "Nobody."

To which she then said, "I find that hard to believe. Someone put you up to this. If you tell me, we can maybe make this entire process go a lot more smoothly for you."

I found her quite closed-minded and very condescending, but who was I? I was nothing more than a low-level pawn without a college education.

It got worse. Rather than offering help in filing for conscientious objector status, the XO began finding different ways to bring me down through his narrow interpretations of the UCMJ (Uniform Code of Military Justice) as well as his secret and illicit suggestions as to how I could facilitate a discharge. He ordered underlings to report on their conversations with me. He told the administrative personnel, "...if it's the last thing I do, I'm going to see him in prison..."

He began following me around — even to the point of potentially endangering the ship by leaving his maneuvering watch station to check up on me. In private, he suggested to me that I become a disciplinary problem by going Away Without Official Leave (AWOL), and he outlined the process that would lead to my discharge. Under his persecution, I lost all of my stripes and was left without pay for many months. This man's behavior frequently made me think of my mother. He didn't get physically violent with me, but his stalking, lack of boundaries, and abuse of rules left me feeling psychiatrically and emotionally tortured.

My first five years in the Navy showed me I was more than my mother thought me or expected. I was an outstanding sailor. As I began my sixth year in the Navy, I was an experienced non-commissioned officer (E5) who had the time in service and was possessed of all requirements to be advanced to E6 (I had the recommendation of the *Benjamin Franklin's* commanding officer to be advanced, I had passed the written test, and had made it past the Navy-wide selection committee). I had qualified in submarines on three different ships. I was a qualified sonar supervisor with the experience of three successful post-overhaul periods and two deterrent patrols. I had a Good Conduct Ribbon and at least one formal letter of commendation in my record. I had never been reprimanded or disciplined in any way. My career had been exemplary from boot camp right up to this moment. However, I had also just insulted this Executive Officer's entire way of life. He had to make an example of me. I was not under any delusions — if there were to be a piece of this equation that would be bent or broken, it would most certainly be me.

Although I'd had no thoughts about doing any of the following on my own, the XO's suggestions amounted to this: I was not going to gain conscientious objector status, so my only path was to find a way to be discharged. If I were to go AWOL three times, he would have to consider me as a liability, and I would be discharged. He often made it a point to apprise me of the status of another sailor attached to the other crew of our ship, who had followed this path (and ended up being processed for discharge). He pointed out that even if I chose to stay in the Navy, my life would be a living hell because I had already tipped my hand (by asking for the change in status). Essentially, he told me I had but one choice: seek a discharge any way I could manage it. He told me it would be best for the others if I were not a part of the crew. He didn't want me on his ship and told me so. He told me all these things during multiple meetings behind the closed door of his stateroom, and he told me he would deny having said anything along these lines if I ever told anyone he had.

I did just what he had suggested. I was gone three times when I should have been aboard the ship or in the "off-crew office." The third time, I had calculated my time away so that I would be gone as long as I could without crossing the magical barrier of thirty days, because that was the determinant between someone being AWOL or having deserted the military. I knew that cutting it that close had its risks, but I thought it could be done. I underestimated how far the XO was willing to go to see me punished. He convinced the one person who could have attested to the difference in my case to lie. He tried me for desertion. I had broken the rules. In that situation, I had been reduced to having a choice between being constantly stalked and persecuted for my ethical beliefs or breaking the rules and being persecuted and disciplined for the same. This was no choice at all. However, I was the one who broke the rule. Then, to rub salt into the wound, he told me he was not going to discharge me, after all. I'm reasonably sure this was simply a mean-spirited lie to make me sweat. I felt the same way as when my mother had refused to take me for my driver's license exam.

Once the XO had completed his emotional and psychological evisceration and had twisted the UCMJ to prosecute me to the fullest… once I had been belittled, embarrassed, and humiliated… once I had lost everything… I was transferred to a submarine tender ship to await discharge. There's no way he could have known, but I had already been down this road. This kind of punishment was not new to me. The setting was different, but the tactics were hardly unfamiliar to me. Nonetheless, he wanted to leave nothing to chance. Before the *Polk* left for patrol, as a parting shot, the XO saw to it I was detained. He didn't quite see me go to prison, but I was confined to the submarine tender and ordered to do extra duty as punishment. I'm reasonably sure it was because of friendships I had made and fostered that a portion of my transfer orders was "accidentally" left out of the official transfer paperwork. I was confined to the sub tender, but the order for extra duty had been mysteriously omitted.

Two days before I was due to leave for good, I got some documents to look over and I was scheduled for a separation physical. What these documents said was that I was receiving a General Discharge. I would not be eligible for veteran's benefits and programs. I would receive a basic discharge stipend (enough to get me home), and that prior to departing the facility I was to turn in my sea bag and any uniforms I had. I had not brought my sea bag back to Charleston with me, so that wasn't going to happen. I had my dress blues and three working uniforms. That was it. In retrospect, I think they used the honor system with regards to returning the uniforms. No one asked for them, ever. I reported the next morning for my separation physical. This marked the first time, in all of my Navy enlistment, that I was ordered to undress in front of a woman. At first, I was a little shy or maybe intimidated, but she reassured me it was nothing she hadn't seen before. It was hardly a physical. She checked for a hernia, listened to my heart and lungs, looked into my ears, eyes, nose, and mouth, and I was done. The next day I would be free.

In the morning, I rose with everyone else, but instead of dressing in a Navy uniform, I put on my civvies. I was handed the last set of Navy orders I would ever receive. I walked off the submarine tender and onto the dock. I walked out by the guard shack and realized I still had my neatly folded uniforms in my hand. I handed them to the guard, who had no idea why I was doing this and no idea what to do with the uniforms. I then walked over to the parking area. My little Toyota Tercel was sitting right where I had left it. I got in, and it started right up. I got off government property as quickly as I was able. I stopped for some gas and a snack for the road. I drove all day long and was home by about 9:30 PM. Cheryl hugged me, and I felt as though I could finally breathe. That nightmare was over.

Thirty-Six

*"With any part you play, there is a certain amount of yourself in it.
There has to be, otherwise it's just not acting. It's lying."*

—*Johnny Depp*

Cheryl and I were never right for each other. Shortly after my discharge from the Navy, our marriage ended. I ended up working as a tobacco store assistant manager, and then as a security guard – both in the Dedham Mall, just outside Boston. That's where I met Elaine. She described having survived her youth with a misogynistic and narcissistic father. Her mother had divorced Elaine's dad, but they remained on friendly terms. After we got married, we moved to her childhood hometown—near Kansas City, Missouri. Partly because of her dad's behavior and partly for self-improvement, Elaine had gone to Texas, after dropping out of college, to train as a commercial diver. Through a connection she had made while in Houston, we were invited to move to the west coast. Her old diving instructor (who apparently had a crush on her) wanted to open a Scuba-diving shop in the San Juan Islands of Washington State, and he wanted her to run it. We were making another move. In a period of just over two years, we had gone from Massachusetts to Missouri, and now we were completing the transcontinental sweep and landing in Washington State. For the first couple of years in Washington, we lived in the picturesque San Juan Islands. While there—and with Elaine's help—I discovered community theater.

In my last two years in high school, I had been involved with a couple of musical theater productions. Through theater, I learned that I could leave reality behind and immerse myself in being someone else. I could become someone who had suffered and continued to be marginalized, such as Riff in *West Side Story*, or someone who was privileged, but still in need of basic human interactions, like Henry Higgins in *My Fair Lady*. I could also combine this with something I had come to love—making music. In addition to marching band and stage band, my theater rehearsals had taken me out of my mother's home for even more hours per week. It would be perfectly sufficient if this were my primary reason for getting involved, but it was not. I got involved with music because it appealed to me, and I got involved with theater because of the musical component. But theater, as an art form, began to appeal with or without the music. Performance allowed me to channel someone else or to express someone else's joy, pain, love, devastation, and genius. These characters could manifest themselves through me, and I could learn from them.

Elaine and I initially set up the dive shop at a small resort on Orcas Island, but moved after one season to San Juan Island. We didn't have enough year-round business on Orcas to justify an investment in a brick-and-mortar shop. Friday Harbor was a better bet. However, in that bustling little tourist town, there was not a whole lot to do between Labor Day and Memorial Day of the following year. Especially outside the tourist season, the place became quite sleepy... almost a ghost town. To get out of town meant leaving the island. To do so required an hour and twenty-minute ferry ride. On top of the higher cost of living on an island, this commute made frequent trips cost prohibitive. There was a cinema, but we also discovered there was a thriving theater community in town. Elaine saw an advertisement for a production of Gilbert and Sullivan's *H.M.S. Pinafore* at the local playhouse. This sounded like fun, so we decided to give it a go.

It would be a grave disservice to the San Juan Community Theater to intimate that what had been built there was typical of most community theater spaces. This was a beautiful space, which had opened just the year before, and *Pinafore* was the first production for the 1990 season. I was impressed with the sightlines and the acoustics. As I was made to understand it, a retired physician and philanthropist, Dr. Paul Whittier, and his wife donated the land (a gorgeous outcropping looking over the harbor) and offered up a challenge to the residents of San Juan

Island. If they could match his financial donation, they would have a considerable amount of capital with which to create a dedicated space for the local talent. The result was a 275-seat purpose-built theater with a full fly gallery as well as support offices, space for rehearsal, and more. We were attending the opening weekend performance of *Pinafore*, and in the program was a call for auditions for their next production. My sleeping interest in theater was nudged and awakened.

I hadn't done any theater for almost twelve years, and the prospect of auditioning was daunting. My mother's voice kept running through my brain, "You have no musical talent—you sing off-key."

And although it was intended to address life partners and not musical auditions:

"You're nothing special."

The second show of the San Juan Community Theater 1990–1991 season was to be an older (thirty-plus years old) cast singing and dancing their way through the musical *Grease*. I was thirty years old—I fit the criteria. The notice said we needed to sing a song. As an audition piece, I chose a 1961 Doo-Wop song originally performed by Dion (formerly with the Belmonts)—*Runaround Sue*. I was cast as Kinickie, and that began a four-year-long association with the theater in Friday Harbor.

Later in the 1990–1991 season, I played the evil dentist Orin Scrivello, DDS, in *Little Shop of Horrors*. Based upon my two performances, I was asked to audition for a little-known musical from the early 1960s. *A Time for Singing* was a musical rendition of the Richard Llewellyn novel *How Green Was My Valley*, and it had not done well on or off Broadway. The primary (if not sole) reason it was being performed was because of the theater matriarch of Friday Harbor, Martha Gubleman. Martha was another influential adult whose acquaintance I was fortunate to make. Her husband Herb and she had been teachers at the Cornish School for the Arts. Prior to that, they had owned and operated a theater in Goshen, Connecticut. They had been active in the New York theater scene, and when they tired of that, they moved to Connecticut and formed the Goshen Players. Martha had fallen in love with *A Time for Singing* and wanted to reconnect with the show. It was an honor to work with her, and I learned a lot of stagecraft during our all-too-brief acquaintance.

Immediately on the heels of *A Time for Singing*, I auditioned for *The Wizard of Oz*. I was never so intimidated as I was on those two nights of open auditions. There were so many talented folks who came out for that show. In the end, I was cast as the Scarecrow. For the longest time, if anyone would ask me what my favorite show had been, I would answer that it was this production of *Wizard*. With each show, there was a new learning opportunity. Each director had wisdom and skills to impart. I made my directorial debut in the very next season with a production of *Harvey* and brought in Martha Gubleman for a cameo. The following season ('92–'93), I got my second directorial opportunity with *You're a Good Man, Charlie Brown*. I was gaining experience and theater stature. I began to be sought out for certain roles.

In the beginning of the '91–'92 season, while I was directing rehearsals for *Harvey*, the Straights of Juan de Fuca Players (the resident company) came to me to propose something they'd wanted to do for a long time. It seemed there was a desire, in Friday Harbor, to put on a production of *The Music Man*, but they felt they lacked an actor capable of pulling off the title role. Martha was slated to be the director, but she was also mentoring a younger woman in theater direction. Therese Finn was to be the primary director and, with Martha as her mentor, they felt they could pull it off if I were willing to portray Professor Harold Hill. We put together a whiz-bang production of *The Music Man*, and I became extremely popular. Elaine's grandmother, who was eighty-seven years old, had been brought up in Keokuk, Iowa—one of the towns specifically mentioned in the Meredith Willson script. She made the trip from her home in Missouri to see the show and was one of the first people in the house to stand after the final number. We got standing ovations every night, and this was a crowning achievement for me in theater. In all, I was a part of eight shows over four seasons in Friday Harbor.

Theater had become my life, and my life was theater. To support my rediscovered passion, I worked at whatever I could to bring in money. In addition to the dive shop that Elaine and I ran, I also managed a privately-owned motel, worked for the local phone company, and worked odd jobs including landscaping. I got into a program to train as an EMT and then took up that vocation on a volunteer basis. This training included college-level courses that were listed as being a part of a local nursing program. Suddenly, it clicked. I knew what I wanted to do. I just didn't know how to go about it.

Thirty-Seven

*"First, they ignore you, then laugh at you,
then they fight you, then you win."*

– Mahatma Gandhi

After his first read-through of the manuscript, my cousin Michael Jolin, who held a PhD in psychology, suggested to me that I should include more about my sister Lori in this memoir because my memories involving her were actually a huge part of my early life. At first, I hesitated. I didn't want this to be about her. After giving it considerable thought, I decided to follow his suggestion. My mother and my older sister Chuckie were both a part of my life. Lori was also a part of my life, and she often embodied a link to the abuses I suffered at my mother's hand. Lori was a secondary antagonist and often was the sole reason for some of the punishment I received. She was certainly present for most of it because the proximity of our ages placed us in the same home at the same time. But there's something more. Despite her not suffering to even a remotely similar degree — the humiliation and emotional, psychological, and physical abuse to which Chuckie and I were subject — she still suffered. Lori suffered because, more than any of the other siblings, she was the most like our mother. Lori and Mom had that unrelenting need to control. Nothing was ever because of them, nor was anything ever their fault. It was usually someone else causing them to have to be the savior or the martyr. It was a difficult position for a young girl to find herself.

My younger sister has had a colorful life. She was married at least three times over a period of not more than fourteen years. I've seen a photo of her with her second husband, but I've not had many interactions with him. I've exchanged emails with spouses two and three and have spoken, by phone, with her first husband. I last saw Lori, face-to-face, at a family gathering in 1995. It had been an additional twelve or thirteen years since I had previously seen her, and I hardly recognized her due to all the cosmetic procedures she had in that span. My previous encounter had been in the early 1980s when she sublet an apartment from Cheryl and me. I had suffered indignities at the hands of my sister before the apartment fiasco, but with that, she had affected other people's lives and livelihoods and left me holding the bag. I vowed I would never again allow her close enough to do anything similar.

My mother had a far greater influence on Lori than I think many of us, especially Lori, ever knew. She had seen Mom's aggressions and abuses on the three older siblings. She heard arguments between our parents. She had been the beneficiary, more often than she would be willing to recognize, of 'the favorite' status she enjoyed with Mom. But what did she learn from all of this? Reading her book, she appears to have interpreted what she experienced in a manner diametrically opposed to the interpretations and memories of her siblings. She saw all of these egregious and violent abuses levied on her siblings as personal attacks on her by our mother. Is it possible, looking at her young life through this lens, that she saw (especially) the emotional and psychological abuse as favoritism or even as love? It was as if she lived in a child's opposite world.

Lori was the fourth of our parents' five children. She was a decade (or more) younger than Faith and Chuckie and was closest in age to me. Especially after our youngest sister—Wendy—was born, the two older siblings were charged with looking after and occupying Lori's and my time so that we were kept out of Mom's hair. She was a weird and quirky child and learned that she could make others laugh by being even weirder. She once hung by her knees from a tree branch and ate a banana by dangling it from the peels. She would catch big brown toads and kiss them because they were "so cute." Faith, who was normally—at best—a B/C student, wrote a psychology paper with Lori as the subject and received a rare 'A' for her grade. *Skinny Legs and All* was a 1967 song composed and recorded by soul singer Joe Tex, and that song inspired a theme, of sorts, for Lori. We'd say: "Who's that lady with the skinny legs?" (a lyric from the song), and Lori would try to walk like an ostrich to show off her skinny legs.

Lori was often jealous, conniving, manipulative, obstinate, bratty, and attention-seeking. As a babysitter, Faith was low-energy and boring. Her and Chuckie were tasked with watching Lori and me and alternating days with each one. When it was Faith's turn to watch her, Lori would want to join Chuckie and me in our adventures. She'd get angry if we were doing something (like ice skating) in which she was not capable of participating. I, too, felt the Faith doldrums and would sometimes request to go along with Chuckie and Lori. According to Chuckie:

"[I was] gracious and didn't resent the intrusion, but when the roles were reversed, she would get very angry if you tried to join us. She was hateful even at a young age."

If one of the older sisters had taken her out with them and Lori was bored, she would claim to be sick and ask to go home. If she didn't get her way, she would scream that the older sister (whichever one was with her) was hurting her. She would insist on sticking her hands into the projects or activities of others. I had a chord organ I had gotten for Christmas one year. Chuckie would help me try to figure out melodies from television shows on the keyboard. Lori would come into my bedroom and reach in between us to depress whatever keys she could reach. It was very frustrating.

On another occasion, I had my chemistry set outdoors (I wasn't allowed to use it indoors) and was boiling some water over the alcohol burner. She nearly knocked over the beaker stand (and the beaker with the boiling water) by reaching in. I yelled at her to stop because one of us might get burned. Mom heard me and stuck her head out of the kitchen door, saying:

"You let her do something!"

"You can check the temperature of the water," I offered, handing her a dial thermometer.

"How am I supposed to do that?" she responded.

I began to explain what to look for and she said:

"I know all that." (she didn't).

I showed her how to put the thermometer's stem into the water, being careful not to hold it against the bottom of the beaker, and explained what she should expect to see on the dial. Lori didn't have patience or much of an attention span. She became bored waiting for the dial to show 212 degrees and started looking around. She ended up tilting the beaker over, spilling the boiling water onto my wrist. I was scalded and had a bandage on my wrist when I showed up for a festival band rehearsal the next day. I still have a scar from that.

In yet another odd encounter, I was trying to put together a hatchet head with a new wooden handle. I had shaved the handle slightly to allow the old steel head to slide over it. I was doing something I had seen Dad do in a similar circumstance: I was pounding the lower end of the handle on the concrete steps so that the head would advance downward to its final seated position. When I had just begun, the hatchet head was precariously balanced on top of the handle. Lori kept reaching in. As my hand came down and the handle was about to meet the concrete, Lori pushed just enough for my trajectory to be offset. Instead of moving down the handle, the head fell off. The head of this hatchet was (as all similar tools are) wedge-shaped. The wider and heavier blunt end came down first and landed on the back of Lori's hand. She started to get belligerent with me when I asked her to step away so I could do the job without either of us getting hurt. Pouting, she ran inside the house.

The next thing I know, Mom came out of the house with fists and open hands pummeling me for "attacking Lori with an axe." I showed her the hatchet was still in two pieces (head separate from handle) and tried to explain that she had reached in while I was attempting to make it a whole tool. Mom was having none of that. She grabbed Lori (who had been sniggering behind her) by the wrist and showed me the slightly reddened back of her hand. I confirmed the back of the head had landed on Lori's hand, but Mom came back with:

"You attacked her and tried to cut her hand off with an axe!"

The ridiculousness of the situation overtook me and I burst out laughing. The "axe," as it was now being called, was taken away and the handle became a weapon with which to beat me. Many times, Lori repeated the story of how I attacked her with an axe. Lori had created conflict where there was none, and Mom did her no favors by fueling that fantasy.

It is my opinion that when a child is witness to abuse, but they somehow manage to avoid the same degree and frequency of the abuses they see, they may either begin to feel some sense of guilt and condition their memories to put themselves into the position of victim, or, with the additional leash afforded them by an abuser, they may take on some strange sense of superiority over the abused. Lori did both of these to some degree. I tend to doubt she truly felt any guilt, though, as that is just not something I would associate with her personality, although she may have felt ignored. She also carried forward several of our mother's rigid (and ridiculous) limitations into her adulthood and eventual parenthood. In these ways, Mom passed on some of the learnable traits of her personality disorder to her daughter.

Sometime between September of 1977 and June of 1978, after I left the family home and before Mom sold the place, Lori went into a rage, citing her hatred of our father. She found a cache of family photos and destroyed every one in which Dad had appeared. The type and intensity of that hateful rage was a carbon copy of the kind of behavior we had come to expect from Mom. Lori was fifteen or sixteen years old. In her book she claims:

"To say that I loved my father is an understatement."

But we all knew otherwise.

She was envious of the amount of time he spent with Chuckie and me, and she appeared to believe that he didn't like her as much as the rest of us (with Faith as the possible exception). None of that was intentional, on his part. He loved us all. Without having actual knowledge, she attested to a litany of anecdotes detailing interactions between her and Dad that simply did not happen and could not have happened. She retroactively imagined herself in those situations, but her lack of knowledge showed up in several stories that could not have happened due to physical impossibilities and the restraints of time. She literally injected her presence in place of me and allowed her imagination to become her truth. She wasn't close to Dad, by her own choice. She said she hated him and didn't want anyone to have those photos of him.

Thirty-Eight

"Disillusionment isn't an event, it's a process. It doesn't arrive and do its work all at once, like an epiphany. It is a way of living, a perpetual vigilance, a habit of mind."

—*Philip Kennicott*

I have worked with psychiatric providers and counsellors. Together, we have dealt with all degrees and types of mental illness, so I have a somewhat unique perspective when it comes to that human malady. Also, as the saying goes: "Hindsight is 20/20." I can look back and see my mother's behaviors as sources or major contributors to my behavioral shortfalls. She was not a good parent. But she learned her behavior somewhere... didn't she? Was it only a learned component that drove her to abuse us? Was it a chemical imbalance? Nature or nurture? I know, now, that there are multiple contributors to behavior such as hers.

In 2014, when I first decided to write a memoir, I had no idea that the process was going to take me down so many rabbit holes. I thought I'd just write down my memories. After all, my mother had done that, and Lori had sort-of done the same. It wasn't until my cousin suggested I bring my recollections of my sister into my narrative that I began to understand several key factors in this thing I refer to as my life. In discussing discoveries and enlisting others' memories, I began seeing a family history and family dynamics that were vastly different from what I thought they were when I started.

I have known my sister Lori to be manipulative and prone to exaggeration, as well as outright fabrication. As I've alluded to, it is my opinion that her behaviors tend to point toward some personality disorder and/or mental illness. I have also learned that there is a genetic component to borderline personality disorder. Even if it is simply a predisposition, it can—and often is—passed from one generation to the next. In fact, there are connections between Borderline Personality Disorder, Bipolar Disorder, and Schizophrenia. Some—or all—of the components manifest in offspring, but they may (and often do) skip a generation. Until just now, as the year 2020 draws to a close, I was not able to put a lot of these things together into what is sometimes referred to as a 'Theory of Everything.' One day, after discussions with a psychiatrist and a substance use counselor with whom I had worked, it suddenly clicked. It wasn't any one thing either of them said, but their input seemed to electrify a lot of what I'd been writing about and hearing. My mind was just ripe, at the right moment, I guess.

It occurred to me that with Borderline folks, there's an element of obsessive-compulsive behavior, a tendency toward addiction, a need to control, meanness, and (this was the clincher for me) a sense of loathing, as they see in themselves the negative attributes of someone (a parent) they don't want to emulate. My mother despised her father. Lori despised my mother. The three of them, in consecutive generations, were very much alike in many ways. Mom and Lori each embodied the very attributes they despised in their parent. Bipolar disorder and schizophrenia are connected to this weird matrix, and not all elements are clear. Like so much else in the world of mental health, we just don't know all the interconnections. But it's interesting to be able to track attributes from one generation to the next. Guillaume, Faith, and Lori are perpetrators—and victims—of violence, and they are all related… to me.

Thirty-Nine

"Life is like a book that never ends.
Chapters close, but not the book itself."

– Marianne Williamson

In the decades since all of this came to an end, a lot has happened around and with me. All three of the submarines upon which I was stationed were decommissioned between 1992 and 1999. I made my peace with my mother, and we stayed in contact until she died forty-one years, one month, and four days after Dad had passed. I forgave her, but I will never forget her part in this trauma. When I was fifteen, I had thought she would ultimately kill him. I don't think I was wrong; she was the cause of it. Of this I am certain. The question, after all these years, has been answered: I wish it had been Dad who had survived.

Cheryl and I didn't last. After I was discharged from the Navy and I was faced with having to live with her on a full-time basis, I realized she was definitely not the life partner I had hoped for. If only her parents had acceded to our original plans, the intensified heartache caused by the end of a marriage might have been avoided. She sensed me slipping away and, without telling me, she discontinued her contraceptive pills. She also suddenly quit smoking — something I had been asking her to do for a couple of years. I should have been better about reading the signs. Despite infrequent relations, she became pregnant just as I was planning my exit. This made the whole thing much more complicated.

Cheryl and her second husband did a marvelous job raising our son. He's a lovely human being, and I have three beautiful grandchildren as a result. He — and they — would not be in the world were it not for Cheryl's parents. I have to admit that their religious views resulted in the presence of these beautiful people on the planet. I later met and married Elaine, with whom I spent twenty years. My second son came from that relationship. That marriage, however, ended terribly, and a year or two after that divorce, I found myself in an on-again/off-again relationship with Gretchen. This also did not end well. In retrospect, I can see aspects of the personalities of Cheryl, Elaine, and Gretchen that point to me having sought out someone, as a partner, with behaviors similar to my mother. I had no idea I was doing that. I couldn't see the forest for the trees. My relationships were based upon a truly warped understanding of what constituted love. Violence is not love. Passive-aggressive behavior is not love. Gaslighting is not love. Abuse is not love.

There are a lot of things, from those years, that I often reflect upon and from which I have tried to learn. While writing about these memories, I've come to realize other things about myself and have tried to determine how I got to be the way I am. Am I self-pitying, like the Navy psychiatrist said? Aren't we all—just a little bit? I think if I am, to any extent beyond the norm, it's likely because there was so little maternal love and caring during my formative years that I had no one else to empathize with me or to concern themselves with my fears and insecurities. What little piece of love—for myself—did I find that helped me to get through all of this? Were some of my sisters able to find something similar? I don't have answers to any of these questions.

I have often thought about and reflected upon the Polk's XO's words. He told me I would not amount to anything. That without Jesus Christ in my heart, I would fail at everything I tried. I have worked for a company installing bank alarms and was trusted to be alone, inside bank vaults, sometimes with millions of dollars in cash. I sold cars and was top salesman on more than one occasion. I started my own company and did quite well with that. After the Navy and a cacophony of occupations, I settled on nursing and have succeeded in many of the myriad specialties within nursing. I bought a home on acreage and so much more. I wouldn't call any of those failures. I'd call them successes. I remain an atheist.

I've looked back at those last several months in the Navy and have discovered still more about myself. I had done really well for five-plus years. I was a model sailor right out of the blocks. I picked up most things quickly and had a good memory, so I could implement the things I learned. Asking to be designated a conscientious objector was not unreasonable. What was unreasonable was the XO's reaction to my request. He took it personally, and that was neither his job nor his place to do so. Was he in the wrong? One would have to say he was not totally wrong on all counts. Some of the things I did were not true violations, but by manipulating the UCMJ and interpreting it as narrowly as he did, he painted me as a dangerous criminal who needed to be locked up. I wasn't, and anyone who knew me then—or knows me now—would say as much.

Did this XO, who later aspired to become a Wyoming State legislator, stretch credulity and honesty with some of his actions and interpretations? Absolutely. Was he stalking me? Do I think he set me up for failure? Was he wrong to suggest I should go AWOL? My answer to those questions is an unequivocal "yes." He handled the whole thing quite poorly. Maybe it made him feel better about his place in the world. Maybe he lashed out because, by the simple act of thinking, I became a threat to every aspect of his life. Do I consider him to be a hypocrite? Surely. Did he treat me as "a good Christian" would? Two words: "Hell No!"

In my youth I experienced so much that it sometimes felt surreal and at other times totally unreal. All I had to do, though, was to look at the newspaper clippings from the '70s and the paperwork I had with me when I left the Navy to bring me back to the facts as they were, and those facts were very real. I came to despise the effect a .22 caliber rifle had on our family. It didn't matter that it was obtained outside of the law. If anything, that fact reinforced my position on guns. If my dad could buy a gun in a state where a Firearms Identification (FID) card was supposedly required for gun sales and he didn't have the requisite clearance, then gun control was a myth. The rash of AR-15 and AK-47-type mass shootings that have plagued the U.S. show that availability, regardless of legality, allows for and promotes gun violence.

I can't be the only person to have seen the man behind the curtain. Being more of a dove after having served in uniform, I can sure surprise some folks when discussing politics and the military. As a post-middle-aged white man who served in the military, conservatives expect me to be one of them. I'm not. Upon learning all of this about me, there's a nearly comical process of back-pedaling that goes on. I've done the right things. I should believe as they do... but I don't, and that's difficult for some to understand and/or accept.

All of the adverse events and turmoil from my teens through my time in the Navy didn't just happen. I don't subscribe to the idea that I am solely responsible for having brought these things onto myself. I also don't think providence or chance had anything to do with those experiences. I certainly do not consider my lack of faith as a conduit for bad things to happen. There was something about me, though, and the way I approached the world that put me into certain situations from which the outcome was often bad. But what was it? Is there someone to blame? And was it because that person was just plain evil? If so, why were they evil? I don't think that's all of it either. We are the result of how we deal with our life experiences. I was going to say that a lot of how I reacted to the negative experiences in my life was just my gut. But that's not totally true, either. I simply learned how to react.

Forty

*"You can spend minutes, hours, days, weeks, or even months
overanalyzing a situation; trying to put the pieces together, justifying
what could've, would've happened...
or you can just leave the pieces on the floor and move on."*

– Tupac Shakur

On the 30th of September 2017, I married Alycia—a beautiful, witty, intelligent, and totally enjoyable person. She's also more than 25 years younger than I am. Mom joined Chuckie, Wendy, and me via a video call from the wedding venue, as she was unable (or unwilling) to travel. Faith had not had any interaction with Mom for around ten years and didn't participate in that call.

Alycia met my mother while we were visiting New England on the occasion of Aunt Dottie's funeral in 2016. While there was limited interaction between Alycia and Mom on that occasion, I recall the brusqueness with which Mom had treated my bride-to-be. Alycia saw it differently. She recalled one of the first things that Mom did was to pat my tummy, saying I had gotten rounder. She didn't appear, to Alycia, to be the terrifying woman I had described. In fact, she seemed like an amiable grandmother type.

The more time they shared, the more Alycia began seeing—through a veil of laughter—the older woman's lack of self-confidence. She kept to herself; she seemed almost timid and frail in Alycia's eyes.

To Alycia, Mom's apartment appeared stark, tiny; everything had a place, and nothing was out of place. While talking at the kitchen table, she might have appeared, to the outside observer, to have been outmatched by the larger personalities in the room (Chuckie, Alycia, and me). It seemed to affect how she acted—not trying to keep up necessarily, but to assert a sort of control in the room, which showed she had a place there. The thing that stood out the most was her laughing at Alycia's attempts to accurately pronounce the terrible Woonsocket-area locutions documented in a local "dictionary."

The situation of Aunt Dottie's death brought into focus a dynamic that was quickly becoming obsolete. Since the death of their sister Rita in 1963, the remaining Longtin clan had basically maintained a form of status quo that lasted almost 40 years. Then, in 2000, Aunt Mary suddenly passed due to a form of infectious meningitis. Mom was particularly distraught with her death. They were born only a couple of years apart and had always been very close. They had agreed to a pact whereby they would not die peacefully; they would both go out screaming and kicking. Aunt Mary's death was very quiet—Mom was the sibling chosen to "pull the plug." Then, in

2005, Aunt Rose died, followed by Aunt Shirley in 2007. There was a bit of a break until 2013, when Uncle Rene passed. Those last two also hit Mom hard because both were younger than her.

This left just Aunt Dottie and Mom. Because she was my godmother, I got semi-regular reports from Mom about Aunt Dottie's health (particularly her mental health). She was in her declining years, and although she had been the oldest after 1963, she had outlasted them all... all except Mom. On the date of Dottie's passing in 2016, Mom became the last living member of her immediate family. This had a sobering effect on a woman who very rarely showed emotion. She was the last standing Longtin.

For a woman I had described in such beastly terms, there was a softer side. Mom always loved to laugh, and we were there in the room, on that occasion, to help with that. Alycia noticed this readily. Mom was trying to be demure, but she was never good at doing that. Despite knowing I didn't agree with her religious views, she still made me aware of her opinion regarding divorce and remarriage... as odd, out of touch, and hypocritical a perspective as that was.

Mom enjoyed singing—whether along with a recording or a cappella. She also enjoyed games. When we were kids, she would often participate in card games or board games. These would usually include Faith and Chuckie, but sometimes (as I got older), I might be included as well. After her kids left the house, she would host game nights with Aunt Dottie and cousins Beverly and Sharon often in attendance. She could (and did) instigate major laugh fests—often at the expense of one or another of her guests. Many times, the giggles had to do with a bodily function or an attribute she found comical. Our visit with her in 2016 was no different.

A little over a year after that encounter, and two weeks after our wedding, I found myself heading back to New England. This time, it was for Mom's funeral. She had succumbed to a hemorrhagic stroke while showering. In a manner consistent with her lifelong need to be in control and her (likely ideologically imposed) gymnophobia, her last words to Henry were: **"towel... towel..."** I got the call from Wendy while I was driving on a Thursday afternoon. I made the arrangements as quickly as I could, but she died in the wee hours on Friday, before Chuckie and I could get there. The six Longtin siblings had lasted 37 years together. Then, in a span of just 17 years, all six were gone.

Chuckie, Wendy, and I were joined by Faith and her husband Dickie at the Woonsocket apartment Mom had shared with Henry. Lori was made aware of her death but had made clear she wanted nothing to do with the family. Arrangements needed to be made, and a service had to be planned. Mom was always a Catholic, and there was never any doubt she would have a Mass of Christian Burial. Her service was to be held at All Saints Church in Woonsocket, where she and Henry attended weekly Mass.

Among the many things we spoke of, the topic of her eulogy came to the fore. I think it was a unanimous decision to have me deliver said tribute. This made me feel uncomfortable in at least a couple of different ways. For one, I was not the closest to her; that would have been Wendy. Wendy had a troubled youth, and Mom and Henry had helped her through those difficult times. Wendy had always vowed to help them when that eventuality played out. She likely would have been too emotional to speak in public. Faith had not spoken to Mom for a really long time, and with her meekness, she would not have been the best choice. The decision as to which one of us would speak essentially came down to Chuckie, who thought it better that I deliver it.

The second point of discomfort had to do with a difference in religion—or, to be more precise, religion vs. non-religion. I joked that I might burst into flames if I stood in the pulpit of a Catholic church. I had a couple of days in which I needed to compose my remarks. I needed to tread carefully. The final speech was one of respectful tribute. I included a hint about discipline that probably only one other person recognized, but made the overarching theme one of loss and love. The speech was written on a hotel lobby computer and not proofed. I made a few corrections and addenda by hand. I would bring this with me to the pulpit.

Eulogy for Mom

It's been said that life is not about the destination; it's about the journey. During Mom's lifelong journey, she touched the lives of countless souls—some were family, but there were many, many more. How does one describe this journey and all of those journeys with which hers intersected? I could come up with some witty metaphor, but in reality, it was a zoo—and Mom was a sometimes zookeeper.

Mom's tastes and interests varied widely. For instance, she loved the music of Marty Robbins, Anne Murray, Andy Williams, and Robert Goulet. She and Aunt Mary went to Providence to hear Frank Sinatra in concert. But she was equally fond of Simon and Garfunkel (although some of their lyrics embarrassed her) and the Irish Tenors.

She had some favorite songs she would sing at home, like *Dunderbeck's Machine*, *The Bump on the Log in the Bottom of the Sea*, and *There's a Hole in the Bucket*. Seasonally, she might have raised her voice to sing *Mele Kalikimaka* or *The Twelve Days of Christmas*—but not the usual one. She liked the Hawaiian version made famous by Frank DeLima—the one with "Forty stinkin' pigs" and "One Myna Bird in One Papaya Tree."

Mom instilled in her children a love of reading, which was a lifelong passion of hers. One instance of inspiration came while Mom was pregnant with Wendy (I was just a little guy). She was seated in the living room chair with a book propped up on her (very large) belly. I have to admit, at that point, I wasn't paying attention to what she was reading because I was trying to figure out how she had gotten so fat so quickly!

The dictionary provided a source of both entertainment and learning. Mom would introduce us to new words and increase her own vocabulary at the same time. A recent comment about me indicated my preference for "$5 words." Mom... thank you!

Crafts and creative endeavors were also a part of her life. She tried her hand at numerous things, including cross-stitch and sewing. She made a lot of clothes for my sisters and many gifts. My sister Chuckie was inspired to try her hand at all kinds of textile arts. On one occasion, Chuckie and Mom were seated in the living room—Mom doing a cross-stitch project and Chuckie knitting. Enter Dad. Mom broke out her best hillbilly accent to proclaim, *"Don't it do your heart a heap o' good to come home and find yer women folk a-sittin' and a-stitchin'?"* Dad did not appreciate the humor.

She also dabbled in home décor and would have people help carry it out. Faith's husband Dickie often helped out around our home. Once, while painting a room, Mom offered Dickie something to eat. He stepped out of the room and began taking off his painting overalls. Mom was very concerned that she was about to get a "free show" and halted Dickie's strip-tease. It wasn't until he assured her he was appropriately covered underneath that he was allowed to proceed.

I remember Mom planting a garden just about every year. One year she planted onions. Now, I've always been fond of onions and, as a boy, I was also fond of grossing out my mother. I pulled up an onion and washed it off in the kitchen while she was cooking. I then proceeded to eat it as most "normal" people would eat an apple. Mission accomplished.

We all know that discipline is part of a parent's job. With multiple children in the house, that task grows exponentially, so parents often have to develop some shortcuts. Playing the odds, Mom figured that if one of my sisters screamed, it was likely due to something I had done. If you were within earshot, you might hear the scream followed by a slight pause... then: *"Brian!"* Wendy figured this out and would raise the occasional false alarm so she could revel in the consequences I would face. This behavior would come back to haunt Wendy in later life. Mom would hear Henry yell and, after that brief pause, she'd shout *"Wendy!"*

For those of you who wore black today [finger wag]... Mother would not have approved. A few other gems: *"You kids behave!"*—to which she once received the response: *"I AM being have!"* Another: *"Do you want to get hit?"* Of course we didn't. Her cleverosity (yes, that's a word... Mom said so) was overwhelming!

Mom's sense of humor was quirky and often bizarre. She allowed her adult children and nieces to dress her as a sumo wrestler or as Pope Faith. Some of you may remember *"Punch this Pilot."* She also set a rather strange precedent by creating a family tradition. She gathered a bunch of useless junk, including some pretty strange items, and gave it as a birthday gift—which was dubbed a *"Smedley Box"* by Dickie, who was the first recipient. Another interesting laugh generator was her greased watermelons at summer cookouts.

Mom was never one to follow sports of any kind. But she certainly had a soft side. If Henry was unable to follow a game himself, Mom would listen to the game on the radio and take notes so she could bring Henry up to date when he got home.

Our cousin Donna summarized thusly: *"The first words that come to mind when describing my aunt are 'STRONG,' followed by smart, funny, giving, kind, thoughtful, and loving..."*

Mother. Grandmother. Great-grandmother. Great-great-grandmother.

So now we say goodbye to mother, grandmother, and aunt. You raised your own family and helped shape the lives of many who are present today. Your journey is done, but so many other journeys—in which you played a part—continue. You were loved, Mom, by many.

On behalf of my sisters and myself, and for all the extended family members: We love you.

The Catholics like to have a wake for their dead. They advertise it now as "Visitation." Mom had (of course) made all the arrangements through her preferred funeral home, and we all gathered there the night before her funeral. Something I hadn't even thought about was how she would be dressed. That became a discussion among my three sisters, and I bowed out. Because of the suddenness of her demise, her dentures had not been with her when her body was delivered to the mortician. They had to use wax to support the structure of her mouth. It looked weird, but she lay there, peaceful and still. Both her piercing eyes and her mouth were closed. A lot of people who visited, including family and friends, had nothing but nice things to say. My sisters and I were seated off to one side so that people could express their condolences to all of us at once (at least that's why I think they did that).

Cheryl and her husband came to the wake. The two of us had not seen each other or, in any other way, communicated in over 30 years. The idea of she and I meeting made our son Matthew quite nervous. She was pleasant, though, and even introduced her husband. As the visiting hours ended, we were each given the chance to say our individual goodbyes. I walked up to the coffin and, placing my hand on her right shoulder, said:

"We've been through a lot, old girl; this is it. This is the last time for us."

I patted her corpse on the shoulder and left. I was done.

At the church, we said our official goodbye as a family. Cousins and their families gathered in the cold, nearly empty church to share in the sense of loss. Not only had they lost an aunt, but they were also saying goodbye to an entire generation of family. To be honest, it was a day of great relief to me. Chuckie and I walked out of the church together. There was no overwhelming sense of grief or loss. She was gone. She was cremated, but her burial place is listed as St. Paul's Cemetery in Blackstone. My cousin Donna created some beautiful, turned-wood urns, made mostly of cedar—one large one for Henry and four smaller ones for each of us.

Wendy, although the youngest sibling, had taken it upon herself to be the de facto family leader. We allowed her this indulgence. She became extremely agitated with Chuckie and me. The two of us had been excluded from the more intimate discussions happening around the kitchen table, so we sat in the living room recounting our experiences and memories… by ourselves. Wendy overheard and chastised us as though we were her children. From that point until now, the family has been even more fractured than it was before. Mom's death had done a number of things: as mentioned, it was the end of the Longtin family. It was also the end of an era that some of her children didn't really mind. It is often said that funerals bring out the worst in people. I don't think that's as universal a statement as some might think. In this case, however, the death of the matriarch further splintered the family she had presided over for nearly 70 years.

Almost two years after we were married, Alycia and I took our long-planned honeymoon. We went to Ireland and Scotland. Mom had always loved the traditions of the Irish and had always wanted to visit Ireland. She never made it while she lived. My "share" of her ashes went with me, as I had already decided to leave the portion of her remains relegated to me in Ireland… but where? Chuckie pointed out that she had often mentioned Galway. I tried contacting officials at the Galway Cathedral but never really got a response. I pushed forward. Alycia had a small, polished stone engraved with Mom's name and her dates. I dug up some soil at the base of a tree in full view of the Cathedral. Her ashes were left there, along with the stone, and I brought back some of the disturbed/displaced soil. Mom had made it to Ireland at last.

Afterward

"*In any kind of entertainment, we are not compelled by the ordinary.*"

—*Craig Good*

My parents and all of my siblings have been included in accounts reported in print media, so I have not felt compelled to hide any of our names. My sister, Lori (who now goes by Lorijane), chronicled some life experiences in her self-published book. This is relevant because I have not tempered, nor have I conditioned – in any way – the telling of any of my memories that may include Lori. The two of us have described several events that appear in both her account and mine, but in dramatically different ways. I have had the advantage of tapping into the memories of my two older sisters, and I feel what I've put forth are the more commonly accepted and realistic versions of events about which we have both written. I have incorporated those memories into these pages as most of us remember them, and my descriptions of events involving Lori are put forth without explicit permission from her. I also felt these things needed to be addressed because her versions invalidated and diminished a lot of the suffering that others among us actually had to deal with.

347

At the times these incidents occurred, I was chronologically and developmentally older than Lori, so those parallel memories were formed in a different manner for me than they were for her. In my opinion, her versions are strongly influenced by her tendencies toward fabrication, confabulation, and mendacity— tendencies she displayed from the time she was a small child. I understand that Lori and I didn't get along; there was never any doubt about that. The further I examined my life (as in writing this book), I realized that although sibling rivalry is a known phenomenon, our relationship was somehow worse. I began searching for reasons that I could never have known at the time. I came to some painful realizations.

A parent can reduce the tension between siblings, or they can incite and worsen such discord. Children look to parents to learn everything from tying shoes to working out problems in a civil and appropriate manner. Children can also learn hatred, connivance, and divisiveness from a parent. I mention my sister Lori a lot because she and I were close in age and we grew up at the same time. While I incurred a decidedly greater degree of my mother's physical, emotional, and psychological abuse, I didn't realize the effect that was having on my younger sister. She not only witnessed the severely punitive treatment Chuckie and I received, but she was an unwitting tool for my mother as well. Because Mom used Lori as a kind of weapon, and because Lori witnessed the aggression, she suffered a very different facet of mother's cruelty.

Lori ended up a lot like Mom. I think she privately realized this, but she was loath to admit it. Lori has always sought separation from Mom and has also sought to convince people she was very different from our mother. As a result, Mom was portrayed, in Lori's book, as monstrously more amoral and violent than she really was, and Lori portrayed herself as a solitary heroine or martyr. There is no question Mom was an abuser. She was, however, not quite as malevolent nor quite as dangerous in the ways my sister described. Lori injected herself into the victim role in a lot of her memories. While she may not have actually been the victim, she was often a first-hand witness to the violence, and that obviously took its toll on her developing psyche.

I point all of this out not necessarily to debunk what I think are exaggerations and untruths in my sister's accounts (doing so would require a separate book), but more to show just how deeply we all were affected. Lori was not the recipient of the majority of the physical violence her book describes—within the memories of all of her older siblings, this is irrefutable. Her recounting, however biased, shows that she remembers a number of the vicious attacks. She was not subjected to the physical, psychological, and emotional abuses levied directly on her older siblings—the rest of us feel Mom was especially easy on her—but she bore witness to those attacks and was involuntarily complicit. While I think Lori may have wildly embellished or totally mis-told her variations to improve the entertainment value of her book, she nonetheless confirms and corroborates many of the incidents I remember.

Although Lori's confabulations and exaggerations are likely a part of her behavioral issues, they may also have a basis in neurology. Mary Karr, writing in *The Art of Memoir*, references neurologist Dr. Jonathan Mink, M.D. He explained to Ms. Karr that with intense memories, children "often record the emotion alone, all detail blurred into unreadable smear." Maybe Lori remembered the emotional stressors but didn't remember details. Maybe she put herself into those roles because she didn't remember who was actually suffering. Maybe she is also just malevolent and narcissistic. The truth may lie somewhere between or be a combination of the extremes. I have no doubt, however, that this is the direct result of our mother's effects upon her children.

I still get reminded of my past experiences in unexpected ways. In 2020, just prior to the COVID-19 debacle, I was cast in a community theater production of *The Smell of the Kill* by Michele Lowe. One of the characters, when directed by another to hold a third at gunpoint, asks:

"What do you aim for? ... the head?"

and the other responds, "or the heart."

I had what I presume is some sort of mild PTSD response when I first heard that in rehearsal. The lines cannot pass my ear, now, without eliciting a response. It mirrored the discussion I had with my dad back in 1976, and the coincidence stunned me.

This is how the Blackstone Street house appeared when it was placed on the market in 2020. Aside from a few minor changes*, it is essentially the same as when we lived in it. It was white when we first bought it and we painted it a dark, greyish blue at some point.

*The brick planters in front originally contained the lilac bushes I was accused of permanently damaging. Windows have been upgraded. There were several oak trees that no longer stand. The back door (at the back of the left side of the house) was where my mother ran from my father on that fateful day. The small, stone structure outside that door is a "dry well" used to drain the washing machine.

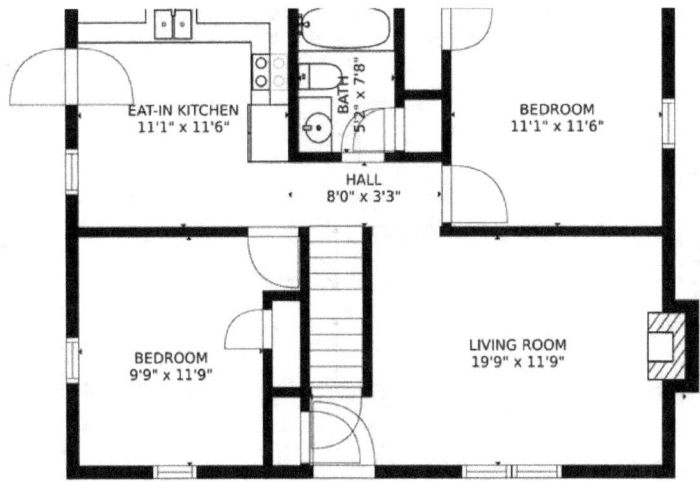

Here's a layout of the house on Blackstone Street. This is the downstairs. The bedroom off the kitchen was Lori's and Wendy's room and later became my mother's sewing room. The bedroom by the living room was our parent's room. The hallway was where Dad ended his life. At the other end of that hallway, by the kitchen, was where I caught the skillet on my shoulder.

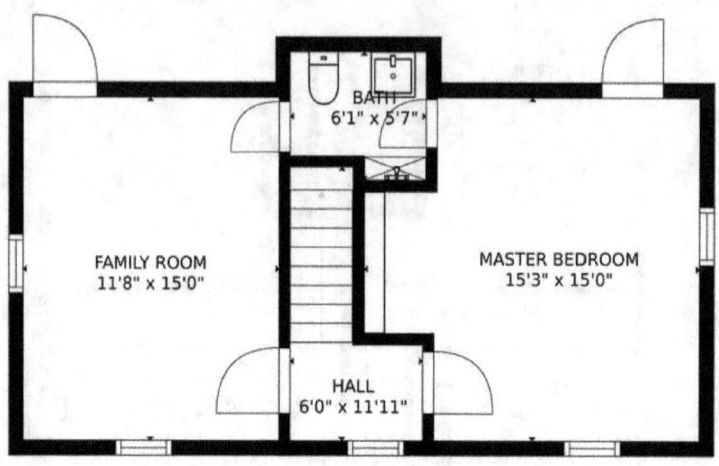

FAMILY ROOM
11'8" x 15'0"

BATH
6'1" x 5'7"

MASTER BEDROOM
15'3" x 15'0"

HALL
6'0" x 11'11"

...and this is the upstairs. The room labeled as "Master Bedroom" was my
bedroom from 1965 until I left for good in 1977.
The half bath was added in 1965-66.

My bedroom (Master) from 1965 to 1977. The room was finished in ¾″ shiplap
pine. Dickie and I did all the work, including building the barn style door (left) to
access the storage area behind, in the winter of 1976-77. It smelled of pine ever
after. The window to the left of the bed was my entrance point when Mom
locked and bolted the doors to keep me out.

Chuckie's and Faith's room from 1965-69. Lori moved into the storage space (door on the right) in 1968 or 1969 and, after Chuckie left in the summer of 1970, Lori's bed was moved out into the main part of the room. Wendy's bed was eventually moved to this room, as well. Panelling went up in the spring of 1977, after my room was finished. Mom couldn't afford more of the shiplap pine (like that used in my room) and settled on panelling.

Second section of The Woonsocket Call and Evening Reporter from Wednesday April 9, 1975 covering the marching band's return from Washington, D.C. two days prior.

Charlie Francis c. 1957

The Longtin siblings c.1990 – from left: Mary, Mom, Shirley, Rene, Rose and Dottie.

The five Francis siblings: From left: Faith, Lori, me, Chuckie and Wendy.

Late spring 1981.

Brian Francis

"Little Brother"

Sister Chuckie holding author

1995 –Aunt Dottie's and Uncle Eddie's 50th wedding anniversary celebration in Woonsocket. It was the last time all five Francis siblings were together. Although Lori was present, she chose not to take part in our bit of theater. The remainder of us mocked Mom's use of kneeling in a corner as punishment in front of the extended family.

VOL. 168—NO. 85—85TH YEAR WOONSOCKET, R.I. FRIDAY SEPTEMBER, 1976 36 Pages—PLUS SUPPL.

Man Shoots Wife, Kills Himself

Blackstone Woman in Fair Condition

Death In
Blackstone

The body of Charles H. Francis, 48, lies in the blood-spattered hallway of his home at 133 Blackstone St. Blackstone, this morning after he apparently took his own life after shooting and wounding his wife.

Blackstone Still Stunned By Shooting

By FRANK VISGATIS
Call Staff Writer

BLACKSTONE — This small community is still reeling from a double shooting yesterday morning that left a father dead and a mother in critical condition after a family squabble.

Neighbors, friends, police and fire officials, and others, still can't believe what happened in a quiet Blackstone Street neighborhood shortly before 9 a.m.

Pronounced dead at the scene was Charles A. Francis, 48, a laborer and maintenance man. His wife, Faith A. Francis, 44, is listed in "stable" condition today in the intensive care unit at Woonsocket Hospital.

According to police, Francis shot his wife twice before turning a .22 caliber, bolt action rifle on himself in the couple's neat, two-story home at 133 Blackstone St.

Mrs. Francis suffered two gunshot wounds in the back, as she ran toward a neighbor's house. One bullet, police said, exited from her chest after shattering a rib and imbedded itself in her right arm. A second bullet also struck her in the back but shattered and caused metal fragments to splinter.

Police said Francis also shot himself twice. Both bullets entered his chest. He collapsed in a hallway of the first-floor and died minutes after police arrived.

Continued on Pg. 2   Double Shooting

 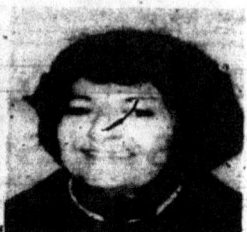

CHARLES A. FRANCIS   FAITH A. FRANCIS

Double Shooting Stuns Blackstone

Continued from Page 1

Patrolman Eugene Desjarlais, one of the first officers at the scene, said Francis was unconscious but breathing when authories arrived. He died within minutes.

According to reports, the couple had been estranged, but Francis recently moved back in with his wife and three children. The children were in school when the shootings occurred.

Early yesterday morning Francis reportedly put a sum of money—about $400—on a kitchen table and told his wife he wanted a "minute of your time."

From preliminary information, police said there apparently was little conversation between the couple and Mrs. Francis left the room to shower and dress. When she came out of the bathroom, Francis was standing before her with a rifle.

According to authorities, Francis repeated his earlier statement about wanting "a minute of your time," but the woman began screaming when she saw the gun. One shot was fired but struck a door, police said. The woman ran from the dwelling. Her husband followed.

Kenneth Robinson, a neighbor, was welding in his yard at 137 Blackstone St. Two more shots rang out and the woman ran across the front lawn toward the Robinson house.

Police said she knocked on the door and when it was opened by Mrs. Robinson, the woman mumbled, "Charlie just shot me." She then collapsed in the entry.

Police and Fire Chief John Greene this morning said that Robinson's instant response "probably saved her life." Robinson and another neighbor, Mrs. Pauline Salome of 134 Blackstone St., wrapped Mrs. Francis in a blanket and rushed her to Woonsocket.

"This is an unbelievable thing." Sgt. Lucien Lizotte said "They might have been having a family problem but this department never once had to go to their home on a domestic complaint call. They were a quiet, well-liked couple."

"It is a real quiet, nice neighborhood," Patrolman George Buskirk said, "and never do we get complaints from there."

Police said Francis was a "well-liked guy who always stopped for coffee in the morning at Arnold's." He worked in Rehoboth at a large farm and had once operated a cab company in this town.

The Blackstone Street neighborhood is a typical, tranquil, residential area, comprised of working people who seldom bother with each other. The Francis family has occupied the house for about 15 years.

"To show you what kind of a neighborhood it is, and how typical, when Mrs. Salome ran to help Mr. Robinson it was the first time the two had ever really met." Desjarlais said. "When they were riding in the Robinson car to Woonsocket Hospital, Mrs. Salome said to Ken, 'this is an awful way for neighbors to meet for the first time.'"

Police this morning said calls are already coming in at the station from townspeople offering to help the three children. Last night the children stayed with an aunt and uncle.

Officers and firemen this morning talked of the tragedy while taking some telephone calls in the station.

"You know," Chief Greene said, "this is a very small, tightly knit town. Charlie Francis, for example was Mike Eldridge's uncle. Eldridge is a selectman. Greene said the tragedy affects "everybody."

"It's tragic," Lizotte said, "none of us can really believe it happened—what could have made him go that far."

www.ingramcontent.com/pod-product-compliance
Lightning Source LLC
Chambersburg PA
CBHW061134120626
46546CB00005B/1775